Major Bob Unvarnished

Why We Keep Making
the Same Mistakes

Millennial Mind Publishing
An imprint of American Book Publishing
American Book Publishing
P.O. Box 65624
Salt Lake City, UT 84165
www.american-book.com
Printed in the United States of America on acid-free paper.

Major Bob Unvarnished
Why We Keep Making The Same Mistakes

Designed by Jana Rade, design@american-book.com

Publisher's Note: *This publication is designed to provide accurate and authoritative information in regard to the subject matter covered. It is sold or distributed with the understanding that the publisher and author is not engaged in rendering legal, accounting, or other professional service. If legal advice or other expert assistance is required, the services of a competent professional person in a consultation capacity should be sought.*

ISBN 1-58982-263-3

Bevelacqua, Bob & Bryan Fugate, Major Bob Unvarnished
Why We Keep Making The Same Mistakes

Special Sales

These books are available at special discounts for bulk purchases. Special editions, including personalized covers, excerpts of existing books, and corporate imprints, can be created in large quantities for special needs. For more information e-mail orders@american-book.com, 801-486-8639.

Major Bob Unvarnished

Why We Keep Making
the Same Mistakes

Bob Bevelacqua
and
Bryan Fugate

This book is dedicated to the best soldier I ever had the fortune to serve with, Master Sergeant David K. Thuma.

I miss you, Dave.

Therefore I say: Know the enemy and know yourself; in a hundred battles you will never be in peril.

When you are ignorant of the enemy but know yourself, your chances of winning or losing are equal.

If ignorant both of your enemy and of yourself, you are certain in every battle to be in peril.

Sun-Tzu, **The Art of War**
Translated by Samuel B. Griffit

Preface

I have written this book for the average reader, not the elite, highly educated walking thesaurus with a PhD. In order for the reader to appreciate my analyses and understand my background, I have written this book from the perspective of tactical vignettes that I or my close friends have experienced—in other words, been there, done that!

The problem I have with most analysts is that, while they are well-read and educated in their subject area, they have never gotten their hands dirty, they have never stood on the floor of the arena bloodied by battle after having been knocked to their knees.

A brilliant man once said that there are two kinds of people who study the stars. I believe this applies to most professions, be it a fireman or a terrorism expert. There are astronauts and there are astronomers.

Astronomers have degrees in astro-science and study the stars through massive telescopes—they are well-read and very articulate. They can tell you the composition of a star a billion light years away.

Astronauts strap their butts on a huge rocket filled with tons of explosive fuel and launch themselves into space traveling thousands of miles an hour. They are not real sure they will get back in one piece—but they have BEEN in space.

I always strive to be an astronaut—enjoy the ride.

Bob Bevelacqua
Baghdad, Iraq
August 2004

Foreword

In every human's life, there comes a time to put into words what we feel in our hearts. This is Bob Bevelacqua's time. Bob chose a profession that most men shy away from; one requiring physical stamina, mental discipline and soulful compassion. Bob's heart is not only tender for the suffering; it is stout for impossible tasks. It is the heart of an officer in the Army Special Forces. This is a book written by a patriot, a soldier, a leader — it is a book that is both a journey through hard times and an analytic look at what created them. Bob has captured lessons learned, in some cases his own mistakes and lays them out before you in a manner that leaves behind ego and arrogance — learn from them. His no-nonsense approach to solving problems, coupled with his ability to communicate with people in many languages, served him well in the military and has allowed him to once again serve his country in Iraq. The wake-up call from 9/11 affected all of us; it also focused Bob Bevelacqua's fierce patriotic spirit which guided him back to his true love, serving his nation. You will relate to his passion, sense of humor, and frustration in dealing with our world's complicated events and our sometimes ineffective foreign policies. Bob tells it like it is because he recognizes the gravity of the situation in which we currently find ourselves; a war on terror. Bob's first appearance before the public on CNN and later on Fox News as a military analyst provided proof that his analysis was what all of the us wanted; unafraid and unvarnished truth — now we have it in writing.

Lt. General Jay Garner (U.S.A. retired)
Washington, DC, September 2004

Chapter One

On the Front Lines of Freedom

U.S. Army Rangers

How do you describe Ranger School? Well, basically, Ranger School is a life appreciation course. For nine weeks you walk, you don't sleep, you get very little food, and you constantly go through an evaluation process: leadership skills, individual skills—all the skills associated with small unit patrolling. While this is going on, the taunting and the harassment don't stop, either.

The most stressful part of Ranger School was knowing that you have to get a Ranger Tab on your sholder. Trust me, you do NOT want to be an officer in the United States Infantry without a Ranger Tab. You're looked upon as a pogue or a slug. Everyone looks at your shoulder to see if you have the Tab. If you watch officers when they meet for the first time, it's like two dogs on the block that start sniffing around each other. First thing they do is look at the left shoulder of the other guy's uniform to see if they have a Tab, then they look at what decorations are over the "U.S. Army" tag on their left pocket, finally, noting whether they have Airborne Wings. Do they just have an Expert Infantryman Badge (EIB) or the more coveted Combat Infantryman Badge (CIB)? This is how you take the measure of an officer without even talking to him or her. You can tell where he's been, what schools he's been through and generally pass judgment on how tough and hard core he is (this doesn't always work).

The concern in Ranger School isn't really surviving or losing a bunch of weight, which you do. (I went into the school at 185 pounds and came out at 150–155.) It's knowing that if you don't get the Tab, you don't get the respect. That's what the school is all about—that's the bottom line. So why does the Tab carry so much significance? The reason is that Ranger School is so miserable an experience that at times I think most people would rather be sitting safe and comfortable on a prison farm somewhere in Louisiana.

Ranger School, when I went through it, had four phases: city, mountain, desert, and swamp. The city phase was at Fort Benning, Georgia. The course consisted of two weeks of patrolling and learning how to do basic small unit tactics at the squad level. The physical training (PT) in the city phase was horrendous; you would get up in the dark hours of the morning and go on long runs. If you fell out of the run, you got a major minus report—two major minus reports and you were history. Major plus and major minus reports were turned in at the discretion of the Ranger instructors. I learned all of this too well because several times I was on the verge of being booted out myself.

By reading this far, you may have formed the impression that I had a tough time with a lot of different things. It's because I'm a non-conformist; I really don't know how to fit in. The maverick in me probably brought me to Fox News because I didn't like what I was doing at CNN, but that is a story for later. I'm only telling you about it now because it is a constant theme in my life.

The second phase was the mountain phase in Dahlonega, Georgia, where you do a lot of mountain climbing and a whole lot of walking hills late at night.

The next phase was in the Utah desert at Dugway Proving Grounds. We did a lot of long-distance patrolling in a moonscape-like environment. Finally, the last phase was at Eglin Air Force Base in Florida. There we did extensive patrolling in swamps with alligators, snakes, and bears, along with other kinds of creepy creatures that make your skin crawl.

I recall a late night patrol in the swamp when I started to lose it—I began to hallucinate. It was probably 02:00 in the morning and I think I had gone forty-eight hours with no sleep. You could only sleep in short stretches, maybe two hours at a time, if you were lucky. The days would bleed into each other and you would totally lose track of time. Hallucinations are caused when the integrative function in your brain becomes too taxed—the picture in your mind of what is happening may be more dissimilar from reality than usual. As you lose more sleep, or continue to receive less-than-adequate amounts of sleep, your neurons become even more taxed and your brain may begin to generate even less coherent images, possibly resulting in temporary insanity. In extreme cases lack of sleep may cause death.

On that patrol, the night was pitch black and we had "taken a knee" to rest while the patrol leader was doing a map check. The rule was that you stayed close to the guy next to you and watched him the whole time because it's easy to break contact with each other at night. When he got up and started walking, you got in behind him. I kept an eye on the guy, he didn't move, I stared some more and he didn't move. The next thing I knew I was being shaken and somebody was yelling at me, "Hey, get up! Get up, man, we're movin' out." What I had taken as the guy next to me was a bush! So I got up, fell back in with everybody, and we moved out with me acting like nothing unusual had happened.

We encountered these things called wait-a-minute vines. They are called that because when you bump into them, it takes you a minute to get loose. Everybody got tangled up in these vines and when you are drudging through waist-deep water and smashing your shins against cypress stumps which leads to an infection called cellulites, life just sucks. After that, the real fun starts as you watch your leg implode with plus-two pitting edema—your body begins retaining water like Hoover Dam. We had all this going on and we dared not complain.

I remember stopping and watching one man on the patrol pull out his ID card. Ranger students had quarters taped to their IDs so they could make emergency phone calls if they got separated or lost. This guy tried to stuff a quarter into a tree and push buttons like he was waiting for a soda to come out. We had another guy that stopped in the middle of crossing a small stream because he was waiting for a giant fish to go by. I mean, it wasn't in the water—it was in front of him. All of us were pushed to the outer limits of what we could endure and still be effective.

I think Ranger School really prepared me for the gut checks I was going to experience later on in my military career, and in my civilian career for that matter. For those of you who don't know what a gut check is, it's an event that you go through that is extremely miserable and causes you to do some soul-searching. You wrench your gut out at times—you can't hold down food or water. It's your classic bad day. I was pretty sure at the time that Ranger School was going to be my last gut check in life because it was way over the top of anything I had yet experienced. Not so fast, not the case.

I had the distinct pleasure of graduating from Ranger School and having my Ranger Tab pinned on by my hero, Dick Meadows. Dick was an incredible Special Forces legend. He was a Son Tay Raider, the story of which needs to be a Hollywood movie. If anybody's going to make movies about daring wartime adventures, they need to make a movie about this.

The objective of Operation Kingpin was to rescue as many as a hundred U.S. POWs that intelligence said were at the Son Tay prison camp, only thirty-seven klicks (kilometers) west of Hanoi. Shortly before midnight on November 20, 1970, at Udorn Air Base in northern Thailand, fifty-six Green Berets boarded three rescue choppers for the mission. They flew over five hundred kilometers to Son Tay accompanied by two C-130 Hercules aircraft. Major Meadows was onboard the lead chopper that actually crash-landed inside the compound.

But you know what? The intelligence was bad—there were no prisoners there. While on the ground they killed several hundred North Vietnamese and Russians, no big surprise there, and, I believe, several Chinese. The assault force was extracted from the area without losing a single person. The entire raid took twenty-three minutes. Later in this book we will get around to talking more about bad intelligence.

To say I was proud that Dick was there to pin on my Tab would be a serious understatement. I was the baseline definition of gung ho at that point in my life; I was "Hooah" to the max. Let me explain both expressions to you. "Gung ho," which comes from Chinese, is better known as a rallying cry dating back to the Marines in World War II and Korea. "Hooah," which we would joke about, really has no meaning, other than to be motivational and reinforce a statement like, "Hooah, roger that, understand, sir, gung ho!" "Hooah" was used in every other sentence as a very common expletive. Guys would finish a sentence with "Hooah!" when asked if they understood an order. It was much more respectful than the "F***in' A" widely used in Vietnam. When on camera during the invasion of Iraq, all the soldiers shouted the word to show the folks at home they were pumped and motivated. On Fox News, Geraldo Rivera was especially good at provoking shouts of "Hooah!"

My Hooah was dampened a bit when I got my first assignment, the 8th Infantry Division (Mechanized), "The Crazy Eights," stationed in Germany. I didn't want to be mechanized anymore, I wanted to be a light fighter (light infantry). I had the urge to jump out of airplanes and helicopters. Being a ground-bounded Mech slug had no appeal for me because it just wasn't "Hooah!" This feeling didn't last long after I was transferred to Germany, but that's the way it was at the time.

The Fulda Gap, 1988

The 8th Infantry Division (ID) was headquartered in Goppingen, southwest of Stuttgart, in southern Germany. After being there a while, I was enjoying the 8th ID despite my earlier misgivings. Living in Germany was the real Army. You possessed a sense of mission in that you knew you were here to prevent the Soviet Union from roaring through the Fulda Gap and invading Europe, you were here to stop the whole world from just collapsing to communism. The domino theory was alive and well.

My part of the general defense plan (GDP) was in the Hofbieberspohl, square in the middle of Fulda Gap. We would go up to our designated area and do terrain walks with our battle books that showed exactly where our vehicles were going to be positioned when the attack came, where our fighting positions were going to dig in, where the obstacle belts were, and where we expected to see the Soviet 8th Guards Army, including three motorized rifle divisions and one tank division, come across. If that kind of land combat ensued, it would be epic, indeed. We all prayed to God that the day would never come.

One more thing about the Fulda Gap, which nobody talks about; rumor has it that it was shielded with nuclear mines. If the Soviets succeeded in overrunning us, and they would, those mines would detonate with unimaginable consequences. Another interesting thing was our French "Allies," who had already withdrawn their forces from NATO military command in 1966. Do you want to know why they did that? It is likely that, as the Soviets were punching deep into West Germany, the French would fire their nuclear-tipped Pluton missiles to air-burst over the Russian troops. Do I have to draw you a picture of this? We would be there, too. It was a great strategy for the French. They would get a two-fer by blowing the hell out of their ancient enemies, the Germans, as well as the Russians. Actually, it was really a three-fer; the U.S. forces in Europe would be killed as well. Great, huh?

Here I would like to dedicate a little time to some of the most influential "negative" characters in my life. One was my company commander, whose name I won't mention, and the other was my battalion commander who shall remain nameless as well. My company commander was a true-to-life slug and pogue. In the first eight months of his command he never came to PT with his company. Now this is pretty pathetic. When a leader fails to lead his own men in physical training in the morning, how can he expect to lead them on the battlefield—something that would be far more difficult than morning PT?

After dealing with this guy for well over a year, we had a new battalion commander come in. This gentleman was the most anal-retentive, micro-managing neo-Nazi you never wanted to work for.

At this point in time, I was befriended by another individual who was instrumental in helping me out in life, our own battalion S3 (operations officer), Gary Cavender. Gary taught me that sometimes it's more important to learn how not to do things than it is to learn how to do things; and in addition, he helped me learn how to quell my temper.

I definitely learned a lot and I had some great noncommissioned officers (NCOs), or sergeants, there to assist me with the learning the Army processes as well—I owe a lot to them.

I have one fond memory from the 8th ID that was an early indication I didn't fit into the traditional Army and that I needed to go someplace where guys think outside the box like I did.

We held tactical exercises at Baumholder, which was a maneuver center in Germany where various units conducted tactical exercises. On this deployment, one of our missions was a platoon-level exercise that consisted of attacking a reinforced squad on a hilltop. In a mechanized infantry division like the 8th ID, a platoon had four M113 armored personnel carriers, each with a 50-caliber machine gun mounted in the commander's cupola just forward of the cargo hatch. My platoon had about twenty-five men.

Our mission was to go to the top of the hill, up a long winding road, attack to seize the objective, and then secure the hilltop.

I hated driving a vehicle on a battlefield, especially through wooded, hilly terrain, because you were just a bullet magnet, and because those vehicles were nothing more than rolled aluminum—we are talking recycled Budweiser cans here. They won't stop a bullet bigger than a 7.62 mm, so if the enemy has anything at all substantial in size, (a rocket propelled grenade (RPG) is good enough) they were going to open us up like a can of peaches.

Several other platoons did this exercise before me; I was maybe sixth or seventh in order. Everybody else got their butts kicked. I knew that the only way to do this wasn't by driving my "Winnebago of Death" up this eight-hundred-meter hill. I decided it was time for something totally different, a truly unconventional approach.

I told my platoon sergeant what we were going to do. We were going to drive our tracks to a predetermined point, exit them, leave the tracks at the bottom of the hill, and then we were going to carry our 50-caliber machine guns up to the top of the hill and attack the strong point—dismounted. Hah! Let me tell ya! You want to talk about guys looking at you like you got an eyeball growing out of the middle of your forehead, well, everybody's jaw dropped and they said, "Sir, you're friggin' nuts!"

And you can't blame them, when you think about it. Aside from having to carry their M16s, their helmets, load-bearing harness, water, and ammunition, I was asking them to carry four crew-served 50-caliber machine guns. A 50-caliber, when it sits on a tripod, is very heavy—we're talking in excess of 130 pounds per gun, not to mention the bulky ammunition that goes with it.

The mission had to be broken down among my twenty-five guys. I left the Platoon Sergeant back with the tracks. Each track has a driver and a track commander (TC) and I took the rest of the guys with me.

We negotiated the open field part of the approach successfully and crossed into the wood line. There we dismounted our guns and moved out on foot. We were stumbling over steep, uneven terrain through thick trees with the guns snagging on branches. I realized soon enough that my plan wasn't working. So I said, "Okay, everybody, get in the road." Now this you don't do—this was a tactical, high-risk chance that I was taking. But, the opposing forces, commonly known as the OpFor, were so accustomed to having tracks drive up the road to attack the objective that I figured they would kick back, relax, and listen for the sound of the tracks, not a platoon of hard-heads carrying their 50-cals.

An M113 with a 275-horsepower (hp) diesel engine going up a hill, filled with seven guys makes a lot of noise. Walking carrying a 50-caliber machine gun is like walking on cotton in comparison. I knew we wouldn't make any noise at all, so I figured we could move right up the road undetected.

It was a cold, wintry night and it was most likely the OpFor were in their vehicles with the heaters running and everyone fast asleep. There were a couple of vehicles providing perimeter security for the squad on the hill. They were set up on the inner edge of the woodline in overwatch positions—they were watching for tracked vehicles not grunts with 50-cals. We found each vehicle on the way up. We simply walked to the rear of the vehicle, opened the crew compartment door, and "shot" everyone inside.

The evaluators loved it. My guys were no longer pissing and moaning because they realized this was a good plan.

As we made our way farther up the hill, we grew more and more fatigued. The weight of the guns was really starting to bear down on the guys. Once again, they started to say how stupid this was and that we really shouldn't be doing it. "The lieutenant doesn't know what he's doing, he's a brand new lieutenant," that sort of stuff. In fact, I really was not a brand new lieutenant. I had been a lieutenant for a couple of years serving in the Georgia Army National Guard. I just had this compelling feeling that what I was doing was right. I shouted "Shut the hell up" a couple of times to the gripers to keep things moving.

Slowly we made our way to the top of the hill like a giant anaconda, and arrived on a piece of high ground overlooking the objective. Keep in mind that this was being done at night, but the moon lit up the objective pretty well. I put the four guns into an overwatch position which meant they were in a location where they could engage the objective without endangering the assault force. This allowed the assault force to take down the objective while reducing the chance of fratricide, or "friendly fire" as the media calls it. I got the guns set up off to the right-hand flank and then moved the assault force off to the left. The guns were to initiate on a verbal command from me. Once the assault force had breached the wire obstacle surrounding the objective, I was to shoot a green star cluster in the air. This was the signal for the guns to shift their fire allowing the assault force to exploit the breach and take down the objective

I called up my senior squad leader. He was on the guns. I said, "Open fire!"

When those four 50-cals opened up on the objectives, the OpFor were in shock. My battalion commander, who was on the hilltop at the time, was also caught off guard.

When we opened up with the 50-cals, they drew all of the OpFor's attention. Once they started focusing on us, we begin picking them off as they tried to return fire. Meanwhile, the assault force came in from the left flank of the objective, cut through the wire, got into their trench line, and quickly killed everyone.

I called up the platoon sergeant and he drove up the hill with the tracks. We cross-loaded the dismounted 50-cals onto the top of the tracks and got into a 360-degree perimeter. We had taken no losses.

After that, we could pretty much do no wrong. I had really gained some rapport with my guys. The mission went so well that it dawned on me that I didn't think like everyone else. I was unconventional in my approach to warfare.

The progression in my thought process was confirmed when I met with Dick Meadows a year or two later at his river house in Florida. As I told him the story he began to smile, especially about the men complaining and questioning my tactics, only to congratulate me at the end. This was the support I was looking for—Dick Meadows' seal of approval.

One of the last large exercises in Europe at that time was called Caravan Guard. The REFORGER series was starting to wind down. REFORGER was a large exercise in which forces were deployed from the United States to Europe where they would link up with pre-positioned equipment. We would then go through a mock defense of Europe with our NATO allies, against the invading Soviet hordes.

Caravan Guard was a scaled-down version of that exercise, and instead of using our tracked vehicles, we went out and dismounted from trucks. I was a company executive officer (XO) but I found myself in charge of the company as the acting commander, because my spineless company commander broke his foot so he wouldn't have to go on maneuvers, he knew the mission was dismounted. God forbid he lead his own troops on foot. So he stayed in the rear with the gear and I took the company to the field.

Caravan Guard was a good lesson for me because I realized you cannot trust what everyone tells you, that you have to check, you have to supervise.

This was also when I began to suspect that my battalion commander was a stark raving lunatic. This impression was confirmed in a later incident, when he tried to punch out one of his company commanders.

We deployed to the field and took all our gear—night vision equipment, weapons, rucksacks, ammunition, and things of that nature. We loaded up on trucks and drove to a northern part of Germany.

Sensitive items are pretty important things in the United States Army. A sensitive item can be a weapon or an expensive piece of equipment, such as night vision goggles.

When you are in the field, you conduct what is called a sensitive items check. You must have everything you are responsible for and know where it is at all times. God forbid you lose a weapon and somebody else gets their hands on it, especially a civilian.

Toward the end of the field problem, my platoon sergeant arrived on the scene running way behind schedule. His first act was to conduct a complete layout of sensitive items. Lo and behold, a set of night observation devices (NODs) was missing.

Now these were a damn expensive model, AN/PVS-7, about four or five thousand dollars each, and they were state-of-the-art NODs, American ingenuity at its best. These are the ones that make a soldier look like a cyclops.

We went through the normal process of having everyone check his gear and dump it out with no luck, and then I had to make my report to the battalion commander. Well, the battalion commander reacted in a very hostile fashion because he realized that he had to tell his brigade commander that he was missing a sensitive item. It would have a negative impact on his command and show his inability to control his people.

After having my butt handed to me in the field and being told that I was not going to survive this, I went back to my guys and, without being the complete maniac that my battalion commander was, I had the men conduct a very thorough search. We searched the countryside. We traced routes we'd taken, we searched vehicles, we left no stone unturned. About three-quarters of the way through this process, the soldier who was missing the NOD finally confessed and said, "Well, sir, I never brought 'em to the field, I left them in the arms room. I've been saying I had them the whole time because I am embarrassed." So we actually weren't missing anything.

This infuriated the battalion commander even more and resulted in me being relieved. That's right; I was relieved of my command. I was sent to Echo Company which was the improved tube-launched, optically tracked, wire-guided anti-tank missle (TOW) vehicle (ITV) Anti-Tank Company, the same type of unit I had served with in the National Guard. The battalion commander pretty much wrote me off as a leader.

Following Caravan Guard he proceeded to run the battalion in a rather tyrannical fashion. He made a hell of a lot of enemies. But you know what? Gary Cavender was right. It's more important sometimes to learn what NOT to do, than it is to learn what to do.

Toward the end of my tour, the 8th ID was notified that it was slated for deactivation. It was going away. We were folding up the colors, retiring the unit, and everyone was going to be cast to the winds. But fate decided otherwise when Iraq chose to invade its neighbor, Kuwait, in a surprise attack. This was in August 1990. After that, it became quite obvious we were heading for war. A massive build-up was being set in motion, so the battalion commander asked for volunteers who wanted to transfer to the 3rd Armored Division and deploy to the Persian Gulf for war.

All the officers in the battalion were gathered into a classroom; the battalion commander explained the situation and asked for volunteers to go with the 3rd Armored Division to Saudi Arabia. I thrust my hand into the air and I knew—*I just knew*—everyone behind me had their hands up, too.

You know what? Less than half the room had their hands up, and I said to myself, "What a bunch of chickens! All talkin' smack on a daily basis about how, yeah, I'm ready to go to combat, and I can do this and I can do that, but when it's time to put up, they shut up." The Army has a term for these kind of people, REMFs, or rear echelon mother f***ers, and that's what they were—in my humble opinion.

I remember talking to my unhappy commander, who was a first lieutenant although typically company commanders are captains. He had the position because he was pretty squared away. I remember commenting to him how surprised I was that so few officers had volunteered without realizing that he was one of those who had not. He said to me, "Hell, I don't want to go, I don't want to go to war."

I said to him, "Why not? Why are you in the United States Army?"

I can't fathom why someone would want to be in the Army and not want to serve his country in combat and do what he was supposed to do, what he is trained to do—I don't get it. I really didn't get it.

I was very happy to leave my battalion after all that. I was glad to transfer to the 3rd Armored Division *Kaserne* (Barracks) in Friedberg, Germany.

The 3rd Armored Division was, at the time, one of the most lethal armored divisions in Europe. It had been newly equipped with M1A1 main battle tanks, Bradley fighting vehicles, and the new M800 series five-ton diesel cargo trucks. It was definitely fit to fight. I was very impressed. I believed, when I arrived at the 5th Battalion, 18th Infantry, which was part of the 3rd Brigade; the officers were different from those in the 8th ID. They seemed to be a little more focused, a little more serious. Sure, they were getting ready to go to war, but the caliber of officer actually seemed to be better than what I was used to. I suppose that since 8th ID had been targeted for inactivation a lot of the slug officers were assigned there. I figured before anybody had been officially notified, they had started to send the better quality officers to the 3rd Armored Division.

I had my in-briefing with my new battalion XO, Major Tom Sitnick, whom I was indirectly working for as the battalion assistant S4 (logistics officer). Normally, battalion S4s don't have assistants. My new assignment didn't sound too exciting, but I decided it was a lot better than watching the war on TV from the good old U.S. of A. This was going to be the Super Bowl for the Army and I was not going to be sitting on the bench.

Major Sitnick had a great reputation from the Ranger battalion as a veteran of the Grenada conflict—a real hard charger. He was very physically fit, a good looking guy, and he impressed me with his no-nonsense attitude.

When any officer gets into a battalion, a new unit, he tries to do something that will cause him to stand out, or to make a name for himself and earn some kind of notoriety. If he doesn't do that, he's not going very far in his career. This was what I was struggling with; what could I possibly do to prove that I was an integral member of the team. I needed to prove that I was ready to get into action and fight. I had to wait for the proper moment and seize it as soon as I could.

My first challenge came when I was told the battalion had some shortages. I looked at the list of shortages; items they needed in order to go to war. Just tents, spare parts, tires, extra water containers, fuel cans, things of that nature. I asked Major Sitnick, "Sir, how many trucks can you get me?" He replied, "How many do you need?" I said, "Well, get me about seven Hemmets." Now a Hemmet or HEMTT (heavy expanded mobility tactical truck) is a large vehicle, around three meters tall, and it has eight wheels. It is about ten meters long and has a cab that looks like one of the vehicles you'd see at an airport moving airplanes around; a low profile, squared-off cab.

I got seven of them and headed to my old battalion. Why? They had an extreme amount of excess equipment, and when a unit inactivates they are required to turn in all of their equipment and get rid of everything that is excess.

I was really doing my old battalion a favor when I showed up with those trucks and started grabbing everything. You name it, we grabbed it: M113 track pads, spare tires, extra tents, sets, kits, and outfits, camouflage nets, fuel cans, and water cans. We grabbed tons, literally tons of stuff, including a spare CONEX shipping container, the kind that you see going across the ocean on ships and on back of trucks rolling down the highway.

When I reappeared back at my battalion with the loot later on that evening, the battalion commander told the battalion XO he was very impressed. That was the first step I made to show that I really wanted to be a part of the team and that I could make a difference.

In the three or four weeks that it took us to prepare for overseas movement, we packed up everything we owned. Every piece of equipment—tanks, computers, field desks, you name it—and we rail-headed it to the port of Bremen. Our troops moved to the Rhein-Main Air Force Base near Frankfurt so the Air Mobility Command could airlift us to the Gulf. We flew out of Germany on a C-141 Starlifter—the first time I'd been on a C-141 since Airborne School.

Preparations for War

We arrived in Saudi Arabia in early January 1991. When I first stepped off the plane, it was pretty comfortable weather. It was probably in the lower-to mid-seventies. I remember thinking, "This is what it must have been like when they first arrived in Vietnam." I always associated combat with Vietnam because as a kid, as an adult, and later as a lieutenant it was the war we studied and learned about. I remember stepping onto the tarmac of al Kharj airbase, watching a couple of heavy lifters come in and land, and I recall thinking, "We are really mustering for a major battle here and it will be something that hasn't been seen since World War II, a mechanized war. You don't deploy armored divisions as a bluff. When you deploy them, you're going to use them." Bluffing with a billion tons of equipment just isn't cost effective—this was for real. We can wait around for all the U.N. resolutions in the world, but once the heavy equipment is on the move, we are committed. You know it and your opponent knows it.

As the battalion closed on Saudi Arabia, we moved to the Port of ad Dammam, where I set up shop for the next month. As the assistant S4 logistics officer, I was responsible for bringing in, receiving, and accounting for our equipment as it arrived on ships from Germany. Some of the equipment came in on RORO (roll on, roll off) ships. These vessels are so big you can just drive your vehicles on and off them. They have large side ramps that come out of the mid-ship and they also have large ramps that come out of the stern of the ship.

The other type of ship we had was from the Merchant Marines. They are center-loaded cargo ships, meaning that everything has to be picked up by a crane and then lowered into different cargo holds within the vessel's hold.

These take a lot longer to offload, and I stayed in the port insuring our equipment moved into the proper holding areas where we could inspect it for damage caused during shipment. Once a company had the majority of its equipment checked in, they either loaded it on a HET (heavy equipment transporter), which is a heavy vehicle designed to move a tank, or a Bradley fighting vehicle, or they simply drove their wheeled vehicles to an assembly area.

The air war against Iraq started on January 17, 1991, and lasted for forty-three days. I was in the port, quartered in an M113 medical vehicle with my supply sergeant when it started. Our track had litters in it which made great bunks for catching forty winks. Now I sleep naked, which normally isn't a problem. However, when you have to get out of your bed and suit up in a protective over garment against chemical attack, you can be at a disadvantage. This is a lesson learned: sleep like you are going to fight.

I was lying in bed on the top litter. The cargo hatch that I was sleeping under was cracked a little bit so I could get some air. Just as I was about to nod off, in the distance I heard a real deep, kind of drone, *BRMMMMMMMMM*. Then I heard the sound that I will never forget for the rest of my life. *AAAEEEUUUUUUWWWWWAAAAA*. It was the air raid siren. We had been told that when the air raid siren came on, it meant that a Scud attack was imminent. When the siren sounded, my supply sergeant woke up, placed his transistor radio to his ear, and announced at the top of his lungs, "Sir, we're bombin' that MF."

I said, "Sergeant Harris, I think that MF's bombin' us back!"

The Iraqis had plenty of Scuds they had gotten from Russia. They generally fired them from mobile trucks. The technology for aiming a Scud is not very good and they are notoriously inaccurate. The problem is, however, they could carry chemical, biological, or even nuclear warheads and we had to take them seriously. With a range of six hundred kilometers they can be fired at just about any target in Saudi Arabia.

Now they were firing them toward our port area. For the first time we saw our Patriot missiles go into action. The Patriot weapons system caught a lot of flak in the press, unjustifiably, in my opinion. The Patriot was not designed to shoot down incoming missiles; it was designed to shoot down enemy aircraft. I firmly believed the Patriot did a great job being adapted to an anti-Scud role. Certainly the Israelis appreciated them.

We watched CNN that day in one of the large storage buildings on the main dock. We watched our president tell the world that the air campaign had started. Our operation was no longer Desert Shield, it was now Desert Storm. Even though ground troops were not yet engaged, you could feel the urgency at the port and sense that the atmosphere had changed. People were very mission focused now that we were, in fact, at war. Since Saddam Hussein had shown no sign of pulling out of Kuwait or negotiating a peace deal, that meant a huge ground war was inevitable, and we all knew it.

Scud attacks occurred quite often. Probably the most comical one and the one that shook me up the most occurred when I am was in the latrine —my brother-in-law Mark Meadows still laughs about this story. Now, as you may know, latrines in Saudi Arabia were great. You really have to appreciate this. This was an outhouse that was built out of half-inch plywood, 2x4s with holes cut in them, and you sat down suspending your derrière over a barrel of flammable liquid. They were screened-in, but forget about privacy. People could walk by it and see you with your bare butt hanging out. You sat on top of a regular toilet seat that was built over a fifty-gallon drum that had been cut in half and was sloshing with a mixture of diesel fuel and oil. So I was trying to do what nature told me to do and as I was sitting there, all of a sudden a siren went off.

AAAEEEUUUUUWWWAAAAA.

"Holy sh**," I said to myself, "we're under Scud attack."

Well, at this point, they had become routine, so I just casually put my protective mask on, sat there, and watched a couple of guys run by headed toward a tracked vehicle seeking cover. The best place to be in case of an attack is definitely in an armored vehicle. What I didn't realize was that 150 meters off to my right, on the other side of a large building, was a battery of Patriots. The Patriots were launched to engage the incoming Scuds, and when a Patriot is fired, it sounds like very large explosion, *WHOOPMMPPPP*. I was still sitting there in the latrine with my mask on, looking like an idiot, when a couple more of these large explosions went off just to my right. Well, I think it's safe to say that this situation assisted me in finishing what I needed to do; I got dressed and ran back to my vehicle. I know it all sounds funny, but I was rather shaken up. That is probably the closest I came during a Scud attack to thinking that things weren't looking too good; that we actually had impacting warheads in our immediate area.

One more thing, and I don't want to go off on a rant here, but picture women living in a combat zone—not a pretty sight folks. Primitive conditions like I just described, and it gets much worse than that, I believe combat is no place for women. Say what you like about me, but I believe that, in general, men are hard-wired mentally and physically to tolerate wartime conditions and women are not, period.

A Rant

Reliving this experience requires a rant. Allow me to digress for a moment and address a couple of issues. Be all you can be...except a warrior. Whatever happened to the spirit of the bayonet? Whatever happened to right arm night? Being able to go out with your boys and get drunk? Well, the military has been neutered, that's what happened. It's been trickled down to a social experiment. It's politically correct. It's a gentlemen's club, it's the zero defect environment times ten. It's don't ask, don't tell. It's women serving in combat. It's everything except what it was originally created to be: an organization of men that have the ability to meet the enemy on the battlefield and defeat them.

I would rather have a platoon of drunken brawlers than I would a platoon of people that joined the Army because of college grants. We are recruiting some real Poindexter geeks and all they do is sit around and play computer games. I would rather have the rejects from the football teams, the guys that stay after school because they have bad attitudes and get in fistfights; that's who I would rather have in the Army. They can then be shaped and molded into leaders. Leaders are not born, they're made. They're made by discipline and leadership experiences, hard discipline and hard leadership, not this pampering and catering that we've got going on at basic training. Keep in mind that I am not referring to the Special Operations community or the branches of the combat arms—specifically the infantry—they remain hard core, but there are some real slugs within their ranks as well.

I knew we were sliding downhill when it got to the point that you could no longer use a four-letter word in a forum with other officers without getting reprimanded. God forbid that you should talk about women in a manner that was sexually inappropriate among a group of guys. The camaraderie we used to have that made us what we were, gets diluted and then gets washed away, and it's uncalled for.

I think General Patton put it best: "The Army is a team. It lives, eats, sleeps, fights as a team." This individuality stuff's a bunch of crap. The bilious bastards who wrote that stuff about individuality for the *Saturday Evening Post* don't know anything more about real battle than they do about fornicating.

Well, I bet General Patton's spinning in his grave at about 800 revolutions per minute. The Army of One, under Chief of Staff General Shinseki, is the new individualistic approach to being a soldier, "I am an Army of One." No, you're not! You're nothing by yourself. There is no organization in the Army that I know of today that teaches individuality and individualism and being an effective fighting force as one man. This is us catering to Generation X, the Pepsi Generation, and the Nintendo Generation, kids who can't pass the PT test standard. So we lower the PT test standard. That's right; we actually made it easier for the guys that were in the age category of 17–21 years old to pass the PT test. But whose standard increased in difficulty? Who had to meet a harder physical standard? That's right, the older age group, 32–36 year olds. I actually had to train harder to stay physically fit than a kid coming out of high school or college. That's ridiculous! If you can't meet the standard, folks, we'll just go ahead and lower it for you.

My wife enlisted in the Army in 1999 and went to basic training down at Fort McCleanan in Alabama, to be a member of the Military Police Corps. She was physically fit, having run a couple of marathons and she always worked out. She actually fell out of shape when she went to basic training because basic training is no longer designed to weed out people. It's designed to expose recruits to military life and allow them to integrate into the service. Short of being a three-hundred-pound blob of protoplasm, you can get through basic training. In fact, you don't even have to qualify with a rifle. Your unit will take care of that responsibility and will make sure you pass a PT test as well.

One of the things that really floored me was that in both basic training and advanced individual training, my wife was not required to run any kind of land navigation. This was replaced by seven days of Army values training.

The seven Army values—thanks to General Reimer, who was just another brilliant guy, for this crap. The Soviets couldn't have infiltrated the Army with a spetsnaz operator and done more damage than General Reimer has done. Sorry for the digression, but I want you to understand some of the growing pains the Army has gone through.

After the battalion had received most of its equipment, it formed-up in long columns and headed out to the tactical assembly area. Our tactical assembly area was southeast of the town of Hafar al Batin, just south of the pipeline road close to the Iraqi border. That was where our battalion was to complete preparations for the invasion.

With the exception of one piece of equipment that was on the last ship to come in, everything arrived. My job as assistant S4 was to wait on that last piece of equipment—a quarter-ton trailer that contained nothing less than the battalion commander's and the sergeant major's personal effects. So we couldn't go anywhere without that trailer.

My driver, Private Aguilera, and I stayed behind. I didn't know Aguilera, in fact, I didn't know most of the guys in the battalion, because I was still new to the unit.

We had a deuce-and-a-half (two-and-a-half ton truck) that we were going to use to pull the trailer and for those of you who aren't familiar with a deuce-and-a-half, they were designed in the 1940s and haven't changed a whole lot over the years. Although I think the one we were driving had actually been built in the 1960s. You could say that it was a very well-seasoned vehicle, but at least the transmission wasn't completely stripped.

The ship we were waiting on, the *Mangalia,* finally arrived. This Romanian-built tub had a problem with one of her engines and couldn't achieve a maximum speed of four knots, which is about five miles per hour—not exactly water-skiing speed.

We had to wait for this ship to limp into port so we could get our trailer and get the hell out of there. Wouldn't you know it, from the bottom deck of the ship, the last piece of equipment to get off-loaded from the bow section was our trailer. I mean we waited until the last minute to get this piece of…junk.

Aguilera and I hooked up the trailer and we headed off to the tactical assembly area. I didn't know exactly what the grid coordinates were, but I had a general idea. Now, the camp was at least an eight-hour drive away, if not farther, and I was doing all this with a Michelin tire map that I'd bought in Germany because I needed a map of the area and we didn't seem to be able to get maps. If you've ever seen a map of Saudi Arabia approved by the military, they are really beautiful. They look like wallpaper with nothing on them. There were a couple of contour lines for the entire country, that's about it. At least they weren't cluttered up with all those unpronounceable names and roads.

Really, the official maps were useless. I mean you move a map sheet the size of the hood of a pickup truck and it has no terrain on it. The only thing you'd have is the latitude and longitude lines; because they didn't have maps that had universal transverse mercator (UTM) grid coordinate lines that we typically used. So I bought a Michelin tire map. It was, I believe, 1:1,750,000 which is a very large-scale map. An inch on this map is almost fifty kilometers, and that's what I was using for navigation. The battalion XO had drawn a circle on it, giving us the general area of where we were headed.

Another Rant

In reliving this I feel the need for a rant. Anecdotally, I would like to say that American soldiers have the best problem-solving skills in the world. Our guys make the best of any possible situation. A French officer would keep ordering better maps from his bureaucracy and never get them. A German officer would accept the official maps he was given and not question them. A Russian officer would assume that all the available maps were counter-informative; all the good maps were state secrets. The Brits? Well, they would simply muddle through by drawing new maps as they went along. Only an American would use the Michelin tire guide to fight a war. I know I have used some stereotypes here, but think about what it's like to have a multinational force like the U.N. carry out a military operation. Americans DO think, plan, and execute differently—and I think, better—when it comes to fighting a modern war. It's not that the Europeans don't know how to fight, it's just that their political systems have largely emasculated their armed forces. If the going gets tough anywhere in the world, it has to be the U.S. military that finishes it.

So we were finally rolling down the road, we were finally moving. I was psyched. I had live ammo in my magazines and I was carrying an M203, which is an M162A rifle with a 40 mm grenade launcher on the bottom of it. I was ready to deal out some death and destruction, baby. Hah! Not quite.

We got maybe two hours down the road; there were convoys moving up and down the road, there were camels and desert and sand—you could just feel the excitement in the air—and then it happened...*BOOOMMM!*

Our right front tire blew out. Aguilera grabbed onto the wheel...I tell you, a deuce-and-a-half is a good-sized vehicle. Two and a half tons of truck moving at fifty miles an hour, pulling a quarter-ton trailer and the right-front tire blows out—that is a little pucker factor for you. So much for dealing out death and destruction.

Aguilera wrestled the vehicle off to the side of the road, no problem. Do we have a spare tire? Yep, got a spare tire. So we pull it out, change the tire, no problem, we're up and rolling again.

We get about, I don't know, another hour down the road and *BOOOMMM!* The LEFT front tire blows out. So now I'm thinking, "What we've got here is obviously the battalion hangar queen," which means this truck does nothing but sit in one of the depots and never gets worked on. It was a piece of crap and there was nobody out there who could assist us.

This time, we don't HAVE a spare, so we basically just sat there. I don't have any comms, I can't talk to anyone, so I have to wait until another convoy drives by.

Luckily, we did have another convoy come by from a National Guard unit; I believe it was out of Massachusetts. These guys were more than happy to help, and they had a wrecker. They towed us to a convoy center, a service station. A team of mechanics hooked us up, gave us a new tire and a spare. We ate, we were fat, dumb, and happy and we started moving again. After a few more hours of driving, nightfall was upon us. We arrived at Riyadh, hooked a right, and headed up the main road from Riyadh going toward King Khalid Military City (also known as KKMC or "Emerald City") and Hafar' al Batin.

By now it was dark and we were getting pretty tired. We had been driving for awhile, I think maybe five or six hours. We took a right when we should have gone straight and things changed. All of a sudden, we were no longer on a hardball road, but were on a dirt path. It was like Rod Serling appeared in front of the truck—"Welcome to the Twilight Zone."

I said, "Aguilera, pull the vehicle over. Where the hell are we?"

"Sir, I'm not sure."

"Okay, bud, we're going to bed. When the sun comes up, we're gonna figure out where we gotta go. We got plenty of time, there's NO rush to get there, so let's get some sleep."

After three uncomfortable hours of trying to sleep in the cab of the truck, we got up the next morning and could see where we made the wrong turn. The country was extremely flat, so we just back-tracked onto the hardball road and started toward our destination again.

We were maybe two or three hours up the road when I started to smell smoke. Our rear axle had caught on fire. I have no idea why, but it seemed like the drive train on the last two tires of the truck had caught on fire. We pulled to the side of the road, got out a fire extinguisher, and hosed it down.

Now Aguilera, who was a mechanic, was scratching his head and speaking in Spanish. Some of which I could make out; none of it sounded good. So I said, "Okay, Aguilera, whadda we gotta do to fix this?"

He replied, "I think we just gonna hafta drive slow."

What could I do but laugh? "OK, bud, hah!"

So we drove slow, I mean we drove like six miles an hour, the *Mangalia* could have passed us!

Finally, we came up to a barrel on the side of the road that had an armor symbol painted on it, which is a triangle with a big "3" in the middle, 3rd Armored Division, and an arrow pointing to the right. I said, "Aguilera, take a right."

We took a right off the hardball road and drove out into what looked like a scene from *Lawrence of Arabia*. Nothing but sand for as far as the eye could see.

When you're out in the desert, it's very similar to being out on the ocean. You could see something at a distance, you're not sure how far away it is, and you estimate, well, it's probably going to take us ten or fifteen minutes to get there. Some forty-five minutes later you realize that whatever you saw was pretty far away.

So we headed toward this small mass of green that was out in the middle of the desert. The 3rd Armored Division didn't have time to paint its vehicles desert camouflage. The majority of our equipment was still green with its European coat of paint.

We drove toward the mass and we bumped into a part of our brigade support area. The guys there were able to give us directions to our battalion.

We were pointed off in a different direction to another small green mass. We got to it, and lo and behold, it was our battalion. Major Sitnick was very happy to see us and, of course, we told him about the trip, all the anxiety and everything. We dropped off the trailer and that's when I received my first introduction to desert life.

The division was dispersed across a huge area of desert. If I had to estimate, I'd say it was maybe fifteen to twenty kilometers square. Each brigade had its own area where it had deployed its battalions in a defensive posture.

Maintaining dispersion among vehicles was essential, because you don't want to get everything piled up too close. Let's face it, if we do receive indirect fire from Scuds, mortars, or artillery, and we're parked hub-to-hub, we would have a lot more damage.

The distance between units was several kilometers. You could see them off in the distance and it was easy to navigate because you had a general idea of the direction you needed to go.

I lived in a hex tent, which is a small four-man tent, with the battalion S1 (staff officer or adjutant), his assistant, and myself. So there were three of us in the tent.

Sand got into everything. It got into everything you owned, including your body. Every crack, every orifice had sand in it. There was no way to get away from it. We're not talking sand like Miami Beach. We're talking about a fine, powdery sand that you get in your sleeping bag. Even when you go outside and shake your sleeping bag off and hit it for a little while, it doesn't seem to go away. It's still there.

We had the ability to keep some of the blowing sand out by closing the tent flap, but because we had a sand floor we bascially lived in the sand. Our uniforms were constantly covered in it; it just gets into everything.

When we ate, whatever we ate, powdered eggs, real eggs, Chef Boyardee, no matter what it was, even a plastic-packaged MRE (meal ready to eat), it had sand in it.

The bathrooms in the field were no better than they were in garrison. We had the same type of outhouses that were built when we were in a static position and flies were into and onto everything. I particularly don't care for flies, especially when I know they've been hanging out at the outhouse and they wanted to come over and sample my eggs that morning; this is cross-contamination at its best.

We had a short period of time to prepare and I had always thought that when I went into combat I'd have a good concept, a good plan in my head. I expected that we would receive a good Operations Order (Op Order), that we would have a good back-briefing, that everyone would have a detailed plan in his head, and we would all be on the same page when the crap hit the fan. I would know exactly what was going on and what my role would be. Not so, not the case. You'd think after having sat in the desert for several months and knowing that we were about to go to war we would have had ample time after we received the Op Order to give instructions to our men. We needed time to disseminate the information to everybody; have them memorize, plan, and have a good idea what we were getting ready to do. Well, that didn't happen.

The night before we went to war, and I still can't figure out why this happened, I was told we were short nine hundred protective suits. I needed to go scrounge up nine hundred chemical protective over garments (CPOGs). We also called them mission oriented protective posture (MOPP) suits. I said, "You've got to be kidding me."

They said, "No. And oh, by the way, try to get as many boots as you can as well."

"Roger that, sir."

We drove to Log (Logistics) Base Echo. Log Base Echo was a city of CONEX containers. There had to be a mile of nothing but containers, stacked ten to twenty meters high and thirty to forty rows deep. All the different classes of supply were there. The Army has ten classes of supply and we were going to drill through them and get chemical protective over garments.

One of the things that is very interesting in the supply world is how paperwork functions. You have to have request forms, they have to be properly filled out, you have to have approval, and then you go to the supply sergeant and you beg, on your hands and knees, and hope you haven't pissed him off lately so you can get what you need.

I was fortunate because I had the opportunity to work with a fine E7 who was the S4 (Logistics) noncommissioned officer in charge (NCOIC). Sergeant Leroy Frasier was a wheeler and dealer extraordinaire. You talk about somebody who could make something happen. Leroy didn't look like the most squared-away soldier in the world, and he wasn't the most articulate one, either, but this guy knew the supply system and when he moved, he was a rogue; he was like a rogue shark, like a great white. I mean he moved out. He knew how to sniff out a bargain. There was no woman in the world that I would put up against him in finding a bargain somewhere, because Leroy knew where they were.

So I said, "All right, Sergeant Frasier, what are we gonna do?"

He said, "Well, you're gonna sit over there and talk with the officer in charge and I'm gonna go over here and get us what we need."

I said, "Okay."

So in about two hours time he came back with three or four HEMTTs filled with chemical protective over garments, all packaged up in their sealed containers. "Did we get all nine hundred?" I asked.

"Roger that, sir. I made it happen."

I said, "Okay."

We headed back off to the battalion with what I thought was going to be an extremely difficult task accomplished. When I asked Sergeant Frasier, "How did it go, how'd you get 'em all?"

He replied, "Let's just say I seized the initiative." He made it happen. This is another great example of why the American Army is the best in the world.

After we got back to the battalion and finished distributing all these chemical protective over garments, we had to do late-night refueling. Our support platoon leader, Lieutenant Bernie Willeford, was a giant of a man from North Carolina. He was six foot four inches tall, 230 pounds, a big guy, a big football player. I believe he was a West Point grad; Bernie was in charge of the support platoon and he was doing all the late-night fuel runs with his guys. M1 tanks suck gasoline. It doesn't matter if they are sitting stationary, they will burn through tons of diesel fuel. We were topping off all the tanks because we knew the next day we were moving out.

We got up that next morning after almost no sleep and I went to the battalion Operations Order meeting. When I got back from the meeting, I was getting ready to brief our guys in the combat trains. The combat trains included the Battalion Maintenance Collection Point, with its maintenance vehicles, the battalion aid station, the fuel trucks, and the Administrative Logistics Operations Center (ALOC). We were a mini task force element known as the combat trains.

I was getting ready to brief our guys and the battalion S4 was there; we shared duties and he was a pretty decent guy. He was actually very good to me. We were there doing our thing and were about halfway through the Operations Order when we got a call over the command net, "Regulators, mount up!"

I said, "You gotta be kiddin' me! It's time to go to war? We haven't even given the Op Order to the troops."

So, the cardinal rule of allowing enough time for your men to digest their information, and brief their guys was definitely violated.

We mounted up, fell into battalion formation, and we moved out. We started driving north. When in doubt, attack! Drive north! (This is an inside joke within a small circle of military leaders.)

So this was part of the Hail Mary move. The Big Hail Mary Pass. We were all massed on the eastern side of Saudi Arabia and at the commencement of the war; we all shifted to the left.

The Invasion

The battalion traversed probably forty kilometers on its first movement up to the border and we spent the night just south of the border. We got briefed by our air liaison officer who, I believe, was French, but I can't recall his name. That night, at 01:00, the Air Force was going to drop a 15,000-pound. Daisy Cutter, or Big BLU-82, just across the border from us. I stayed up to watch that drop. There was a very impressive, large, orange flash off in the distance and a loud rumble and I just knew I didn't want to be anywhere near the point of impact. These bombs were dropped from C-130s and were designed to clear minefields using the tremendous overpressure of their explosions, but they turned out to be a weapon of psychological impact.

Early the next morning we moved across the border and encountered the infamous Iraqi berm. It was a large dirt berm of packed sand, probably six or seven meters high and twenty meters thick. It had been breached during the night by our combat engineers and we drove right through the breach. That's when we first started to see exploded vehicles.

That was about it for the next two or three days. All we saw were burned-out vehicles. The Air Force A-10 Warthogs and Army attack helicopters had just raised hell and indirect fire had really ripped everything up. We didn't see any actual combat until the last day of the war.

After we did the big Hail Mary move, we ran up almost to the northern part of Kuwait on the Iraqi side and made a right-hand turn and started to come into the defensive positions of the Republican Guard. We were supposed to be hitting the Tawakalna or the Hammurabi divisions, which unknown to us at the time, had packed up and were moving out of the area.

As I am reliving this…

Just because they didn't want to engage in combat with us raised a great question; why did we let them escape? We had air superiority and we knew they were pulling out with their transporters, high-explosive anti-tanks (HEAT) ammunition fully loaded. They had all their tanks on heavy movers and were running down highways. How come we weren't busting them in the butt with artillery and indirect fire and calling in air strikes?

I would love to know what happened behind the scenes that caused that decision to be made. What dope deal was cut between Saddam

Hussein and the United States of America? Rumor had it that a head nod was given to Saddam Hussein by our State Department to invade Kuwait. Why was that? Is it because we didn't have any military bases in the region, we had no presence? If we let Saddam invade Kuwait that would allow us to flow forces into the region, and get bases established. Saddam would then effectively pull his forces out of Kuwait once he knew we were going to attack, and the majority of his military would surrender. In fact, almost all of his officers that were on the front line fled a week or two prior to the commencement of hostilities and Saddam was allowed to pull back his most prized forces. Was that the deal that was cut, so we could have a base in the Middle East? I don't know; it sounds plausible to me.

I suppose the Kurds in the north and the Shiias in the south would like to know the answer to that as well. The unmolested Republican Guard slaughtered them in large numbers.

The real frustration is that we turn right back around, some ten years later, and go do the whole thing over again. I mean, you talk about history repeating itself. History doesn't repeat itself, my friends, we just keep making the same stupid mistakes over and over again.

When we were told to cease-fire, that the war had, in effect, stopped. I think we were surprised and a little disappointed because we were just starting to get engaged. We had a couple of tanks that had direct fire engagements with T72s (Soviet main battle tanks) and also with a BMP (Soviet armored personnel carrier with a 73 mm gun), and a ZSU23-4 (Soviet truck-mounted, quad-barrel 23 mm anti-aircraft system). So we really felt like we were starting to commit to battle when the whole thing stopped. The question of, "Okay, so why are we here?" came to mind. If I am not allowed to fight, why did I come all this way and go through what I've been through just to let the bad guys escape?

Once the cease-fire was put into effect, we moved into a tactical assembly area. I guess you could call it a tactical defensive position, but we really weren't defending against anything.

At that point things became dangerous, because we had free time and we were not in a position where we could conduct training. One of the most dangerous things about Desert Storm was all the unexploded munitions that were scattered about the battlefield. We had training on just about everything and anything in the Army but one of the things that I had NEVER received any training on was what unexploded munitions looked like. We had not forseen the fact that they would litter the battlefield.

On April 2, 1991, we became very familiar with unexploded munitions and what they can do.

It happened in the combat trains. It was in the morning and the battalion XO and I were having our morning coffee on the hood of his Humvee (better known as a "Hummer" in the civilian world). It was probably 06:30 and we were right next to our tent on the far edge of our security position. The vehicles were all around us in the combat trains in a circular position. In the center of the trains was an M577 which contained the ALOC. An M577 is a large tracked vehicle that looks like a pregnant M113 and it has a big cargo net coming off the back of it and a bunch of antennas; it looks like an antenna farm. We were sitting there having coffee when off to our rear came an M88, which is a huge tank recovery vehicle. Its massive frame and engine allows it to drag incapacitated tanks off the battlefield. It is also big enough to pull down monumental statues.

The M88 was driving around behind us in a circular pattern, and we never really paid much attention to it. It finally stopped probably a hundred meters away from us. The mechanics started walking around it, doing something. As we are talking, all of a sudden, we heard a loud explosion and time froze. The only thing I could compare it to would be when you first step out of an aircraft and throw your body into 135-knot wind of prop wash. Everything just went into slow motion—like a scene from *The Matrix*—I lifted my head up and looked over Major Sitnick's back. His back was to the explosion and I saw the smoke of the blast and a body about two to three meters in the air dropping back down to the ground. I was sure that I actually saw the shrapnel that flew toward me and hit one of our mechanics in his ribs, throwing him to the ground. I can just see it happening again and again, watching the pieces flying through the air.

As I stood there and my brain began processing this information, Major Sitnick, who was a real war veteran, turned and ran toward the sound of the explosion. He was gone. I sat my coffee cup down and started to move toward the blast and then finally started to run as I realized that we had guys who were hurt and we had to do immediate triage.

There were four guys on the ground. One was dead and I think he was killed when his body hit the ground. The other two guys were pretty busted up, lots of broken bones.

When you stand there looking at the scene of bodies lying all around and burned flesh—you know this guy: you talked to him the day before—if you sit there and pay attention to that, you don't really process the fact that you have to do something to help. If you stand there and dwell on it, you can get stuck in a kind of zone, or you get droned out, and I saw that happen to a few people. It caught me initially when the blast went off. But I had to snap myself out of it. The sad thing was that the kid who got killed was only nineteen. The two NCOs survived their wounds and the third guy, I think, was only hurt superficially.

What had happened was they had been policing up the battlefield on their own initiative. They came up on a gator, which was a bomb that releases several bomblets, designed to kill vehicles. These were duds, they hadn't gone off, and they were strewn all over our assembly area. We had marked them off with tape so soldiers would know they were there. These guys drove over them with an M88 thinking they were going to blow up; thinking that they were not nearly powerful enough to take out an M88 or even cause any kind of serious damage to it—that's what they thought. After they had driven over them they figured they were inert. They picked them up and put them into a pile. The kid who was killed was dropping the last bomblet on the stack and when he did, the whole pile exploded.

That happened after the war was over and it was, I believe, the only combat fatality we had in the battalion. It just ended everything on a real sour note. It made me respect and fear unexploded ordnance—a lesson that later saved my life.

Soon after the war ended, I was asked by Major Stinick, the battalion XO to go back to Log Base Echo and King Khalid Military City, some 240 klicks to our south, to do a re-supply run and pick up critical supply items that the battalion needed. We were running low on a number of spare parts. The major told me, "Bob, Route Blue has been cleared, take Route Blue."

"Okay, sir, no problem."

I was in a Humvee and along with about six other vehicles, and we headed off. I didn't have a map, other than my Michelin tire map and a GPS that at times told me I was in Istanbul. It was not the most accurate system in the world at that time. They were brand new and there were still some bugs.

So we headed due west to what we thought, throughout the majority of the war, was a ditch filled with oil, but in fact, it was a hardball road, a tar road—so much for satellite imagery and the weenies that interpret it.

As we headed west, we picked up the tar road and headed south. This worked almost all the way up to the border. Then the road made a sharp left-hand turn and headed out to the east. We continued to head south, on a dirt, unimproved road, which meant you basically had a trail on the sand that had been used by hundreds of vehicles until it finally gave in and became a road.

We headed south on that. This was supposedly Route Blue, which had been cleared. After another hour or so of heading south, I came upon a triple-strand, staked-down concertina obstacle with tangle foot, which is like barbed wire and a series of anti-personnel mines that seemed to run all the way to the coast, which was probably sixty klicks away. This obstacle belt ran, we estimated, another 120 klicks or so to the west.

I didn't have a whole lot of choice at this point. I could either turn around and go back or I could attempt to get through the obstacle belt. I decided after doing an initial assessment, that I could cut my way through the wire, pull it off the road, and, from what I saw, it was a very hard-packed surface road which meant no mines. There was no evidence of any mines at all and a majority of the mines we'd encountered up until that point had been all surface-laid. In other words, you could see them.

I cut the wire, pulled it off the side of the road, and then I walked down the road to a point where you could tell that this first obstacle belt ended. I felt pretty comfortable in ordering the convoy on ahead.

I walked back to my vehicle and we proceeded through the obstacle belt. We drove for maybe another half a klick and there in front of me was the mother of all minefields. "Holy crap!" I muttered softly to myself, thinking no one else could hear. I thought we had breached the minefield. We hadn't. We had come up on a series of mines that stretched as far as the eye could see and they were probably laid out in a belt fifty meters deep. There were several different types of mines. There were anti-personnel mines, Soviet toe poppers. There were Italian plastic anti-tank mines, too, that are almost impossible to detect with a mine detector, also some tilt-rod mines and Chinese anti-tank mines. The majority of these mines were surface-laid. Possibly they had been buried at one time, but the wind and blowing sand had uncovered them.

After observing the situation, I had an idea of where the heaviest concentration of mines was, so I directed the vehicles off the hardball road we were on, because it was heavily mined. I drove off to the left-hand side of the road maybe twenty-five meters from the obstacle belt and stopped. I got out of my vehicle and I gathered some of my guys around and said, "Okay, this is the plan. I'm gonna find the part of the minefield that has the fewest mines in it and I'm gonna take these mines out and I think, in theory, that if I shoot them, they'll blow up. Once they blow up, we may get a sympathetic detonation of other mines and, hopefully, clear a path."

I took everything off that was metallic, which is the first thing you do when you go into a minefield. I had my M203 40 mm grenade launcher, my helmet, and my flak vest and that was it.

I searched around and found a path that only had about six mines that I had to take out. I didn't mess with the anti-tank mines at all. I went for the anti-personnel mines because I felt that we had enough room to either straddle or bypass the anti-tank mines in a zigzag fashion.

I got into a prone firing position on the ground and pulled my helmet down over my head as low as I could get it, drew a bead on the first mine, and shot. I hit the top of the mine, which looked like a mushroom sticking up out of the ground; it was green and about three inches tall. When I hit the top of the mine a chunk of it shot right back at me, hitting me square in the forehead. If I had not adjusted my helmet, I would have bought the farm. At that point I realized that I needed to change my technique. Instead of shooting directly at the mine horizontally, I thought I probably should get a little bit of a downslope shot. So I got up and took a knee. I turned around and looked at my guys and they were sitting there staring at me. I know what they were thinking, "You sure you know what you're doin'?" Now if I was asked that question, I would have answered, "Hell, yes, I know what I'm doin'!" Deep inside, I was thinking to myself, "Bob, do you have any idea of what you're doin'?"

I was probably six or seven meters away from the first mine. The mines were designed to blow up and out and I felt that if I could get back far enough away from the shrapnel pattern I'd be all right. So I took another shot at the mine. The wind was slowly blowing so I was swaying a little bit on my knee. I missed with the first two shots. On the third shot, without expecting it, I hit the mine and it blew up. That shocked everyone.

I felt a warm, tingling sensation on my thigh and didn't want to look down, because I knew I'd been hit by a piece of shrapnel and was bleeding. Well, I was not bleeding. What happened was I had an uncontrolled release of my bladder. I'd basically wet my pants, in front of my men. It was an incredible thing because I had absolutely no control over it. It was my body's reaction to the explosion. And no one, and I mean no one, said anything to me when I walked back to my vehicle after clearing the path. They all saw it, they all knew that I'd wet my pants. Of course, keep in mind they were hiding behind their vehicles while I was doing this, so no one was going to—excuse my French—f*** with me over the fact that I had wet my pants, which I have absolutely no problem owning up to now—or in the future. Go out into a minefield and blow up the mines yourself. It's a significant emotional event.

After this first mine, I moved on to three or four more, had great success, and got to the point of where it was one shot, one kill, and the mines blew up.

I finally breached though all the mines, and walked the path. I felt comfortable enough and guided the first vehicle through. I walked in front of it, with it following closely on my heels. The rest of the vehicles came through and we got back on the road. If you want to know how leadership works, or is supposed to work, in the U.S. Army, then this is as good a story as any. Now I knew Route Blue had been cleared. It was an experience for the books.

After we had driven for maybe thirty minutes or so, I started to think about what I had just done. I started getting uncontrollable shakes. My right leg and my right arm just shook uncontrollably for probably a minute or two. I got the jitters and then it went away and I didn't think about it. It does trigger a strange response in me. I can really empathize with some of the guys who've suffered from shellshock. I can't imagine being exposed to indirect fire, close-in explosions for a long period of time. It has to be just devastating to your psyche, to your body, to your soul.

After sitting around the desert for a couple of months, we received notification that the unit was to be inactivated.

My second division in a row was being pulled out from under me. We prepared for redeployment back to The Federal Republic of Germany.

We packed up all our stuff and we stood around in a huge parking lot; imagine a huge parking lot of tanks, Bradley fighting vehicles, and Humvees out in the middle of the desert, acres and acres of them. We were standing around, all the battalion officers, the battalion XO, the S3 (operations officer), and the battalion commander and somebody said, "We stopped too soon, we will be back. Business is not finished here. We will be back."

Another Rant

Whoever said that was absolutely right. Absolutely right! It was a flawed political decision that caused the premature end to the war that should have ended in Baghdad. We would have been seen as liberators. I personally took thirty POWs and processed them. I listened to the interrogations of some of the tankers who we had encountered and engaged in direct fire.

They hated Saddam Hussein. They hated the leadership of their own military. Two weeks before the ground war started, the officers disappeared; they were pulled back to Baghdad. This gets me back to my point of why were they allowed to retreat? The men had no leadership. It was just the enlisted guys and when we listened to these guys and some of the stories they told, we couldn't believe them, but we knew they were true.

In one of the Iraqi division's headquarters, the officer on duty at night would have a soldier come in to his office and he would sodomize him. We asked about this because we found a trash can filled with used prophylactics and we wanted to know what had been going on. The story finally came back to us that this was what the staff duty officer would do to his solders at night. ...Talk about a way to affect morale.

So I think Saddam was ripe for the plucking back in 1991. His army would have turned on him in a heartbeat because he had really just dumped on them, left them in the field; they had no respect for their leaders and probably would have killed them. It was a missed opportunity all the way around.

After Desert Storm

After the war, I went on to the Infantry Officer's Advanced Course at Fort Benning, Georgia. That's when I learned what professional jealousy was all about. It was amazing, the animosity that was created between the soldiers and officers that served in the Gulf and those that didn't. To the ones that didn't serve in the Gulf, the war was a joke. "You guys didn't do anything, all you did was drive a couple hundred klicks and everything was over."

I don't want to get into those conversations because, really, I don't like confrontation and I don't feel like I have to validate what I have done in combat. There were lots of veterans, Vietnam veterans and others that say the Gulf War was a joke. Our guys got CIBs, Combat Infantryman Badges, and they didn't deserve them. Well, you know what, for the guys that got killed and for the guys that had to kill people and got the shit scared out of them, what can be worse? You can't compare one man's fear and bravery in battle to another man's. I'm proud that I have a Combat Infantryman's Badge, but I will not brag about it or use my experiences to gain me any favors. Anyone who has to belittle other people because of their experiences, well I believe, they have a chip on their shoulder and there's something in their closet that they are hiding— John Kerry comes to mind.

I want to just leave it at that.

Chapter Two

My "Haitian Vacation"

Preface

As this book is being written Haiti is once again falling into chaos and turmoil. After years of work, loss of life, and several hundred million dollars nothing has changed—why did we even bother?

I was inserted into Haiti as a special operations officer in September 1994. The story of my experiences there provides an interesting and informative lesson for those who may return to Haiti again some day and for anyone who finds themselves having to stabilize a nation. As we can see from recent headlines, the situation in that beleaguered country is no different now than is was ten years ago. Even the names of the major characters have not changed that much. In 1994, Jean-Bertrand Aristide was considered to be the savior of the nation, its rescuer from the oppressive rule of a cruel military dictatorship. Today that situation is reversed. It is Aristide and his cronies that are regarded as the oppressors, torturers and killers. The fact is that Haitian society has *always* existed for the benefit of the elite and the suffering of the multitudes has always been ignored. In the past, economic growth and investment from abroad was encouraged, however weakly. Under Aristide, foreign investment has dwindled away and is now virtually nonexistent.

Our lack of attention to economic development in the lands that we pacify is a consistent thread of our policy. This characteristic ignorance in our attempts to establish peace and democracy in foreign lands after we occupy them is echoed in Afghanistan and Iraq. Based on my experience in Haiti, it was already possible to see the emergence of this persistent problem ten years ago. Freedom, democracy, and peace cannot exist in a land crushed by poverty, illness, ignorance, and hopelessness. Here is my story about Haiti and my lessons learned. In the timeless lyrics of Bob Dylan as sung by Janis Joplin, "Freedom is just another word for nothing left to lose." Thus is set forth the theme of this book.

Haiti, the Beginnings

I reported into the 3rd Special Forces Group in July 1994, at Fort Bragg just after the Fourth of July weekend. My first thought was, *God, this is a busy place!* Everybody was running up and down the hallway from the "B-Team" headquarters offices. There were Special Forces teams deploying to Africa and others readying for training missions within the United States. You could just feel the place bursting with activity.

Fort Bragg, of course, was very familiar to me, having been my Special Forces training base in 1993. This sprawling 130,000 acre military reservation is home to the U.S. Army's Special Operations Command (USASOC), Civil Affairs (CA), and Psychological Operations (PSYOP) Command, XVIIIth Airborne Corps, and the famous 82nd Airborne Division.

I reported to my company commander, Major Doug Wisnioski, "The Wiz," as he came to be known, and saluted.

"Captain Bevelacqua reporting as ordered."

He smiled and said, "Have a seat."

"Is it always this busy around here?"

He laughed, "Yeah, it is."

Doug had just taken command a month or two prior, but he had been in the Special Forces for quite some time. He was now in the 3rd Special Forces Group (SFG), having served in the 7th and the 10th Groups as well. The 3rd SFG's area of responsibility was all of the Caribbean and the western part of Africa.

Doug's experience was extremely broad in scope. His sergeant major was a very experienced noncommissioned officer (NCO) who represented the best of the Special Forces. What you would normally find in a conventional line company would be a first sergeant, who was an E8, but in the Special Forces, it was a sergeant major, who was an E9. Sergeant majors are extremely experienced NCOs who have been in the Army normally for at least eighteen to twenty years and they are literally the generals of the enlisted force and you don't want to screw with them.

When I reported to Doug in his small corner office at the end of the building, the first thing he asked me was, "Are you married?"

"Yeah, I just got divorced and I just got remarried."

He laughed "Good, you got that out of the way, because in the Special Forces the divorce rate is at least 50 percent, one out of every two guys, their marriages just don't make it and it's probably higher than that."

After that we made small talk and he said, "You're reporting to ODA336." My team was an Operational Detachment Alpha 336. The Operational teams or A-Teams are the heart and soul of the SF groups—typically we would be the first units on the ground in any deployment. Finally, I was in a unit that "rated."

After the Wiz's welcoming speech, I walked down the hallway and introduced myself to my new team.

ODA336 was made up of a real cast of characters, each of whom would be invaluable in our deployment to Haiti. Everybody had a nickname. There was "Nick," the new guy or "Nasty Nick," depending on the mood that he was in. Nick was probably five feet ten or eleven, kind of stocky, a little chubby, sandy brown hair, had a great sense of humor, and smoked a carton of Marlboros a day. We're talking the unfiltered kind here. Nick was the senior engineer on the team so he was responsible for either blowin' things up or buildin' 'em.

Nick's junior engineer was a gentleman by the name of Mongo. Mongo was a converted Hell's Angels motorcycle club member who decided to get back into the military after he had a break in service, after serving in a Ranger battalion. Mongo told a lot of Ranger Bat stories. Mongo was built like a brick outhouse. His body frame was that of a prizefighter; he probably weighed 220 pounds and stood about six feet tall. He had blonde, long wavy hair, and he had a great way of talking like the boxer Ray "Boom Boom" Mancini—"I'm a fightah." That was Mongo. He also had the ability to multiply three-digit numbers in his head and give you an answer in a matter of seconds. This was very useful when calculating formulas for explosives and other different types of charges for demolition. He was also Nick's nemesis and they fought like cats and dogs.

Next on the team was our senior weapons sergeant, code-named "Joey Buttafuoco." No, Joey wasn't Italian, he was actually an African-American. This guy was extremely physically fit, more so than Mongo, except he was streamlined. He had the skin tone of a Cherokee Indian and the high cheekbone structure of a Native American. His very fine skin made him a really good looking guy. He wore a flat-top haircut, short style, and was a real no-nonsense operator, but he also had a great sense of humor. He spoke excellent French, which would prove to be very useful on our deployments to both Haiti and Africa.

Our senior medic had few redeeming qualities, almost no personality, and very little sense of humor. But, he was a good medic and had a good bedside manner. He was very capable and confident. We just called him Art.

Art's assistant and sidekick was fresh out of the Special Warfare Center (SWC) Q Course and had a number of different code names. In Haiti he was called "Mengele," which was not exactly the name you wanted if you were a medic because it was the name of the infamous Nazi death camp doctor, Josef Mengele. But, it was all tongue-in-cheek. He was also called "Cornholio," and I guess he got that from the *Beavis and Butthead* TV show. But Mengele, or whatever you called him, was quite the character. He was built low to the ground, had a small frame, probably five feet six or seven, weighed 140 pounds, could run like a gazelle, and would not back down from anything. Mengele was extremely determined to stand his ground against all oppressors. He was also a skilled medic.

The Q Course, more commonly referred to as Swick, every year has about 850 men that were selected for the medical training, but only about 600 actually made it. Medics have the longest training of any in the SF, everything from the "Goat Lab" to actual internships with the busiest trauma labs in the States. They are a fully qualified emergency medical technician (EMT) when they leave the military.

Then there is our senior communications (commo) man, code named "Vince," nickname "Dr. Pepper," Vince was unique. Usually he was the most solid guy on the team for providing advice and guidance and being there for me as a detachment commander and that was a good thing. But, when Vince went into his infamous shut-down mode, he became the largest distraction on the team, and really at times was my nemesis. I have to say, all in all, Vince was usually the voice of reason and truly did provide key assistance when it was needed. Vince stood about six feet tall, had a thin body structure and frame, maybe 155–160 pounds. He had short brown hair, and was a pretty serious guy. He could also go toe-to-toe with Nick on the consumption of cigarettes. More importantly, he definitely knew his commo gear.

The junior commo man, "Nutley," as in you're a nut, had a very strange sense of humor. He was a good commo man, always upbeat. Nutley always saw the glass as being half full and was instrumental in keeping up morale and providing some entertainment for the team while on deployment.

But, Nutley had a bad temper, as I personally found out. I don't think there was a guy I have described that, when pushed to the point of mass saturation for aggravation and BS, didn't have a tendency to go nuclear-ballistic. I include myself as the detachment commander in that description. The only guy that didn't have this quality, and he should have, was the team sergeant. A Special Forces team sergeant is a cat of a different breed. These guys were typically the Jacks of all military occupation skills within the Special Forces. They had on a number of teams for several years, typically were jumpmaster qualified and HALO (parachute high-altitude, low-opening) qualified. Some were SCUBA (self-contained underwater breathing apparatus) qualified, they had been through the Survival, Escape, Resistance, and Evasion (SERE) course, and they were skilled in all the different duties of being a Special Forces NCO. In the Special Forces, the officers did not make it special; it's the noncommissioned officers who did that.

These desirable qualities and traits, however, didn't exist in my team sergeant. I got one of the worst team sergeants you could ask for. Now this guy, code-named "Tango," was very physically fit, and I guess that's about where it stopped as far as his redeeming qualities. He possessed little to no common sense. Tango was the type of guy who walks up to a door that says "Pull" and proceeds to break the door down because he can't get it open when all he has to do is pull it instead of push it. Tango was also the kind of guy that couldn't see the forest through the trees and I'll explain that in further detail. He was a real paisley wallpaper personality kind of guy. He was totally white or opaque in his personality and color of skin. He had just gotten to the team probably a month before me, so they were getting to know him and I could tell by the way that the guys were all either talking about him or talking with him that Tango just wasn't going to fit in.

The team was short on personnel as most teams in the Special Forces were. I only had eight guys and we should have had twelve. I was missing a couple of key positions. We didn't have a team technician, who was typically a warrant officer, we didn't have a team intel (intelligence) sergeant, and we didn't have a junior weapons sergeant, either, but you go with what you've got and you make the best of it.

Our first deployment as a team occurred in August 1994. We deployed to Fort Campbell, Kentucky, to conduct team training and were there for two weeks. We had a chance to get to know each other. We spent two weeks in the 5th Special Forces Group isolation facility, also known as an ISOFAC. An isolation facility was what a team moved into prior to deployment on a mission. It was just that. It was an ISO-lation FACility. It kept you away from everything and everyone that didn't have anything to do with the mission. The facility was broken down into a number of different rooms, or holding chambers, where the team could conduct planning for their mission, house their equipment, do combat equipment checks, go through pre-deployment checks, palletize their gear, and prepare for deployment. While we were there, we trained on a mission that simulated a snatch of one of our team members who had been captured. We worked with a local indigenous force leader played by one of my NCO buddies from the Q Course, David Gibbs. We planned for this mission, which called for a fairly lengthy infiltration over broken terrain, through large erosion ditches, across streams, and things of that nature. Finally, we came to a facility where guards had been holding one of our guys and then we basically conducted a raid.

On our first night of the infiltration, Tango and I decided to put the team into a clandestine patrol base to get some sleep—two or three hours worth. We sat in a straight column of twos back-to-back. One man stays awake and monitors the radio during his shift and awakens his relief when his shift is done. I am sitting on the end of the line with no one on my left and I feel something press hard against my left leg and then cross over my boot—oh shit, it's a BFS (Big F***in' Snake)! Well slap me in the mouth and call me a pussycat. I leaned over to Nick and announced what just happened and the general mood of the team was, "Let's move out ASAP, who the hell needs sleep?"

It was experiences like this that would bind us together as a team, and more importantly, we had a chance to work together, to do planning, and see how each of us worked under situations of physical stress, sleep deprivation, and giant snakes. For the most part, everybody performed well, even Tango. It was then that I realized I had a pretty solid team and we just needed to do some work together, refine some standard operating procedures, and we would function just fine in a real-world combat situation. This was also the first time that I gave a heads-up to the team that something was brewing in Haiti and that we may have a chance to go into combat.

After returning to Fort Bragg I bumped into one of my old buddies from the Q Course, Tony "Schwammy" outside his B-Team headquarters. Tony was the Bravo Company commander. We talked a little bit. He told me something was definitely up for Haiti and that he was involved in the planning process. He said he would be coming back and giving us some follow-up information if the green light was given. I would deploy with his company. We would be attached to the 2nd Battalion of the 3rd Special Forces Group. Normally, we were in 1st Battalion, but a task force was being put together that really didn't follow the organizational lines of the group; it was more like an ad hoc organization. The Army had a real bad habit of doing this, just throwing sh** together and seeing if it worked, instead of going with a typical task organization that a unit had. Actually, we had picked up this technique from the German *Wehrmacht* in World War II. It didn't work all that well for them either, did it?

The word came down pretty fast, and I was told that I had to meet with Schwammy over in his company with some of the other detachment commanders that were being assigned to this task force, code named "Task Force Raleigh."

In regard to what was happening in Haiti, Jean-Bertrand Aristide, a Roman Catholic priest, had been elected president in 1990. Less than a year later he was overthrown in a military coup by General Raoul Cedras. This revolt triggered U.N. sanctions and warnings about human rights abuses. The big problem for the U.S. was the TV pictures of Haitians crowded on the most unbelievably flimsy rafts and boats trying to float to the U.S. mainland. Many of them didn't make it. The outcry was so loud that the Clinton administration finally decided to do something about it.

The idea was that Cedras needed to be taken down and Aristide restored to his position as president.

We met in the Bravo Company orderly room and Schwammy came in with his B-Team. The B-Teams were the company headquarters personnel responsible for the isolation, launching, and recovering of their Special Forces teams. They came in with a number of yellow packets, target information packets (TIP). These packets were typically put together by higher headquarters and contained all the necessary information about the assigned targets. All of this came in a mission folder. This was the beginning of what became known as Operation Uphold Democracy.

Schwammy gave us a quick rundown. There was going to be an invasion of Haiti and some of us would be attached to the Ranger regiment. We would go in as part of a joint task force (JTF 180) commanded by the XVIIIth Airborne Corps. Elements of the Ranger regiment were to be inserted with us. We were assigned specific targets that we were required to either neutralize or stabilize. The target packet I was handed was for a town called Les Cayes on the southern Caribbean coastal side of the southwestern peninsula, or "claw" as it was known. This would be the first opportunity that I would have to use my French that I'd just learned in six months of language school. Haitians speak French, and those who don't speak French speak Haitian Creole, which is, I'd have to say, altogether different than French.

We went into isolation in our own team rooms and prepared for deployment to Haiti. We were going to be launched to an intermediate staging base, an ISB, at Guantanamo Bay, Cuba ("Gitmo"). We had orders to prepare our gear and equipment for palletization and be prepared to move out within six or seven days.

The 3rd Special Forces Group didn't have an isolation facility like the 5th Special Forces Group, so we turned our team rooms into an isolation facility within our company compound. I opened up our TIP and pulled out of the packet a great number of photographs, obviously taken by human intelligence sources that were on the island, aerial photographs taken by reconnaissance aircraft, and overhead satellite imagery. Also included in the packet was a written assessment of some of the characters that we would encounter. This was the intelligence we would have to go on. We were given instructions to go to the main police or military garrison and either gain their support or establish control over them. In Haiti, the military is known as the *Forces Arméese d'Haiti* (FAd'H) and was really a national police force. Another organization called *Front Revolutionnaire pour l'Avancement et le Progrès d'Haiti* (FRAPH) was feared by the populace as a political death squad.

The main garrison in Les Cayes was believed to contain 250 soldiers and policemen. Additionally, they had the ability to recruit a militia from the streets; they had actually been seen marching around. They handed out weapons to these guys and, bang, they had 400–1,000 militiamen.

I had an eight-man team and we received two additional bodies, "Pat" and "Goofy." Pat was a very large guy; he became the junior bravo, which was a weapons sergeant. He was about six feet two, a good-looking guy, dark hair, well-built, very muscular, very serious, an intent guy with a great personality. So, he was welcomed to the team. Goofy was a former Wolfhound from the 27th Infantry Regiment out of Fort Ord and quite the character. Goofy had reddish brown hair, very stocky, a deep southern drawl, and spoke perfect French. Goofy's job was the official jack-of-all-trades—I really scored by getting these two guys. Now we were up to ten men, really lean and mean.

We began the planning and preparation phase for going into the garrison. The orders we had were vague to say the least. We were told to go into the garrison and establish rapport with the military and notify them that a new sheriff was in town, "We're here to work with you, not against you." Determining whether or not they wanted to fight or if they were gonna be cooperative was the issue. How do you do that?

Well, you do it by sticking your butt out on the line and giving armed Haitians the opportunity to act hostile toward you—to shoot you or in some other way initiate hostile contact. This was what the manuals call a semi-permissive environment. Instead of just doing what we were supposed to do, and declare them the enemy, declare them the bad guys, and go in and kill them, we had to go in and see if they wanted to kill us, and, if so, return the favor. If this is designed to save lives while satisfying the political correctness spewing out of Washington DC it's rather pathetic.

Our planning focused on how we were going to move into a 250-man garrison with ten guys and establish contact with them? If we were fired upon, we had to return enough firepower to convince them that resistance was futile. The way we planned to do that was with the help of an AC-130 Spectre gunship. For those of you who haven't seen an AC-130 in action, it is literally the wrath of God on earth. When you walk upon the earth with an AC-130 providing cover for you, you are a giant. So we pre-plotted targets for the AC-130 and the plan was to use both indirect and direct fire. The AC-130 would light up a couple of targets that we had pre-designated with its 40 mm Bofors and its 105 mm cannon. We had 81 mm mortars and M60 machine guns that we would set up in an overwatch position. This position was near the garrison site where we could see the compound and lay fire on it if the reception team received any type of resistance. Since I was on the reception team, it basally meant after I was dead and they drug my stinking carcass out of there we were authorized to dust everyone...hell of a plan! A real semi-permissive environment.

That was our plan and it didn't get any fancier than that. We were not talking about shooting from the hip anymore. The things we had to coordinate, rehearse, and practice were brought sharply into focus. We practiced room-clearing techniques and securing the soccer field for our forced entry into Les Cayes. We were setting down in a CH-47 Chinook helicopter in the soccer field with one Humvee and then driving over to the garrison. The garrison was probably half a klick down the road. The soccer field was surrounded by an eight-foot-tall cement wall with bleachers on one side and two small openings on the other, as are most soccer fields in Haiti. The idea was that in the event of a soccer riot, the crowd could be controlled at those small openings. The portals in the wall were just big enough to allow the Humvee to pass through. This was our plan.

We began to palletize our equipment and went to the arms room to draw our weapons. Vince drew an M24 bolt action sniper rifle, as he was sniper-qualified, as well as an MP5. The MP5 is a "P" version which is a small Bullpup model we call the "chatter gun." Everyone else drew the standard M16-A2 rifle and a 9 mm pistol for a sidearm. Joey Buttafuoco drew a Sten gun, which was an old British weapon first used in World War II. He also drew an M24. Mongo, of course, drew the M60 machine gun for us—"Dah, okay, boss," Jimmy says as he checks out his gun—*God help me,* I muttered to myself. There were not a lot of M60s left in the inventory, so we were happy to have it. This gun was something that puts out good suppressive fire, 7.62 mm with a great effective range, allowing engagement of targets at 600+ meters. Tracer rounds are inserted into the belts so you can see where your fire is going. With a cyclic rate of fire of 550 rounds per minute, you could establish a wide kill zone pretty quickly.

We also drew the two 81 mm mortars that we needed. Most of all, we got lots of ammunition, frag grenades, M-72 LAWs (light anti-tank weapons), some AT4s (shoulder-fired anti-tank missiles), claymore mines, C4 plastic demolition explosives, and *beaucoup*—there's my French—5.56 mm rounds for the M16s.

As we palletized our gear, I was not overly comfortable with the plan because it seemed like we were missing a lot of information, but I knew we had more time to plan once we got to the initial staging base in Gitmo.

I went home that night to celebrate my birthday, which is September 11. I told my wife that it looked like we were going to leave tomorrow. We had only been married a couple of months and it was hard to believe I was getting ready to leave for an indefinite period of time. We were told we would be home within a year. We ordered pizza. I didn't sleep well at all.

I got up the next morning, got dressed, laced up my boots, and told my new wife, "I really can't believe I'm gettin' ready to do this. You know, a week from now, I'm gonna be at war." I patted my dog, Yukon, a Siberian husky. He was just a pup, maybe four months old, and I climbed into the truck with my wife and she drove me to the post. It was incredible the amount of small details you recall, surrounding a huge event.

After I said goodbye to her, which was probably the hardest part, I could feel the sense of camaraderie and concern in the other team members, because we all had just gone through the same thing. Most of the guys were married and had kids and when you say good-bye to the ones you love, it's a gut check and it's a reality check; there is that great unknown looming on the horizon. There was also an incredible sense of excitement and commitment about what we were getting ready to do. The air was filled with so much freakin' energy you could cut it.

We palletized our gear on 463L pallets, which were large, aluminum skids and we netted them, had them picked up by forklifts, had then thrown on the back of large vehicles called family of medium tactical vehicles (FMTVs), and moved to the famous Green Ramp at Pope Air Force Base. We then got on FMTVs and trucked out to meet with the rest of the guys. The Green Ramp facility was on the corner of the Air Force Base right next to the runways where guys went to get 'chuted up' with the help of jumpmasters, to embark on aircraft to conduct an airborne mission. Pope Air Force base was basically surrounded by Fort Bragg and was mainly used as a lift-off point for the 82nd Airborne.

Well, we weren't jumping, we were flying into Gitmo. We boarded our aircraft, which was a civilian jumbo jet with our very heavy rucksacks and were bound for Cuba.

Once in Cuba, we had to set up camp, basically our tent city. We were maybe a kilometer from the runway and we had a large, grassy area to set up our tents, and that was where we stayed in isolation until given the orders to launch.

The 3rd Special Forces Group was in one area and nearby was the 2nd Ranger Battalion that was supposed to go in with us.

We continued to plan and go through different scenarios. We received our ammunition and began packing it in our rucksacks, jamming magazines, vest pockets, cargo pockets, you name it and it carried something. I started to get a little concerned about the size of our rucksacks. The lightest rucksack was about ninety-five pounds, that one was carried by Mengele. The heaviest rucksack was Mongo's at 146 pounds. With a 146-pound rucksack, a Kevlar helmet, a load-bearing vest with all your ammunition, canteens, and your M16 rifle, you didn't move very fast—in fact, you don't move. Then slap on a Ranger body-armor flak vest, with a chicken plate on your front and back and at that point we should have been issued Bradley fighting vehicles! Not to mention that we were doing this in September, which was still very warm, so heat exhaustion and dehydration were all going to be big factors. When you put that "North Carolina tick," which was the nickname for the rucksack, on your back, it becomes a life-sucking parasite, it saps the strength of the strongest men, I don't care if you're a pro-football player for the NFL or Andre the Giant (for you WWF fans) it's gonna suck the strength out of you and it will break the strongest man. Do I need to say more about the ludicrous idea of women in the Special Forces?

This was really one of my big concerns going in, because our "rucks" were just unrealistically heavy, but we had to carry mandatory TOE (table of organization and equipment). We must have redundancy in communications and the radios were early 1980–90 tech stuff. We had very heavy radios that I referred to as boat anchors. You could basically tie a rope to them, throw them overboard, and they would keep a battleship in place. Then you needed to carry a generator in order to recharge the radio batteries. That, coupled with a host of other pieces of equipment that we had to have, weighed us down. All of it got heavy very fast.

While in Gitmo, I asked one of the intel officers if I could get specific information on the buildings in our compound. In Les Cayes, we had probably the second or third largest town in Haiti with a population of about 150–200,000 and a good-sized police garrison. As a demonstration, if the sh** hit the fan when we tried to get into the compound, I wanted to pump 105 mm rounds from Spectre into one of the buildings and cause maximum damage to a specific target.

I was told that this one building in the back of the compound, known as a *magasin,* or storage building, would serve as a good target for the demonstration. It was a good-sized building; it appeared to be a large structure away form the main barracks where the soldiers bunked. We got the information about the *magasin* from the CIA. It turned out to be really bad intel.

Lesson Learned: The day prior to U.S. forces going to Haiti, Jimmy Carter, Senator Sam Nunn, and Colin Powell flew into Port-au-Prince, negotiated with General Cedras, and changed the nature of the mission from an invasion to basically a walk-on. This was why Jimmy Carter was the Nobel Peace Prize winner, because he created a big peaceful environment for us. I should add that Carter seriously invited Cedras to teach Sunday school at his church in Georgia; this man whose hands were dripping with blood. He also joked about "getting cooties" from shaking Aristide's hand. You may wonder what color the sky is on Carter's home planet! What was he thinking?

What was not talked about was the fact that because it was a walk-on, we didn't kill the bad guys. The bad guys were still alive and well in Haiti. They will be for the foreseeable future. The bad guys we didn't kill are the ones committing the same types of crimes that caused the miserable environment that led to people fleeing Haiti in boats. It is still happening. If you think this isn't a problem, look at what is going on in Iraq today. Our slick-fingered politics under the leadership of Paul Bremmer have caused nothing but problems—Jimmy and Paul should get a blood test and get married.

The mission we were now given was to create a peaceful and stable environment for the return of the deposed president, Jean-Bertrand Aristide. A deal had been cut with Raoul Cedras. He was going to be paid twenty-five million dollars and was going to be set up somewhere in South America and the United States of America would rent out his house in Haiti, of course, for which he will be paid money—can you believe this crap?

So this was what the Nobel Peace Prize winner Jimmy Carter did for us. This was a great and wonderful thing he did. But, some of you may get the impression, after reading what I have to say, that this was a big scam and a rip-off that, in the long run, perpetuated a bad situation in Haiti. I hope that you get that impression and I also hope you can draw the connection between what we didn't do right in Haiti that has led to the situation we see there today.

Now, after Jimmy's help, I had to go to the town of Les Cayes, move in with the same group of people I was gonna kill a day prior, eat with them, sleep with them, live and work with them. We were all gonna hold hands and sing *Kum Ba Yah*. We had a complete change of the rules of engagement (ROE); the fags in the JAG (Judge Advocate General or legal office) came in, gave us a new briefing, and told us the new ROE, and we went from being able to basically shoot anyone with a rifle to "Well, you know, if they're not posing a direct threat to you, and if they don't seem to be doing anything that causes a level of concern, then you can't do anything."

So, in other words, I could have five guys walk by me with rifles, we could talk to them, exchange pleasantries, and if there didn't seem to be any problem when they went by me, they could then swing around, open up, and shoot me in the back. And that was what happened. Well, that's just great—hey it's a semi-permissive environment.

So here was a stable and secure environment for you. Now this semi-permissive environment, I'll tell ya, could be just as lethal as a non-permissive environment because you had to wait for the enemy to strike. Make no mistake about it, we had enemies there, only we were to wait and let them open up on us first. You can't initiate, there's no element of surprise, there's no gaining of the initiative; you're basically bait, walking around to be bit in the ass by a piranha. Thank you very much, Jimmy Nobel Peace Prize-Winning F***ing Carter.

So after weeks and months of detailed planning, everything was changed. In a matter of twenty-four hours, we were going to go into Haiti in a totally different configuration. The forces deployment list had changed and units that were going to go in, like the 82nd, had been recalled. JSOC, the Joint Special Operation Command had been recalled, Special Military Units had been recalled, and the 10th Mountain Division was going in with the 3rd Special Forces and was now in charge—Katie bar the door. On the seventeenth of September, we boarded a CH-53 Sea Stallion and flew from Guantanamo Bay, Cuba, to Port-au-Prince Airport. Keep in mind; we still had the same equipment loads, even though we were not going into combat. My rucksack probably weighed around one hundred and twenty pounds so we weren't moving fast. We loaded up the aircraft and took off with 10 CH-53s in our sortie.

Insertion into Haiti

We flew in early in the morning about two hundred feet off the deck at about 130–140 knots. We did an in-flight refueling behind a KC-130, which was a C-130 outfitted as an aerial tanker. I tell you, that was a rough ride. Two birds simultaneously feeding off the back end of a KC-130 at 130–140 knots in a prop wash. It was a pretty fun ride, pretty entertaining. I got some great pictures of it. I wish I had filmed the leaking hydraulic cherry juice dripping on Joey's face.

We refueled and finally arrived at the island; it was probably an hour and a half flight, and we landed at Port-au-Prince Airport. We got all the teams off the choppers, split them up, spread out, and established a normal security perimeter. This was our first chance to get a good look at Haiti.

All my guys who'd been to Africa said Haiti was very similar in the way the buildings were constructed; the perimenter walls around buildings had glass embedded on top of them to keep unwanted visitors out. The walls around compounds were actually mortared in so they provided a little bit of protection. The overall appearance of the island was very similar to what you see in Ghana, Benin, or Côte d'Ivoire (the Ivory Coast), and countries of that nature in western Africa.

We had our instructions. We had to move off the airfield and go into a holding area on the northern portion of the Port-au-Prince Airport. We set up camp there for what we thought was going to be a very short period of time, but it turned out to be several days of sitting in very hot weather and waiting to get our movement instructions. The reason we were held there so long was because General Mead, the 10th Mountain Division commander, wanted to be briefed on what all the teams were going to do in the different towns. He wasn't sure he liked the idea of the Special Forces going out into the hinterlands. This infuriated us as well as our commander, who was the joint special operations task force commander, Brigadier General Dick Potter. Potter was a legend from the Vietnam era and a really fantastic guy to work for, if he liked you. If Dick Potter didn't like you, and you were on his radar screen as being a dirt bag, oh you had a world of hurt coming down. Fortunately for me, Dick Potter was on my side.

We finally got some scuttlebutt that the general's meeting degenerated into a yelling contest and General Potter actually threw an MRE at General Mead's head, which earned an incredible amount of hero worship from us—even if the story wasn't true, we needed someone to vent our anger for us. After that bizarre scene, we were told we could move out to our different areas.

I loaded up with my team and two others on CH-47s and we flew to the lovely resort town of Jacmel, southwest of Port-au-Prince, across the claw on the Caribbean Sea. The population was about fifteen thousand. There were six CH-47s with Humvees sling-loaded underneath them in our flight. We were probably about two thousand feet off the deck and I could see us lining up and coming in on the final approach. We were landing on an unimproved airfield, basically a five-hunrded-foot strip of grass in the middle of an open area. As we circled and got ready to come in, you could see the Haitians gathering around, thousands of them coming out of the town. They were all wearing different, brightly colored clothing and T-shirts, quite visually stunning. Haiti was, by the way, the land of the forgotten T-shirt. If you've ever turned in a T-shirt to Goodwill, you know the yellow ones with the smiley face, "Disco Sucks," different things of that nature, they all went to Haiti. Every T-shirt you ever owned as a kid and had given to Goodwill wound up in Haiti and the Haitians were all wearing them.

As I was watching all these people scurry around and rush up to our LZ, our choppers were getting closer. I have to tell you, the prop wash from a CH-47 is nothing to screw around with. It really got to blowing and we're talking Hurricane Isabelle. Its seventy-five-knot winds blowing down on you will knock you over—I don't care how big you are. As the locals started to crowd around the airfield, we knew we were in for quite a reception. Up until then we really hadn't talked to any Haitians outside of the Port-au-Prince area, so we weren't really sure what to expect. You flick a switch and go from being an invasion force to just a friendly "we're-here-to-make-you-safe" force. We were not real sure how the people were going to receive us. The real world just didn't operate quite that fast.

Our chopper came in, pulled pitch, flared a little bit, landed, and we came off the back of the aircraft carrying rucksacks that were just kicking our butts. We lumbered over and dropped into a circular perimeter around each of our birds. The people started to come closer to us. We were lyin' down in prone positions, in a defensive manner to protect the aircraft and pointin' our guns at them and I realized, *Hey, these are civilians.* This was not a hostile environment, it was a semi-permissive environment; so we had to downgrade our level of defensiveness and we had to show them that we were a little trusting toward them. So I slung my weapon, walked over to the crowd, and took off my boonie cap. My boonie cap had an orange VS17 panel on the inside. The VS17 panel was typically used for signaling aircraft and I waved that at the crowd, smiled, and they went ballistic! Screamin' and yellin' and singin', they were the happiest group of people I'd ever seen in my life. I said to myself, *Bill Clinton, you made the right choice.* I truly believed what we were doing was right. These were happy people that had been oppressed by a very corrupt and brutal regime under Raoul Cedras.

After we got our gear together, met everyone, and talked to the people, I noticed there were a couple of Haitian military types there. These were the guys that we were supposed to kill a week earlier. I noticed that one of them had a nightstick and was using it to keep the crowd back. I told him to stop doing it. I turn around and I told one of my guys, "If you witness a hostile act, I want you to open up and engage on that guy. I don't care if you kill him or if you wound him, take him out." I specifically told the Haitian military guys, "Do not hit anyone again with sticks in my presence." I believe I said, "*Ne frappez pas,*" which is don't hit, don't beat. They got the message. By the way, I firmly believe English spoken loudly while carrying a gun is understood in 127 different languages.

It's amazing what a little bit of discipline and force will do. You punch somebody in the mouth; they tend not to badmouth you anymore. You dish out all the lip service that we typically do as a nation, and they may not badmouth you to your face, but they're gonna badmouth you behind your back, and what does that equate to? An unstable environment. Thank you very much, Jimmy Carter!

The B-Team assembled in Jacmel and got all the other teams together. That's when we decided to push out to our assigned areas. In our case, Les Cayes. Les Cayes was a large city with a population of around 150–200,000 people with a 250-man garrison and a possible 400-man militia force. I was going in with ten guys and I had been worried about this all along. Hello! Ten guys to two hundred thousand people doesn't sound like a real good force ratio to me. At the last minute, I talked to Colonel Boyette, the 3rd Group commander, and explained to him the situation and my concern and he replied, "What do you need?"

"Well, I'd like to have a couple more A-Teams!"

"You got 'em!"

So I got three A-Teams, plus two PSYOP teams. The PSYOPs teams were the guys equipped with loud speakers and a handful of tapes that had messages in Haitian. You just named the message and the guys had it and they could play it out for you.

We also had a Civil Affairs (CA) team with us, which consisted of a seasoned captain and two senior NCOs, to provide assistance for the nongovernmental organizations, the NGOs and the private voluntary organizations (PVOs), in order to build some of that commercial-civilian cooperation we would need to get Haiti back to a stable environment.

Now I had to plan for not just one A-Team, but three A-Teams, the two PSYOP teams, the CA team, (be careful what you wish for) and oh, by the way, two reporters from the *U.S. News and World Report* and two reporters from the *Christian Science Monitor*. Initially, I said, "Nah! I don't want to have reporters with me, because I don't want anybody peekin' over my shoulder, takin' pictures, and evaluatin' what I'm doin' so they can report it back to people in the world what idiots we all are. I don't like that."

The more I thought about it, however, it made sense in that, if they were with us, and we did see things that were human rights violations going on in Haiti and we were making a difference, they would be there to document it.

Lesson Learned: The fact is that Operation Iraqi Freedom was not the first time that media was embedded with the military. I had media embedded with me in Les Cayes, Haiti, in September of 1994. That was true embedding of media—flying in with you and no one in the outside world knew it.

The only thing that was missing was the ability to send live TV images back to the States. That was a limitation of the technology available at the time, but the media was right there with us. The embedded media was great for getting out the proper message in 1994 as it was in 2003.

The plan I had come up with was to fly into Les Cayes, land at the soccer field, drive up to the main compound, and link up with the commander of the FAd'H garrison to conduct stabilization operations. These operations were mainly to be joint patrols giving us a chance to go out and see the people, assess the situation, and report back to higher command authority.

It was early in the morning of September 27 when we brought all our equipment back to the Jacmel airfield where we had landed five days prior. We put all our team's heavy gear, commo gear, and excess baggage into sling nets to attach underneath the CH-47s when they came in to pick us up. I had my two other teams with me, ODA321 and ODA333, both damn good teams.

The CH-47s were coming in on their final approach and we lined up our bundles to get slung underneath the appropriate aircraft. Since we had teams pushing out and getting launched to a number of different areas, Aquin, for example, or flying into the northern part of the southern claw, you didn't want to get your bundles on the wrong aircraft. It's important for everyone to get his equipment. You also had to recognize the fact that if you got your bundle mixed up, you could always de-conflict it at a later time. But the bottom line was, you were still going to have radios, you are still going to have ammunition—provided, that is, you have at least one bundle.

Well, you know, the aircraft that we thought was going to pick up our bundle didn't, it picked up another team's bundle. In effect our gear was going to head north and the other team's gear was going to go with us.

This sent my team sergeant, Tango, into an incredible gyration, and he went out there with a couple of the guys and convinced the loadmasters to swap the bundles and move the bundles around, so what ended up happening was one chopper grabbed an extra bundle and another had no bundle at all. The team that was launched up north had none of their emergency re-supply equipment with them. After I realized what had happened, I chewed Tango's butt out loudly in front of everyone because I had specifically told him, "Don't screw with the bundles, you're gonna end up f***in' one of the teams," and that's exactly what happened. Guys were going into an area where they had no idea what they were going to face, without any of their emergency backup equipment. Not a good way to run a railroad.

After that short fiasco, we mounted up on two CH-47s with two Humvees slung underneath each of them and our emergency re-supply bundles. We started out for the southern claw in a flight from Jacmel to Les Cayes. Air time was probably forty minutes, and it was over the ocean. Beautiful, the Haiti coastline is really gorgeous. If you've ever been to the Dominican Republic, you've essentially seen Haiti, minus some of the poverty, but the coastline was gorgeous.

We flew in early in the morning, and we were at one thousand feet AGL (above ground level). As we got closer to the city, we circled a couple of times and you could see the people start to come out of their homes. Les Cayes was a built-up city, like I said, around two hundred thousand people and when it started to become obvious that we were headed to the soccer field, they begin to flow there. You can't hide a CH-47; you don't sneak up on anyone in a Chinook, not at a thousand feet. We circled around the LZ a couple of times, and both choppers went in simultaneously. We touched down, dropped off our Humvees, and unloaded in the same fashion we had done before. We started to set up a circular perimeter, except this time the eight-foot wall surrounding the soccer field was completely covered with Haitians. They were all sitting there clapping and chanting and watching us. They were carrying palm tree branches, and they were going into, literally, a tribal demonstration to celebrate the arrival of their liberators.

Our group priest, a Roman Catholic, threw holy water on me, making the sign of the cross as I got off the aircraft and that helped establish rapport with the Haitians. They were very religious, they were very

Catholic, and even in the areas that practiced voodoo, Catholicism was widely accepted. So that really didn't hurt at all.

I stepped off the aircraft with two of my guys. They got our Humvees ready, and I did the same welcome routine again. I took off my hat, waved to the crowd, and they went ballistic. They just loved it.

A very stocky and well-built, healthy-looking Haitian lieutenant came walking out of the crowd. His nickname was "Shaba." Shaba had gone through the Infantry Officers' Basic Course with a buddy of mine. He was well-educated, very articulate, fluent in English and, unbeknownst to us, was dealing with a tense situation back in the police garrisons.

I found out later, from another source, that Shaba had spent most of the morning convincing his garrison commander, Colonel Gideon, not to open fire on us as we came in. It was literally a standoff at the eleventh hour. Colonel Gideon decided just prior to our arrival that he wasn't going to engage us.

> **Lesson Learned:** So what we would have had was two aircraft coming in on a non-attack approach with equipment slung underneath, with guys not ready to defend the aircraft while in flight, and with civilians on board. Thank you very much, Jimmy Carter. It's a miracle things worked out the way they did and we didn't get a bunch of people killed by landing unprepared in a hot LZ, surrounded by a thousand civilians.
>
> The Law of Unintended Consequences is never unenforced and it can be ignored only at the peril of the unwary. Once you set a train of events into motion, such as the invasion of a country, you must let the commanders on the ground set the rules of engagement. To set them from remote command posts an ocean away is the height of folly. This is the hardest thing for leadership to do, despite the trials of Vietnam.

When Shaba introduced himself to me I immediately established rapport with him. We talked about the Infantry Officers' Basic Course, his background, and we mounted up in a Humvee to drive to the FAd'H garrison, which was about half a klick down the road. The two other ODAs went into more or less a holding position near the soccer field in case everything fell apart. They had the ability to secure an area for a bird to come back in and egress us—get us the hell out of there.

So I climbed into my vehicle with Shaba, and as we drove down the street a crowd of at least ten thousand built up around us, singing and clapping and celebrating. I waved to the crowd, thinking to myself, *God, I feel like George S. Patton liberating France.* It was amazing how happy they were. Then I started to notice that the males in the crowd were coming over, getting our attention, and motioning to us to *shoot* their police force, to *shoot* their military, to kill them. "Kill them, kill them." "Kill them and make them dead." *Tuez-les et faites-leur les morts.*

I was thinkin' to myself, *Man, they really hate these guys.* It was just incredible. This was not a good sign of things to come.

We drove down the street with a crowd of *thousands* following us and we pulled into the compound. You can just imagine how the Haitian commander must have felt, looking out at his compound, at the people he has oppressed, and in some cases, tortured and imprisoned illegally for the past ten years. Seeing them outside cheering the arriving Americans—that had to be an ominous and uncomfortable feeling for him; to see that and to feel the support we had from his own people.

> **Lesson Learned:** Again, driving the point home one more time, it's a bad idea to liberate a country from an oppressive and dictatorial regime that has raped and pillaged the people and the country and still leave the senior political and military leadership fundamentally intact. These people should have been dealt harsh justice for what they had done. The fact was they knew we had orders not to touch them, but that would not still the fear they had in their hearts about what their own people who wanted revenge would do to them if they had a chance.

The compound we were in was probably about two acres in size and was completely surrounded by a wall. The wall on the back and two sides of the compound was probably two meters tall, maybe less, some type of concrete, and was painted yellow. The buildings were all painted the same piss-colored yellow and peeling badly.

The main barracks was a two-story building that had a flat roof. The building behind it was a three-story building with a flat roof. There was a radio tower between these two buildings. Behind that was another inner compound, and that's where the storage facility was; the *magasin.*

Shaba led me, Goofy, and one other guy from my team up to meet the FAd'H garrison commander, Colonel Gideon. We walked into his office; he was sitting down behind his desk and he looked just like Bluto, the gross fat-repulsive character immortalized by John Belushi in *Animal House*. He was very large, heavyset, with dark-colored skin, a pockmarked face, and a couple of chins. He was sloppily dressed in his uniform with a pack of Haitian menthol cigarettes on his desk. His lieutenants, dead ringers for the Three Stooges, were sitting off to his right up against the wall, and one of them had very piercing green eyes, a good-looking guy with light-colored skin. He did not take his eyes off me. I was thinking at this point, *He's either gay and wants to bend me over the desk or this guy's got a serious attitude problem.* As I came to find out later on, he wasn't gay.

We sat down and went through the niceties and introductions. At this point, I was speaking only in English. The lieutenant introduced the colonel to me, I was introduced to the Colonel, we shook hands, sat down, and started to talk. The colonel was being translated at this time. As we were talking, I expressed to him that I was there to assist them, to protect them from the La Volas, which is a civilian organization trying to create an insurgency against the FAd'H and against Raoul Cedras in order to facilitate the return of Jean-Bertrand Aristide. I was also there to protect the civilians from the military and the FRAPH, which was a Mafia-like organization with some political agendas. So there were dynamics here that required us to create a buffer between all of them to keep them from killing each other.

Lesson Learned: This is why, when I see things going down in Iraq, I roll my eyes and go, "Oh, man, we're gonna learn this lesson all over again." The fact is there is nothing more difficult than sorting out a political situation between rival factions after you occupy their country. This is especially true if the political infrastructure is left basically intact with powerful people retaining their influence. It took years for the de-Nazification process to work its way out in post-WWII Germany, why would we think it would be any less difficult in Haiti—or Iraq?

After I explained this to the colonel and it was being translated, he said in French to one of his lieutenants, "This young captain has no idea what he's in for."

I replied back to him in French, "Would you mind if you let me have a cigarette? I feel the need to smoke."

He looked at me, surprised, and said, in English, "You speak French?"

"Yes, I do, and you speak English?"

"Yes, I do."

At that point, I think all the mutual BSing was over with and the "let's-get-all-the-cards-on-the-table" moment had finally arrived.

So the deal was this. We would move into the FAd'H garrison compound, sleep there, eat there, and run our operations out of there in conjunction with the Fad'H and do joint patrols. Now, keep in mind, this was the Haitian Police Force, okay? They had not been stood down or sent home, so there was still the presence of law, order, and discipline in the town and in the country.

> **Lesson Learned:** Without law and order the Haitians would have done exactly what the Iraqis did: loot their town and carry out old vendettas. The point is, you can hand out justice to the bad guys in the police and military without taking apart the whole security infrastructure like we did in Iraq. There, we immediately disbanded all police and army units. How can we be surprised at what happened with the looting and settling of personal scores? Was the U.S. Army supposed to police a huge country of twenty-five million people? How could that possibly be considered an option? To use an old refrain, what was the Coalition Provisional Authority thinking...what was the military thinking?

Colonel Gideon agreed to work with us and we started to move into the compound.

The first day in the compound, I watched the guards keep the crowds back. The people were real interested in what we were gonna do. They hoped we were going to go in there, have a firefight, and kill all these guys. Truth be known, that's exactly what we should have done, because these guys were a bunch of murdering, robbing rapists, as we came to find out later on. They should have been shot. Thank you very much, Jimmy Carter.

I watched the Haitian military working with the crowd and I've gotta tell you, I had never seen anything like that in my life. I watched a Haitian military police officer step out into the street with a whip. I saw the crowd scatter like gazelles spooked by a helicopter and just run in different directions, and I mean stomp right over kids and knock them over to get out of this cop's way. The crowd was accustomed to having their butts kicked by their police force. We're talking Rodney King every day whether it was justified or not. That's what these people had lived under.

Later that afternoon, we finally settled down and went on to an all-night shift and sent out a patrol. In our first night there we got very, very little sleep and at that point, I don't think I had eaten anything at all. I set up our command post on top of the roof of the second barracks building just behind the Haitian headquarters building. We established our comms link, we had a sat-com radio, and we also had communications with an AC-130 Spectre gunship whose call sign was "Mummy 68." At that time Nasty Nick wanted to be known as "Nicky 68," because he had established comms with the AC-130. I think maybe the fact that Nickki Sixx was a rock star with Motley Crue had something to do with it as well. Picture Nick with the bill of his patrol cap flipped up like Gomer Pile and a Marlboro cigarette dangling in the corner of his mouth with a smoke trail going into his left eye.

The next morning, we got up and continued to conduct our patrols. I had received word from an informant in the street that there had been a murder the night before. We thought we had heard a single gunshot. A woman had been shot by a man disguised as a woman wearing a dress and underneath the dress he had been wearing a uniform. While I was being given this information, the gentleman who was talking told me, "Behind your back is the guy that actually pulled the trigger."

I thought to myself, Boy, this is great. I have a murder that went down last night, the guy who is being fingered is right behind me, and who do I report this to? Do I report it to the local police? The police, of course, being the same guys I had been expecting to kill a week ago and who were in cahoots here? You know, at that point, we had to take in information, process it, and try and determine whether or not it was valid before we said anything, because you could do more damage than good. This was the beginning of my first lesson in low level-source operations—I had a lot to learn.

The Jail

It was on that day that I was told that what we thought was the storage facility in the back of the compound, the *magasin,* on that one acre of land at the rear of the compound was actually the county jail. One of the team leaders had discovered it; his code name was "Greezy Reezy" and he said, "Hey, Bob, have you seen the jail?"

"Jail? What jail?"

He replied, "That building that the AC-130s have as a pre-plotted target, the one we were gonna put a couple of 105 rounds into, that jail."

"Oh, well, there's a good CIA f*** up for you."

I went back and checked out the jail and I don't think I've ever seen anything more grotesque in my life. I mean, aside from just a dead body. As I walked into the jail, one of the reporters was bent over puking his guts out, so I told myself, *This is going to be as bad as bad can be.*

There were several cells in the jail, and we're talking about a very old building, probably eighty or ninety years old and falling apart. In one cell there were probably thirty people and the youngest didn't look any older than twelve or thirteen, but when you're emaciated and you're suffering from disease and malnutrition, you tend to look a little bit younger than you are. The worst case that I saw was an eighty-year-old gentleman. If you have ever heard nightmare stories about third-world, jails this was it. It made your basic Turkish prison look like a "Club Fed" here in the U.S.

Some of the men picked the old guy up off the floor; his back had open ulcers on it that were the size of grapefruits and went right down through his flesh to his bones. It looked like gangrene was setting in. One gentleman had elephantiasis, a couple of guys were suffering from insect infestation, they had open ulcers with flies and maggots in them, and the odor was unbearable. I was knocked back by the stench when I approached the cell.

The reporters were going in, taking pictures, documenting this, and asking me, "What are you going to do? What're you going to do?" I thought, *This is great!* This was why the press needed to be here. They were documenting human rights violations committed by the Haitian military under the command of Raoul Cedras, which was why he needed to be shot in the head with a large caliber weapon not set up like a king in South America—thank you very much, Jimmy Carter!

After taking in this sight, I pulled back, went to our rooftop command post, got on the radio, and requested to speak with Gunslinger 06, which was the group commander's call sign. I got on the horn with him and gave him a rundown of the situation.

At that time, the Haitians had started to issue M16s to their patrols. Most of their patrols were carrying either an M1903-type weapon, which is a bolt-action single-shot weapon or a pistol sidearm, so when they started to hand out M16s, I became concerned. They realized that we were at a heightened sense of security sensitivity because of what we found in the jail and we had to fix this problem. It had to be rectified. Things appeared to be coming a little unstabilized.

I got on the roof that night and later on in the evening I received a call on the sat-com radio and talked to Outlaw 06. That was Dick Potter, the joint special operations task force commander, and I gave him my assessment of the jail and the gross human rights violations. I also described the way the town was being run and the fear the people had of their military. He told me that he was coming down the next morning and we were to expect him.

Around 07:00 hours, Potter flew in with two UH-60 Blackhawks and a CSAR (Combat Search and Rescue) team. That was the first time I met Dick Potter. He exited the aircraft, walked over to me, and took off his helmet. I was in my soft boonie cap.

"Are you Bevelacqua?" he asked.

"Yes, sir."

He took me off to the side and said, "You painted a pretty goddamned dismal picture on the radio last night. For your sake, I hope it's that bad. I did a video teleconference briefing this morning with the president of the United States and gave him an appraisal of your situation."

"General, I almost f***ing puked."

He grabbed my shoulder and said, "Really...? Ah, thank God, that's good."

This was a little bit of peace and comfort for him. You have to appreciate where he was coming from. He took my word on a radio that the situation that I had seen was bad enough to justify an update for the president of the United States. He trusted me that much. That, ladies and gentlemen, is leadership. That, ladies and gentlemen, is not micromanaging your troops, but trusting your troops. He put his reputation on the line for one of his officers that he never met and I'll never forget it.

> **Lesson Learned:** If we had Dick Potter in charge of CENTCOM, instead of Tommy Franks, we'd have bin Ladin's head on a spike right now because the ODAs that went into Afghanistan would've never been given unrealistic restrictions in their ROE. Potter would have had those guys going into every rabbit hole, pulling the little bastards out by their Buster Browns and killing them. That's what needed to happen in Afghanistan—not calling back five thousand miles, asking permission to engage the bad guys—what horse sh*t! Didn't we see how well this worked in Vietnam?

I loaded General Potter in the Humvee and we drove directly to the compound instead of meeting Colonel Gideon, who was by now sh*tting in his pants when he found out that an American general was coming down to appraise the situation. I walked Potter straight back to the jail cell. We had the old guy with the scars that went down to his bones stand up and come to the front of the bars. Now, these people hadn't showered in months and hadn't been let out of that cell in years, some of them as long as four years, so they were really rancid. Potter took one look at him, turned to his Haitian counterpart, a one-star general from Port au Prince that flew in with him, and said "We can *not* allow people to live like this. This situation *must* be fixed immediately." Then he says to me, "Take me to Colonel Gideon."

I walked the general up to Colonel Gideon's office and he laid it out on the line, "This will be fixed." We had representatives from the local court system, the international Red Cross, and the delegate (local political official) sitting in Bluto's office who were being asked, "Who's responsible for the jail conditions?"

When you get a bunch of politicians in a room it's amazing how quickly they start pointing fingers. I thought, *Tom Daschle was good, no way—these guys are pros at the blame game.* Well, we couldn't pin it down to any one guy, but we decided that the judge or the local magistrate was responsible. He put the people in the jail; he was responsible for the condition of the jail. Potter looked at me and said, "Bevelacqua, get this fixed. I want it fixed by tomorrow."

After a discussion with a couple of the representatives there about fixing the jail, and none of them wanting to own up to being responsible for it, I decided that the judge needed to spend the night in the jail. So we took him and put him in a cell, and he spent maybe twelve hours there. We let him out the next morning—he was a new man, imagine that?

The next day, we had food show up for the prisoners. We had blankets show up and, of course, I put my foot down and said, "They're all getting washed."

We had our medics come in and they got shots for malnutrition, they got tetanus shots, they got physical examinations, they were allowed to walk around the compound, their family members were notified and were allowed to come and visit them. To bring in clothing and things from home and just say, "Hey, I'm alive and I'm doin' okay."

Colonel Gideon was becoming very concerned, because he was losing control; this Bevelacqua was a loose cannon on deck. He didn't like this. That was when I realized there was a lot of tension in the compound and it was getting worse by the minute. I was thinking, *If we stay in this facility, Colonel Gideon and his thugs will kill us.* I requested permission over the sat-com radio late that night to break into the World Relief Organization Compound down the road and occupy it.

Schwammy gave me permission over the radio and said, "Roger, break in, do what you gotta do, watch your ass."

As soon as he lifted his finger off the push to talk button, the lights on the USS *America* lit up. We only had one sat-com channel for this entire operation and it was being monitored, unbeknownst to me, by Joint Special Operations Command (JSOC) and by the 2nd Ranger Battalion, sitting on the aircraft carrier USS *America* offshore. They figured if there was any group of guys that were gonna get into a gunfight, it's gonna be us in this town, because at that time, there wasn't anything else happening on the island.

Finally, I had a chance to take a break and sit down and eat my first decent MRE meal and not have to worry about what was going on around me, because we had kind of a lull in the battle. I was talking to one of the reporters from *U.S. News and World Report* and he was asking about the jail. "What are you guys going to do? Are you going to free the prisoners? What's your next step?"

I was explaining to him what we were trying to do and as we were talking, I saw a Little Bird OH-6 Loach, fly down the Rue de Chevalier, right in front of our compound. Little Birds only belong to one organization, and that's the Night Stalkers. When the Night Stalkers are in town, that usually means that JSOC is in town and that means a Special Military Unit is somewhere in the area.

Then I saw a UH-60 Blackhawk come in. It hovered behind the compound, and then flew over to the soccer field and landed. I said to myself, *What are these guys doin' here?*

I got in my Humvee, drove down to the soccer field and was greeted by the ranger regimental commander, a representative from Seal Team 6, and a representative from the Army's Special Military Unit, the Combat Application Group (CAG). No, I am not going to use their real name.

After I ran these guys over to the compound they pulled out some intelligence that I had never seen on Haiti. They had overhead satellite photographs, ground imagery, a real impressive packet of intelligence that I would have liked to have had my hands on myself, considering I was the guy that went in and actually tried to secure the town. But, you know, when you're a Special Military Unit, you get priority on intelligence.

I asked the ranger regimental commander what the story was, why was he here, and he said, "Look, last night, when you told everyone that you needed to break into the World Relief Compound Headquarters, and that you'd discovered gross human rights violations, and you thought your situation was deteriorating, all the lights on the USS *America* lit up and I'm here to offer you some solutions and some possible courses of action."

One of the options was to snatch an individual. Now what was really funny was that the representative from the Army's Special Military Unit asked me to "Take a look at one of these guys standin' on the balcony right now that's lookin' at us." I look up and it's Green Eyes, and he says, "That guy's gonna be a problem. If we do a snatch operation to pull somebody out and interrogate them on the carrier, we want to grab this dude."

He was absolutely right, because Green Eyes was the one who ended up shooting Don Halstead in the back.

It was the first time I had ever operated with guys from a Special Military Unit; no-nonsense, very serious looking, very intimidating guys and I had never considered myself to be, you know, overly physically fit or someone that had the ability to intimidate people. These were the guys

I would not want to bump into in a dark alleyway. The representative from Seal Team 6 was bald, very heavyset, and looked like he could eat nails and piss out a barbed wire fence. The guy just looked incredible. The Haitians were looking at them, as well, thinking, we really don't want to screw with these guys. But some of them didn't have the brains enough to figure out that if they pushed us too far, that they would receive the wrath of God.

I had only about an hour to put together three options for our Black Ops guys that were going to come in from the carrier if we needed them. We put those options together, we discussed them in as much detail as we could, and then they flew away. I'm not sure if any of this had been coordinated with group headquarters, but I would be happy to see them if we needed them and some times it is better to ask for forgiveness than beg for permission.

We moved into the World Relief Organization Compound and made friends with one of the ladies working there, Marguerite was her name, and this was a great compound. It was a two-story structure with about ten different rooms in it. It was surrounded by a wall with broken glass shards on top, and a sliding gate that was very strong, very defendable.

It had a generator, so we could generate our own electricity, which was key in Haiti at the time. They didn't have reliable power in Les Cayes. There were lots of rolling blackouts, which were really being used as punishment by the military. Doesn't this sound familiar? Repressive government tactics. Exactly!

What we wanted to do was make our presence felt on the street and I didn't want to necessarily do it just in joint patrols. I wanted to send out our own patrols, because when you run a joint patrol, when we were moving with Haitians, we were not getting the same intelligence off the street. People were not going to come over to us, befriend us, and give us information against the military while they were standing there. So we put our own guys out, really to collect intelligence and start the beginning of what is known as a low-level source operation. I can't go into great detail on exactly how this was done because it's classified, but basically what you were doing was establishing rapport with the people and collecting information from the street.

On one particular night, one of the patrols was Vince, Goofy, and, Mongo. These were the kind of guys you don't want to piss off in the middle of the night. They were patrolling down Rue du Chevalier when a

Land Rover-type vehicle came speeding down the road. The driver pulled right up to them, swerved over, and attempted to run them off the road. One of them called in a bit later and said, "Hey, we almost got run over by a vehicle that's heading in the direction of the compound."

I said, "Roger, understand, just keep me advised."

It happened again later that same night, and that time the window was rolled down and they could see it was Colonel Gideon and he was drunk. I had Bluto running around with three of his lieutenants, yes, including Green Eyes, shit-faced in a car loaded down with guns. They all had automatic weapons on them.

I said, "Enough of this bullshit. It's time to get ornery." So I call up Schwammy, the B-Team commander in Jacmel, and gave him an appraisal of the situation.

He said, "Roger, understand. If it happens again, defend yourself. If you have to capture the colonel, capture the colonel. If he resists arrest, do what you have to do."

"Roger that."

Well, just short of getting on the horn and saying, "Kill the f***er" to the patrol, I was preempted by Bluto, who pulled up in front of the compound demanding to talk to me. That was the dumbest thing I've ever done in my life. I was in a sleep cycle, so I had just been woken up and I was not in uniform. I walked outside to meet him. Of course, I had a couple of my guys there with weapons. He proceeded to tell me in French that we must have discipline, I had no discipline in myunit, my guys could not patrol by themselves, and we must work together. Basically, I was not doing this properly.

So I took my ass-chewing from him. I said, "Sir, I understand. I think we should talk tomorrow." I looked at one of his lieutenants and he was sober, we made eye contact and I could see he understood the gravity of the situation. At that point, I put my emotions in check and attempted to deflate the tension—I schmoozed Bluto and the car drove away into the dark.

The next morning, I told my guys, "All right, we're going downtown, I've had enough of Gideon's crap." We kept getting intelligence reports about the police station. So we went downtown to kick over the hornet's nest. We went to the local police station which was in the center of Les Cayes, and the officer of day wasn't there, bad for him, good for us.

There were a couple of sergeants at the station and they would soon feel the wrath of pissed NCOs because my team was fired up. We were ready to get into some shit. Vince was out in front with his chatter gun as he marched into the compound, raised his thumb up, and told a seated guy who was leaning back in his chair to get up. The guy jumped up, Vince turned him around, put him up against the wall, and started frisking him. At that point, it became obvious there was a new sheriff in town.

Vince set the tone for the rest of the team. We were going to turn this place upside down, and we proceeded to do it. We found weapons they were not authorized to have, automatic weapons and other things that were considered contraband.

One thing we noticed was in the back of the police station there were some small jail cells. I noticed a bunch of women's shoes in a pile, and I asked, "Well, what's the deal with this?" I received some kind of BS answer.

The word on the street was that whenever the cops brought in a woman and raped her or had sex with her, they kept her shoes as trophies. That didn't sit too well with me or the rest of the guys on the team.

We took some of the weapons, and we did an inventory and chewed ass. While we were doing that, a crowd collected out in the streets. We had gone down there in a couple of gun Jeeps. I had desert mobility vehicles, which were hard-shell Humvees, sand-colored, with 50-caliber machine guns mounted, capable of taking out anything the Haitians had.

On that day, for whatever reason, I took a captain's badge the Haitians had given me and I put it on my battle dress uniform and the night before I had cut my hair almost totally off. I had just a short little pinstripe of hair on the top, high and tight and I had my sleeves rolled up, so when I walked out of the police station, they knew I was the guy in charge. We came out of the garrison and I talked to the crowd on the street. I said to them in French, "When you have a problem, you ask for me. I am the enforcer, I will enforce the law. If you have any problems with the *military,* the FRAPH, the attaché, the gendarme, you ask for me." They clapped, they were very happy.

We drove back to the World Relief Compound and I was explaining the situation to Colonel Jones and a couple of the guys that were there. Mike Jones was a mountain of a man with a reputation to back up his demeanor and personality. He had been dispatched to the area now because it was obvious that Les Cayes was going to be a hotspot. We now had a battalion commander and we also had the battalion XO, Major Ray Helton, who was just a great guy.

A couple of my guys went on patrol, went back to the police station and found out that the lieutenants lived in the apartment above it. So they shook up the police station once again to see what was going on. I got a phone call asking me to come downtown. So, I drove downtown with Major Helton and I went up to the lieutenants' apartment. We confiscated some very lethal weapons, small submachine guns, and a few rocket-propelled grenades that fit on the end of rifles, similar to what you may have seen in *Saving Private Ryan*. These fit on the end of an M1 Garand and launch frag grenades and CS gas grenades. While my guys were up there confiscating their gear, I walked into a Mexican standoff. The lieutenants lived in the apartment that was right above the police station. It was a third-story apartment. I walked in and there were my guys, Vince, Mongo, and Joey Buttafuoco, with their guns trained on the Haitians and the Haitians had their guns trained on my guys, all yelling at each other. I thought to myself, *Wow, this is great! All I needed was for one of my guys to pull a Val Kilmer and announce "Say when."*

I managed to talk everybody down and told them the deal. I was taking all their weapons. The lieutenants said, "If you take everything, they're gonna come in and kill us."

I wanted to say, "Well, you know what? You guys probably need to be killed." Instead, I lectured one of the lieutenants, "Look, your people live in fear of you. Okay? You want to talk about the ultimate racism, this is it. You're all the same race, you're all Haitians, but you've decided to create this caste system where the police force is the all-powerful and mighty and can do whatever it wants, and that's neither right nor justified. That's why your people hate you and you need guns to protect yourselves from your own people. That's why we're here on this island. Now give me your goddamned weapons."

We confiscated all their weapons, took them downstairs, and as I stepped outside the building, Colonel Jones said to me, "Hey, Bevelacqua, when you walk outside, you hold that 30-caliber air-cooled machine gun over your head." So I did.

The crowd went wild. They were all chanting, *"Enforcier, enforcier, enforcier."*

They knew me. I'd bonded with the crowd, and they recognized me as the guy who was gonna make a difference here, which was kind of an incredible feeling to be honest with you. I was really beginning to believe in what we were doing. It was a very just cause.

After we confiscated all the weapons, we went down to the Humvee and Major Helton said, "Bob, we need to leave these guys some weapons, we can't have this situation here, where they have no way to protect themselves.

I disagreed with him, but he had the rank, and in the long run, he was probably right, so we gave them back each a personal sidearm so they could protect themselves.

We drove back to our compound and talked about the operations and the way things had gone. I said to Colonel Jones while we were standing out on the porch that night, "Sir, I think we've just increased the potential for violence and our security posture's probably gonna have to be raised. I think we've created some anxiety, here, tension between the forces."

He said, "You're probably right."

We Take a Hit

That night I wanted to conduct a raid on the lieutenant's home who was in charge of the police station downtown. From what I understood, he had a large weapons cache and we were inventorying all the weapons and collecting them from the military. I had intelligence from a source on the ground concerning where this guy lived. It was probably ten klicks away from town.

It was around 23:00 hours at night, when we drove out to his village and made preparations for the raid. Then Nutley received a call on the radio. He whispered to me, "Hey, Captain B, one of our guys has been shot back at the compound."

"Oh, sh**!"

We mounted up in our Humvees and drove back to the compound as fast as we could. As we approached the wall of the compound, we could hear gunfire, so we stopped, dismounted our vehicles, and moved along the wall of the compound toward the front. It was pitch-black that night, I mean, it was like being ten feet down in a well. There was no illumination at all.

Now I had no helmet, my NODs (night observation devices) were in the Humvee because I was not thinking, and I was rushing. I got to the front of the compound and two shots rang out, I heard screaming from inside the compound, and I was thinking, *Oh, this is not good.*

The distance from the front of the wall of the compound to where I and one of my guys stood was about seventy-five meters. I heard one of our guys inside the compound say, "Hey, I see some guys out in front of the wall. Who the hell are they?"

So now they were training their weapons on me. I had shooting inside the building, I had my team split—half of us on the wall, the other half in the vehicles. The other teams that were attached to me were inside the compound, looking at us and thinking we were the bad guys. At this point the tension in the air was broken by a moment of total laughter, when one of my guys leaned over to me and yelled, "I'd suck a dick for my Kevlar right now."

You have to appreciate the situation and understand what it takes to find humor at a time like this. After collecting ourselves from laughing, I tried once again to make contact with the boys inside the compound. Try to yell a code word or a running password while there's gunfire and shouting going on, it doesn't work. Finally, at the top of my lungs, I yelled, "It's Captain F***ing Bevelacqua!" That they completely understood.

We rushed into the compound to assess the situation. Warrant Officer Red and Joey Buttafuoco had already cleared everyone out of the headquarters building—that's what the gunfire was. That's when I found out that Don Halstead had been shot in the back by what we believed were some guys trying to sneak into the compound that night with a bag filled with grenades in an attempt to kill all of us. Don had been seriously wounded, but he did survive. We circled the wagons around the compound and I spent the night on the roof of the barracks talking with an AC-130 gunship that did a spotlight mission for us. An AC-130 Spectre gunship has a very bright IR spotlight with the ability to light up the countryside and make it look like daylight. You could see the infrared illumination with your NODs, but you couldn't see it with the naked eye, so if you were wearing night vision goggles, you could see everything. It was lit up bright as daylight.

After they lit up the street for us, I moved down to the World Relief Compound and we set up a 360-degree perimeter on the roof that night and went into what you would call a hull defilade, just basically getting into a good defensive position.

The AC-130 reported to me that it had what appeared to be a pickup truck vehicle that moved down the street in front of the police station and stopped in front of the lieutenants' building. There was one individual lying down in the back of the pickup truck and there were a couple of guys that assisted him out of the truck. Evidently, whoever Halstead had shot at, he'd hit. Yes, they were the lieutenants. Green Eyes was behind the raid. That was the apartment he lived in; the same guy that had been eyeballing me during the initial meeting, the same dirtbag the guys from the carrier wanted to snatch.

Later on that night, I coordinated with the group in Port-au-Prince for the insertion of a Ranger company into our position for a show of force. There was concern that the situation was going to continue to deteriorate. You have to keep in mind that this was happening less than a year after Somalia (*Blackhawk Down*). The gunfight in Mogadishu was fresh in everybody's mind; eighteen Americans had died in that battle. The last thing anyone wanted to see was a bunch of Green Berets on TV, surrounded and getting slaughtered. So we coordinated to bring in a company of Rangers.

By now the population of Les Cayes had disappeared. On the night that Halstead was shot, the streets were eerily empty. There were no civilians out anywhere and that was not typical for Haiti. Normally at 23:00 to 24:00 hours at night these people were out, the disco clubs were going, and all that kind of stuff. The streets were bare. It was like they knew what happened. They had heard the shots being fired. There had been enough gunfire for them to know something really bad had gone down at the compound. They stayed off the streets. It was very eerie; it was like a ghost town.

The next morning, around 07:30, we marked an LZ for the Rangers, about 150 meters south of the World Relief Compound. A series of CH-47s were flying in, eight choppers in total, to bring in a Ranger company of about 128 men. A fully-loaded CH-47 could carry up to thirty-three troops. There were no vehicles. We linked up with the Rangers and showed them the path to the compound. They moved in and occupied the FAd'H garrison. By now, the Haitian rumor network had opened up communications and put the word out. None of the Haitian military, with the exception of one or two, showed up for work that day.

Colonel Gideon had been relieved of command by a Haitian brigadier general the day prior, and his replacement was Major Ira, who I compared to a rabbit sh*tting razor blades. That's about how put together this guy was. Major Ira disappears after the Halstead shooting, as did most of the others, including Shaba. So the Rangers came in, we moved them into the compound, and then we commandeered a white-colored two-and-a-half-ton civilian truck we called "the paddy wagon" to move the Rangers around, because we were going to conduct a series of raids.

The first raid I wanted to conduct was on the lieutenants' apartment. Intelligence later told us that we missed the lieutenants by literally minutes.

> **Lesson Learned:** Once again, when I watch what's going on in Iraq, and what happened in Afghanistan, I know exactly what the guys are going through. This is not easy, though it's really nice to sit back home thousands of miles away in your air-conditioned house and do an analysis based on what's happening on the ground, and how the guys continually screw it up. But when you're in there, and your head's in the game, and you're dealing with the fog of battle and massive amounts of information and you have to make extremely fast decisions based on what's in your head, it's a different ball game. This is especially true when your personal butt and those of your men are on the line. The fact that our guys bagged Saddam is testimony to their skills and perseverance—God bless 'em.

We loaded up our three Humvees with a couple of teams (my team and one other team), the paddy wagon with maybe twenty-five Rangers, and we drove downtown. We off-loaded probably one or two city blocks from the objective and went in on foot. I had the point with two other guys, and the Rangers were behind us. I identified the police station and showed them the location of the lieutenants' apartment. The plan was for the Rangers to raid the lieutenants' apartment, go up to the third floor, and clear the building as they went. While that was going on, my team would raid the police station. After the raid, we were told that the lieutenants had left their apartment building maybe two minutes before we arrived.

There were no people in the streets, because they knew there was going to be a gunfight, and, like I said, Somalia was fresh on everyone's minds, so the first person that flicked so much as a booger finger at us was probably going to get shot 163 times. After Don had been shot, we were real serious. To quote one of the Rangers that came in, "It's payback time, sir." We wanted to blow away some people, we really did. I was gonna have regrets for the rest of my life if we didn't kill those damn lieutenants.

We started down the street and separated. My team broke off to the left, the Rangers went straight ahead. Keep in mind that the lieutenants' apartment was connected to the police station. We went into the police station and we didn't so much search it as destroy it. They had a large television set, they had bookshelves with glass, and they had a case on the wall that held the Officer's Duty List—stuff like that had glass. We basically broke everything that was breakable: chairs, tables, desks. We turned the place totally upside down and deliberately trashed it.

While we're doing that, the Rangers went in and started to clear the three-story structure that the lieutenants lived in, one floor at time, using flash-bang stun grenades. If you were in a room when a flash-bang goes off, you were pretty much incapacitated for a couple of seconds, your ears were ringing and you were dizzy; you're just about unconscious and if it went off right next to you, you're knocked out.

So they started clearing the building, the explosions were going off, smoke was coming out, and the Rangers were dumping into the building a couple of fire teams at a time, making their way up to the top apartment. As they were doing that and we were trashing the police station, the rest of the Ranger element that came in on foot secured the block and cordoned it off, so it was secured from any type of counterattack.

I was standing in the street, talking to Colonel Jones while the Rangers were doing their thing. I told him what General Potter had asked me two days before, "Bevelacqua, what do you need?"

I had replied, "Sir, I need another Humvee; I'd like to get a heavy machine gun with it, another 50-cal; we need our own 500 gallon fuel blivit (container that can be slung under a chopper), and we need some more ammunition." It was not that we had been shooting all our ammo, we had shot very little, but I wanted to have enough that if we got into a gunfight, we could circle the wagons like at the OK Corral down there at the World Relief Compound and fight off any force that came against us. Once again, Somalia was in the back of everyone's mind.

While I was talking to Colonel Jones, we heard the heavy *WOPWOPWOPWOPWOP* and two CH-47s came in, carrying a Humvee slung load and a blivit at the same time. The AC-130 was boring a hole in the sky overhead at ten thousand feet in its left bank orbit and Colonel Jones looked over at me, smiled and said, "Bevelacqua, why, I hope you're appreciating this. This is all for you, you're never going to see this kind of support again."

He was right. It was incredible to see how we had become the main effort on the island and, really, for that one week period, we were Haiti.

There was really nothing else that was going on. It had hit the fan in the south, so all assets were getting dumped to us, and it was very impressive. It was comforting as well; that true sense of team spirit and camaraderieexisted everywhere and when you talked to somebody, you could cut the excitement with a knife. It was really incredible.

After we raided the lieutenants' apartment, it was surprising to see how much the Rangers had pulled out of there. Keep in mind, two days prior, when I broke up the Mexican standoff, we had pulled a lot of guns, grenades, and ammunition out of there. Well, the Rangers found it had been totally replaced, there was obviously a weapons cache that these guys were tapping into, so they could have protection. We knew then we had to start looking for caches. That was our next big mission.

The Rangers were in town for about another three weeks and we conducted a series of raids on suspected caches and basically anything that was an automatic weapon. Pistols we weren't concerned about, because the police could use pistols for their personal protection. If we had a police force, they could use sidearms.

We were scrambling to get the police to come back to work, because we needed to get cops back out on the streets. The last thing we wanted was an absence of law and order, but that's what was happening. At that point, we had dropped the hammer so we became the police. The word was put out through the PSYOPs loudspeaker teams that there was a curfew in effect. "Do not be on the streets after 22:00 hours at night. You will be arrested. If you are looting (what the Haitians call *desocage,* which was the taking back in retribution by looting stores) you will be shot on sight." And we meant it.

The first night there were a few people that were out, because they were curious; they wanted to see how far they could push it. We arrested them and took them back down to that same nasty jail that the other prisoners had been living in, most of whom had been released by then. It was quite obvious that the Americans were serious about what they were doing. The attitude of the Haitians was that they really wanted to help us in our mission to create a stable environment, because they wanted Jean-Bertrand Aristide to return. So they were very cooperative. We had no acts of violence, thievery, general disorder, or disobedience. Everybody, everybody was obeying our instructions because we weren't BSing around.

So, in effect, three Special Forces A-Teams, which were 36 men total, and a company of Rangers, a 128-man team, had stabilized a town of 200,000 people with a hostile garrison of 250 and a militia of 400. That's what you call a force multiplier. Okay? No mechanized units, no need for Cobra gunships or any of that type of stuff. It was done by understanding the language, knowing the cross-cultural challenges, knowing the society, communicating with people, and using whatever infrastructure was in place in order to get the word out.

> **Observation:** Once again, when I look at Iraq, I feel for the guys on the ground and I know the pain of what it's like trying to solve this problem. When you're in a town like Baghdad, which is probably putting twenty Les Cayes together, a few million people; the situation is huge, and the challenges are, in some cases, just insurmountable.
>
> I can tell you that the majority of people on television commenting about what's going on in Iraq, how we should proceed, what's being done right, and what's being done wrong, don't have a clue. They don't have a clue. They have never done this type of work before, they really don't know the culture, which in the Middle East is totally different from anywhere else in the world. For them to be standing there on TV calling the shots and saying what's going right, what's going wrong, is, to me, laughable. It's just laughable. Some of the guys we have on TV making comments, Air Force guys, Navy guys, even some of the Army guys that have never deployed, that never went on a real-world mission, have absolutely no business making comments about what's happening in the war on terror or the war in Iraq. It really just pisses me off.

One of the raids that we conducted with the Rangers that turned out to be kind of comical was on the Paloma Ice Factory. At that point, the

CIA was in town and we had an operator that was running an intel collection campaign and doing some recruiting with a briefcase full of money.

> **Lesson Learned:** When the CIA starts paying out money, they're convinced the information they get is legitimate. Well, it isn't always. And, this is another lesson we will learn again in Iraq. This lesson for us involved the soon-to-be infamous, one-armed man.

The agent, code-named "Frenchy," had gotten a couple of sources together. He gathered some intelligence from a one-armed man and said that the Paloma Ice Factory supposedly had a large weapons cache in it. All right, so we were going to go take down the Paloma Ice Factory.

We got together maybe two or three squads of Rangers, altogether about twenty guys, loaded them up in the paddy wagon with my team and a couple of guys from the other team, and set out for the Paloma Ice Factory. It's key to point out now that my company commander, Doug Wisnowski, and the rest of Charlie Company 1st Battalion 3rd Special Forces Group had arrived in country. The rest of the group had been given deployment orders and had arrived in country. So now the entire group was there. Colonel Jones was to move back to his original area of operation, which was up in Port-au-Prince. Colonel Kay, my battalion commander, was to come to town and we were to set up the Forward Operational Base that the battalion, the C-Team, would use in Les Cayes. This would become the main base for our teams in the southern claw.

Now at this point I had more guidance and leadership than I needed. Personally, I think we lost some OPTempo, short for Operations Tempo, meaning your battle rhythm—how fast you can move, how much stuff you can get done. When the new guys came in, they weren't as spun up as we were. Doug made the comment, "You guys were going a hundred miles an hour when we got down there." We were so stoked and pumped with adrenaline that I didn't want to slow down. You have to maintain the initiative; we had to continue to press as hard and as fast as we could.

It is at that point in an operation that you may not see things as clearly and you may make some mistakes. So what the Wiz brought was some pause, some caution, and a clear head for thinking, which turned out to be a good thing.

The Ice Factory

The Paloma Ice Factory was probably two klicks north of our position at the World Relief Compound. It was off the intersection of a dirt road and a hardball road that led into town on the northern outskirts of Les Cayes. It was a large three- or four-story structure, an open warehouse- or manufacturing-type facility.

En route, Vince, aka Dr. Pepper after this incident, decided to discharge "test fire" from his industrial-strength pepper spray in the back of his Humvee. The spray formed a cloud in the street that the Rangers drove through with their paddy wagon. In effect, we had inadvertently pepper-sprayed the Rangers.

I didn't have a problem with him doing a test fire on something like that if you're getting ready to use it, but it probably wasn't the best place or the best time. Now, unbeknownst to us, the Rangers were gassed and pissed.

We pulled up to the Paloma Ice Factory with a truckload of really pissed off U.S. Army Rangers, which is not what you want, and we went into the ice factory. The ice factory's gates were closed; there was a large lock on it and a chain. It was just great to watch the Rangers in action. We had no idea that there was a chain or lock on the Paloma Ice Factory, but these guys had a breaching kit that contained a large set of bolt cutters, some type of chisel, and a large mallet. As soon as the chain was spotted, the platoon sergeant had his guys lined up and said, "Breach team forward." These guys busted that lock, had the gates open, put security on both sides of the gate, peeled off, and then penetrated the facility in about ten seconds. I'm not exaggerating.

I said, "Damn, these guys are good."

Once the Rangers penetrated the front of the facility, we followed behind with our team. The Rangers, the remainder of them, came in and once again cordoned off the area, put out perimeter security, and then we conducted our searches. I went straight to what looked like the office and there was a gentleman there who was in charge of the facility. I told him why we were there; that we'd received intelligence that he had a cache of guns and he laughed and said, "Okay, who told you that?"

I said, "I'm not gonna tell you who my sources are."

"Well, I do have a gun."

"OK, let me see it."

He brought out a shotgun. He had a shotgun because he had some problems with kids coming in and stealing blocks of ice. I said, "Okay, I don't have a problem with you having a shotgun."

So we walked around the facility; there were different rooms we looked into and we checked out areas where stuff could be hidden. It was quite obvious somebody had a vendetta against the gentleman running the ice factory and that we had been lied to.

So we thanked him, we apologized for disturbing his day, and on the way out I talked to a few of the onlookers standing on the street who were watching what was going on. I told them, "This is a good man, he's a reputable businessman, we received bad information from someone that doesn't like him that he kept weapons there."

They understood I did not want to conduct a raid on someone who was innocent. The rumor mill in Haiti, the grapevine, works at the speed of light. The last thing I wanted to do was to get the locals thinking the ice factory manager was bad, was involved with the FRAPH, with the *gendarme,* and that he was hiding weapons. What you have then is a potential mob scene. As far as I was concerned, the guy was totally clean and I wanted to make sure the locals knew it.

We did these types of dry-hole raids for about two weeks with the Rangers and we were just chasing ghosts. We were getting intelligence from different sources; some coming through the CIA and some we were getting on the ground ourselves. It just didn't pan out. Finally, the Rangers decided it was time to pull out. We said good-bye to them, we thanked them, and we tried to get refocused on our mission, which was to create a stable and secure environment.

Several weeks had gone by and I wanted to get focused on catching the guys that shot Don Halstead. We had become involved in rebuilding the community, cleaning up certain areas, and getting the power turned back on. We had a Navy landing craft come in with parts and generators so we could get the power plant back up and running. We did get the power restored in Les Cayes, which was a big deal and we really gained a lot of favor with the local population for that.

We were doing a lot of patrolling. We had one team that was working with the military, we got the police back up and running, we had them paint their buildings different colors, and we got them different uniforms.

They were getting trained at a new police academy in Port-au-Prince so things were starting to really move and you could see a difference in the area.

Bovine's Raiders

But, I was still in that hunter-killer mode and I didn't want to get out of it. I wanted to get the people that shot one of my guys. We had our agent who was collecting information and he came up with a piece of intel that said that the guys responsible for this were holed-up in a sugarcane field on the northwest outskirts of town. Supposedly they were hiding in an old ruined building that was located in a sugarcane field and they had weapons. We were told there were five guys armed with M16s, and one of them was Green Eyes. They were being supported by their family members who were bringing them food and different things of that nature late at night.

Our new information about Green Eyes came from a couple of different sources. Normally when you have different folks that don't know each other giving you the same story, it tends to validate the information and provide proof that it may be reliable. The problem I had, however, was the source verification. One of the guys was the one-armed man whose intel about the ice factory wasn't worth a damn, so my attitude was, *Here we go again.*

I did an over flight of the target area in a helicopter. We flew down the road that went by the location and I attempted to film it with a digital camcorder to get some footage we could look at with the guys and try to come up with a plan, but it didn't work.

Needless to say, I'm not Francis Ford Coppola and the guys actually got a chuckle out of the footage I shot. So we had to get an eye on the objective, but I didn't want us to get compromised. Under the guise of doing an assessment of their commercial infrastructure, we went out to take a look at the large sugar factory that was next to the sugarcane fields. We went out to the factory to see what type of equipment upgrades they might need. We had a soil sample kit that was actually used to do runway impact analysis, to determine the types of aircraft you could bring in and how much weight could be supported. We were going to go out and do a "soil sample" of the sugarcane field and determine the pH levels, and generally bullsh** the factory people. Our purpose was to use this analysis as our cover to do some reconnaissance.

We went to the sugarcane factory, which was a four-story structure and climbed to the top. While the Civil Affairs guys were BSing the factory foreman, we went up on the roof with NODs and a 35 mm camera with extremely large lenses, and we eyeballed the sugarcane fields and the suspected location. We could see the high ground and we could see a clump of palm and deciduous trees located in the middle of the field where the structure was, where supposedly the bad guys were located.

We decided we would take a closer peek and we went out into the field under our cover story of getting a soil sample. We got closer to the location out in the middle of the field and we came up on a little stream. Then the sun started to set and it began to get dark. I remember hearing drums off in the distance, the same drums you hear at a voodoo ceremony. Then we heard a funny whistling, it sounded like a flute and seemed to be close by, yet far away. The hair on the back of my neck started to stand up, because it's just me, my team sergeant, and one or two of the CA guys. I said, "Yeah, we need to get outta here. This isn't a good scene."

We pulled out of the area, went back, and were debriefed by the battalion commander, and decided that this may actually be something.

So we were going to conduct a raid.

This was how I finally got my nickname. Up to that point, I was "Captain B," I didn't have a nickname, I didn't have a call sign, but I was about to get one.

The plan was to use two teams to move out to the area, come in from the south of the high ground across the little stream, and form a large *L*. One of the teams would put down a suppressive base of fire; the other team would assault the target area. But first, before we did that, I would attempt to communicate with a bullhorn and tell these guys "If you're in there, come out with your hands up," yada, yada, yada. If they didn't come out and it was obvious they were in there, we were gonna pump a couple of AT4s (shoulder-fired anti-tank weapons) into the building and basically level it. I didn't care if we captured them. I just wanted these guys dead and I wanted everyone in town to know if you shoot an American, you get killed. That's all that was motivating me.

We got our equipment together, which consisted of M16s with nightscopes, grenades, AT4s, and NODs. Also, I had been issued this thermal sight that had the ability to see great distances and provide excellent imagery at night, regardless of the illumination. It could be completely pitch-black and, because it was a thermal sight, not your typical starlight sight, it had the ability to detect heat from different sources. If there's a human body out in the middle of a jungle, the body will stick out as bright red and the jungle will be black, or you can go black on red; the jungle will be red, the body will be black, whatever you prefer. Now that sight was large and heavy, it probably weighed fifteen to twenty pounds. I carried that because I was going to try and eyeball the objective area and see if I could determine whether or not we had bad guys on the ground.

We loaded up, moved out to the area, and dismounted right next to the sugarcane factory. The battalion commander moved the TAC CP, which is a tactical command post, to one of the small buildings on the outskirts of the sugarcane factory. He sat up comms there and was going to run re-trans back to the group in case the sh** hit the fan and we had to get an evac or anything else. We also had a couple of teams on standby for reaction in case we ran into something we couldn't handle. I didn't think there was a chance in hell of that happening. Once again, Somalia was in the back of everyone's minds.

At about five thousand feet above the objective area, we had a CIA bird, known as an Air Breather, conducting reconnaissance. He had high-powered surveillance equipment similar to what I was carrying, but a little bit more sophisticated. It allowed him to see the whole objective. He was talking to his source, who was located with the TAC CP.

Now, we had the CIA involved, with their assets, and we had a lot of Green Berets, barrel-chested, steely-eyed freedom fighters, really looking for some payback. So whoever was in that target, whoever was holed-up in the ruins of that home in the sugarcane field, they were going to get their heads handed to them.

We started to move toward the objective. It was very dark; there's little illumination in rural Haiti; the sugarcane stood about seven feet tall; it was very thick and similar to a corn patch. We were moving through it when we came to a cut in the sugarcane, like an intersection. We saw this large mass sitting at the intersection and we weren't sure what it was. When we got close, it stood up and we realized it was a cow. So, okay, fine. No problems and we bypassed the cow. She ignored us. We started to come up on the back side of the objective and I gave the signal to the other team to go ahead and get into position.

We were probably a hundred yards from the objective when we laid down abreast to each other in a line and the other team moved over to our right and then came in parallel to us forming a large *L* shape.

At that point with everything in position, I took out the thermal sight for the first time to eyeball the objective. The target was pitch-black and totally quiet. We snuck in. Stealth had been utilized the whole time and we had a great opportunity to really surprise the bad guys. I flipped the switch on the thermal sight, turning it on, and my heart just stopped beating. When I turn it on, the sight goes *scmmmmmmmmmmmm TRRRRRRRRRRRRR* and I said, "Oh, my *God!* This f***in' thing is loud."

Joey Buttafuoco was kneeling down to my right and he looked at me and said, "Could you, hey, sir, could you have gotten a louder f***in' sight?"

"No."

"Well, the son of a bitch is out, you might as well use it."

So I picked it up, put it up to my eyes and, it was one of those things where you see it, but you don't see it. I put it back down and put it up again, and then I said, "Hey, Joey, get up here, man. It may be my imagination but I think I see five guys lying prone around that building up here."

So he picked up the sight and looked at it and said, "Goddamn, you're right. There are five guys lying around the building in the prone position."

Now, unbeknownst to me, my battalion commander was getting a transmission from the CIA asset overhead that was saying the same thing, that I had five guys lying in the prone position around that building. They appeared to be guarding it.

So he called me up and notified me over my radio that intel confirmed we had five guys lying around that building. I said, "Roger, I can see the same thing from my location." We made a tactical decision not to go with a bullhorn option. We were going to take these guys out.

By now my adrenaline was really pumping. I was very excited, my senses were really heightened, and I could feel the tension among the guys. We were going to do this. We were going to kill these guys.

I got on the radio and I told the second team to move into their final attack position which required them to move up the hill another twenty or thirty meters, so they had a clear field of fire. In their current position, they were shooting uphill and couldn't see the objective.

They started to move forward and it was at that point that their movement tipped off the five guys that were pulling security around the building and they sprang into action.

They stood up and it became obvious that these five guys were some big dudes and I mean *really* big, like maybe a thousand pounds apiece and they let us know that they knew we were there with a very loud *Mooooooooooooooaaaauuuu*. That's right, we had five large cows pulling security around an empty building with absolutely no one in it and once again, we had raided a dry hole. You could hear the guys laughing all the way back to Les Cayes. This was when I got my nickname, "Bovine 06." The "06" designation is a number given to commanders as a call sign and my new nickname was "Bovine." It just really fit.

After we determined that it was another dry hole, we made our way back to the TAC CP and the CIA bird took off. When we got back, we linked up with the battalion commander who was laughing. My company commander, the Wiz, was there laughing, too. We decided to move back to the compound, which was only a couple of klicks down the road.

As we started down the road at 02:00 in the morning, we saw five guys walking down the middle of the road who appeared to be carrying stuff. Now remember, we were looking for five guys. So we decided we needed to get tactical again and see what this was. We pulled off the side of the road and let them come a little bit closer. Then we hit them with headlights and told them, "Freeze, get on the ground." They dropped and it turned out they were carrying suitcases and clothing and stuff of that nature. These guys had just been repatriated from the Gitmo refugee holding pens and were being returned to Haiti. They had gotten into Port-au-Prince that night, gotten on a tap-tap bus, rode down to Les Cayes, and were now walking to their homes, which just so happened to be next to the sugarcane fields. They all had paperwork that showed they were in Guantanamo Bay and they had been repatriated; and one of them spoke very good English. He said, "Geez, we heard you Americans were here on the island, but we had no idea you guys were gonna be this serious."

So that was our second little screwup that night and we cursed under our breath about that, but it later turned into a chuckle and we chalked it up as a lesson learned.

Lesson Learned: It doesn't matter how much intelligence you get, how many sources you have on the ground, sometimes it's all about luck, it's all about timing, it's all about coordination, and there's a lotta different things that can happen that can lead to a (un)successful mission. Best laid plans don't always work out. That's why I can't say enough about the guys that bagged Saddam.

Interdiction at Sea

About a month later, in mid-November, we received information that there was an extortion ring on *île des Vache,* or the "Island of the Cows." So how much more appropriate can it be than to give the mission to Bovine to go to the Island of the Cows to figure out what's going on with this extortion ring? We knew they were stealing fish and lobsters from the local fishermen by holding them at gunpoint. They went right up to them in their boats and took all of their money and their catch.

There was a Catholic priest who had been on the island for quite some time. He was part of a Catholic relief organization; he had been ministering to the people there for many years. We were going to visit him and just kind of check out the island and see what was going on.

All of this was going to be done from the USCGC *Maui,* a 110-foot Coast Guard cutter. I have been on boats my whole life and I am very comfortable with them. I know the terminology, I know over-the-horizon navigation on the water, and so I felt very comfortable doing this.

They sent us a RIB, which was a rigid-hull inflatable boat to link up with the team, and ferry us out to the cutter. The island was probably five kilometers south of the coastline at Les Cayes, and it was a relatively small island; it may have been two to three square miles, the population was about three hundred people.

We were going to use the cutter to conduct Mother Ship Operations. We would sleep on the cutter, launch in the morning, conduct our patrols on the island, and then go back to the cutter at night.

We spent our first night on the cutter, and the crew was excellent, they really went out of their way to make us comfortable and we discussed the plan for the next day. We were going to go ashore, move to the location of the Catholic priest, talk to him and try to get a sense and feel for what was going on in the island, converse with the locals, and see if we could determine if there was a problem.

The next morning, after a nice hot breakfast, I conducted my final briefing with the captain of the *Maui* and headed to the fantail of the cutter. "Stand by to launch the small boats" was announced over the cutter's PA system and we watched the Coast Guard prep and launch our Zodiac. I signed for a fifteen-man black Zodiac from battalion with a forty horse Johnson outboard. We loaded up the Zode, went ashore on the island, and beached the Zode on a relatively flat section of beach. It was a gorgeous day; the sun was shining over the Caribbean with a beautiful orange glow. We pulled the boat ashore and made our way to a small path that went through a thick mangrove swamp.

This was like a scene out of *The African Queen* when Humphrey Bogart got into the water; one of those routines. We start moving down a trail and I felt a stinging sensation on my left hand. I was carrying my M16 out to my front and picked up my hand to look at it. The back of my hand had about a hundred mosquitoes on it. So I took my other hand and I crushed the mosquitoes. Then I looked at my other hand and *it* had about a hundred mosquitoes on it. Now I got a burning sensation on the back of my neck. Well, I turn around to tell my guys I'm getting eaten alive. Half of them are doing the Australian peel, turning around, tapping each other on the shoulder, and heading back to the beach.

Ha! So we all went back to the beach and regrouped. Half of us jumped in the ocean to get the bugs off. I had never seen so many mosquitoes in my life.

We needed to pick a different route, so we worked along the coastline, found another path that didn't go through a swamp, and made our way up through some small villages to a marketplace. This was the location of the Catholic priest. His location was pretty easy to identify because he had a large radio tower for communicating with the main island.

We talked with the Father for a little while and found out that the guys running the extortion ring were located on the northwest part of the island and lived in a little fishing village.

We figured we would have to work the coastline again to get over over to that part of the island, about a three-klick movement. So we followed the coastline and it took us about an hour or so to get there. We started asking people questions, and they said, "Yeah, we know those guys, and they're right there." They pointed out on the water and there was a small sailboat with another vessel next to it about a mile offshore. They told us, "The guys who are in those boats are the ones that are doing it."

I thanked them for their cooperation and we beat feet back to the Zode.

We made our way back to the beach, and called the cutter to give them a heads up of what was going down. We loaded the Zode and hightailed it to the cutter. When we pulled up alongside the *Maui*, I noticed the anchor detail was putting the final touches on securing the hook and both the *Maui*'s massive diesel engines were fired up, it was time to pursue the bad guys who were four or five kilometers away.

A 110-foot Coast Guard cutter bearing down on you, goin' twenty-seven knots is quite an imposing sight, especially when you're in a little wooden fishing boat. The captain of the cutter told me, "You know, I can't run interdictions for you, I can only deliver you from Point A to Point B."

"Roger, I understand."

So he piloted us to the site and we put a RIB in the water. Nutley, Mongo, and Nicky 68 got in the boat with my new team sergeant. That's right, Tango had been fired and moved to the B-Team after a huge argument with Company Sergeant Major "Mack the Knife" Clayton. Mack was a true SF baby; he had spent his entire career in the Special Forces and only knew life on A-Teams. Mack had the reputation of chewing detachment commanders a new butt without even batting an eyelash and the Wiz just loved it. These guys were two peas in a freakin' pod, but they gave in to my request and took Tango on the B-Team, a move that the Wiz would later regret. I would like to introduce everybody to the Gentle Giant, my new team seargent, Tango's replacement, code-named "Chewy," short for Chewbacca. You know, the big, hairy, roaring *Star Wars* creature. My Chewy stood about six foot three and weighed probably 230–240 pounds. He was huge. His head was huge, his hands were huge, and his heart was huge. He was really a great guy. So I finally had a running mate that I could turn to when the going got tough. Chewy got in the boat with Nicky 68, Mongo, and Nutley and they headed out to interdict these guys in the fishing boat. Ha! I remember watching this with my binoculars from the bow of the cutter; we had one guy with an M60 on the bow who was going to apply suppressive fire if need be.

My guys yelled at the perps, telling them to get their hands up. They got their hands up rapidly, and once again, English spoken loudly while holding a gun is understood by everyone. After a few minutes of interrogation, the intercept team finally got them in the boat and we left their boats abandoned out on the water. This caused the cutter captain to notify me that we were creating a navigational hazard if we left their boats afloat. So, we arranged for the sinking of their boats.

We interrogated the perps to determine if they were the ones who were extorting money. There were four of them in all—an older gentleman in his sixties and three younger guys.

One-by-one, we pulled them to the side of the ship and questioned them. Some of them gave information, some of them didn't.

It's hard to believe, but none of these guys could swim. We knew that because we played on their fear of the water and they started to sing like church mice. They started to rat each other out and said, "Oh, no, it's not me, it's him. He's running the whole show. Yesterday, he took fifteen dollars from this guy and took all his fish." So as we got information from them, we moved them to the fantail of the ship.

Lesson Learned: Getting information out of someone doesn't mean you have to torture them or humiliate them; however, knowing their fears is very leverageable. I'm sure some people would say we were probably violating their civil rights. No one was hurt, just scared a bit, and we were getting information—this works. You use what works. You have a mission; the mission is to catch the bad guy. If they resist with violence, you kill them. You don't pussyfoot around. That's why the Lieutenant Colonel West story touched so many people. No one could believe that a man who saved the lives of his men was being treated like a criminal because he scared a terrorist. The son-of-a-bitch who should have been put on trial was the JAG lawyer, but let's not leave it with just the lawyer. Where the hell was Lieutenant Colonel West's chain of command? General Ray Odienrno really showed his true non-warrior, political colors by not supporting one of his commanders—typical Pentagon E-Ring BS.

The only guy we couldn't break was the old guy. We tried a number of different things with him, but he just refused to talk. Fortunately, we had found it easy to play the others off against each other. We got them all together on the bow of the ship and begin to tell who told what to whom. Ha-ha! You could just watch the disgust coming across the old guy's face as he realized he'd been ratted out by all the little punks.

The cutter took us back to the docks at Les Cayes. Then we transported our prisoners to the city jail and dropped them off.

Later that day, we gave the crew of the *Maui* a guided tour of Les Cayes including the county jail where we saw our extortionists from the island. The old man had decided to spill the beans because he didn't want to rot in such a disgusting place. I laughed and told him the jail was like a first class hotel compared to the day we had first discovered it.

I told him to enjoy his stay and that he would have his day in court. Nick informed them that they would be served lobster for dinner—we all got a laugh from that comment due to the fact they had been stealing lobster for a living.

That concluded Bovine's mission on île à Vache.

Croix de Bouquet, the Voodoo House

It was late November when I got a call notifying me that Colonel Jones had a situation in a town a few klicks northeast of Port-au-Prince by the name of Croix de Bouquet, which means Cross of Flowers. What had occurred there was evidently a group of bad guys, known as the Zinlandu, had been conducting ambushes on people. They rolled rocks out into the streets in remote areas and hijacked cars and stole money. In one case they had roughed up a couple and murdered an American citizen. I'm not sure, but she may have been working out of the embassy.

Colonel Jones determined that he needed to get to the bottom of this and the only way to do it was to put a hunter-killer team together. He requested that 336 come up to his location and work on this problem for a couple of weeks. We were more than happy to oblige because, frankly, we were getting quite bored in Les Cayes.

I had lost Joey Buttafuoco because he was called back to the White House to receive a medal for his actions on the day that Don Halstead had been shot. Joey and Chief Red had single-handedly cleared out the compound. That was the firefight that we had driven up on that night. He went back to the White House and had a photo op with Slick Willie, I'm sorry, President Bill "I didn't inhale or have sexual relationships" Clinton—yes we all hated him. Joey got himself a medal, which, unfortunately, was only a Meritorious Service Medal. They didn't issue Bronze Stars because "We weren't at war." Hah! Tell that to the guys that are shooting at you, right?

The team loaded up on a helicopter and we flew to Croix de Bouquet and linked up with a team that was already on the ground. We were in a smaller version of the FAd'H compound that we had in Les Cayes. My impression of the team wasn't that good. It didn't seem like they were doing a whole lot to stir things up. They really hadn't aggressively attacked the situation like we did in Les Cayes and you could see it in the town. There were things going on that we would have never allowed in our town, the team had no control.

> **Lesson Learned:** I would compare this to some of the teams that have served in Afghanistan. I know this for a fact because I debriefed one of my buddies that just came back from a tour with the 29th SFG. There are some Operational Detachments in country that stay in their compound, really don't aggressively go out and pursue the bad guys or try to stir things up, kick the hornets' nest over if you will. I saw the same thing in Haiti; it's not the way to win a conflict.

After a couple of days we started to get information from the street that the guy involved in the robberies was actually a high-level voodoo priest and he lived in a house on one of the roads just on the outskirts of Croix de Bouquet.

We went out and did an initial recon of the area; his house was set back with another house in front of it, so you couldn't see it from the street. I talked to a couple of people in the neighborhood and they said, "Yeah, he's the guy you're looking for, and he is known as a *houngan*," which in Haitian is a high-level priest that practices voodoo. His house was set back off the road, and they wouldn't even look at it, they wouldn't motion to it, and when they talked about it, it was in a whisper. This guy was very powerful and feared. There was a little kid who came up to me and said that they sacrificed children in that house. When I heard that, the hair on the back of my neck stood up and I got that same feeling that I had when we found out they were raping women at the local police station and keeping their shoes as souvenirs.

Once again, I wanted to kill these people. I didn't want to capture them. I didn't want to interrogate them. I wanted them dead.

We decided we needed to come up with a tactical plan and conduct a raid on the suspected lair of the voodoo priest. People didn't even want to say his name, they were truly that afraid. He had really terrorized that town and the rumor on the street was, if you backed him into a corner, or got him into an area where he had no escape, he could transform himself into a butterfly or a lizard and elude capture. At the end of this episode, that story came back to haunt us.

Of course, at the time this was all laughable. I mean, we were in the twentieth century and things like that just don't happen. We kept our fears from encroaching in on us by convincing each other this voodoo stuff was all a myth.

I sat down with Chewy and we came up with a tactical plan for getting into the place, conducting a search, and basically shaking it down to see what we could find. Colonel Jones said, "Bevelacqua, I want you to go up there and I want you to stir up some sh**. I want you to kick some stuff over and see what you can find."

That's exactly what we did.

The plan was that the team would come in from the front while another team would cover the back. If anybody pulled out of the house while we went in, the guys on the back side would have it covered and then scarf them up as they exited.

Without notifying anybody, we had an inside source that was providing information to us that proved to be pretty credible. Without tipping anybody's hand, we rolled up for the early morning hit, and we went into the house.

We were in a two-story concrete stucco house, pink in color, square in shape. The second story only had one room and it was an open loft like a bedroom. Walking into the center of the structure, there was a small hallway that was about ten to fifteen feet long and there were open windows going all the way around the structure that provided cross-ventilation and daylight.

As we went in, we didn't see anybody in the open area so we immediately cleared a couple of rooms. The first room was directly to our front. We went in and cleared it; it was a bedroom and nothing was in there. At the end of the open area there was a doorway that led into a separate room. It was obviously set up for religious ceremonies. There were pictures of the Virgin Mary on the wall, there were rosary beads that were painted on the wall next to a portrait of Jesus Christ, and as we went around the room, there were pictures clearly from some type of voodoo rituals. There were sacrificial chickens, different things like that. The feeling in this room wasn't really that bad. It was a little strange, but it wasn't all that bad. At the end of the room on the left-hand side, as we walked in, there was another door. We stepped through that doorway and there was a narrow chamber, the room had a concrete slab at one end that was raised up about a meter off the ground. On the slab stood a statue of a demon, and the demon's name was Backa. It was at that point that I started to get the heebieijeebies. Backa stood about three or four feet tall, had a large mouth, big teeth, large horns on the top of his head, and just looked evil.

The room was painted red. At the end of the room, on the right-hand side of the wall was another passageway that led into still another room.

That room was an obvious temple, yeah, I guess you could say temple. It was definitely a room for sacrificing something or someone. It had an altar set up with the same type of railing you would see in a church when you approach the altar. There was a black railing with a large black iron cross. On one side of the cross was a large skull and on the other side, hanging from one of the arms was a red bottle, or a bottle that was wrapped in red fabric and then wrapped, very meticulously, with white thread. If you have ever seen the movie, *The Serpent and the Rainbow* you'll know exactly what I'm talking about. The vessels were called govi jars. Supposedly, in this bottle, was the possessed or captured soul of somebody who had been killed or murdered. As legend has it, if you break the bottle, that soul will possess you. We were not prone to test the legend.

Off to my back left, I found a little dugout in the floor that was raised up a couple of inches. It was made of concrete and it appeared to be a wash basin. Inside of it was some kind of liquid, it was a really foul-smelling mess with stuff floating in it. I don't know for sure, but maybe it was fecal matter and what looked like viscera or intestines from some kind of animal. This material was just floating on top of the stagnant liquid. It smelled extremely rancid.

I looked up and saw a doorway leading into the last chamber of the house; it was pitch-black, with concrete walls and ceiling. The room was no bigger than fifteen feet long and eight feet wide. On the two sides of the room were slabs that were raised up off the ground that looked like beds. They were made out of concrete. Underneath them was where you put coals and wood and started a fire to heat up the slabs. In between the slabs was a metal pole coming out of the ground with a loop on the top of it that had a chain and shackles running through it. The chain that attached the shackles also ran over to the wall to large eye-hooks embedded into the wall. What one surmised from looking at this was that people were shackled and put on these slabs and tortured by heat from fires started under them.

Then we found the most disturbing thing yet. That was the skull of a young child. We found a coffin that couldn't have been any longer than two feet at most and that really bothered me. It still bothers me that people are sick enough to think that they can actually get power from other people's suffering and that this suffering will keep them safe from harm or make them strong.

It wasn't going to keep them safe from the wrath of ODA336, because not only did we want to hurt these people, I particularly wanted to hurt the voodoo priest and all of his followers. So we took everything in the house that we could possibly move and we brought it into the center room. That's when I discovered that there was a guy and a girl having sex up in the bedroom loft. They had been caught by Chewy while Vince and I were inspecting the torture chamber.

We talked the girl into coming down. She was naked; we made her put some clothes on, and I was surprised by the fact she spoke English. She had an accent, almost like she was from Chicago. It turned out, though, that she was actually from Detroit and she had a real attitude problem. So we start asking her questions. She basically said, "I don't have to answer any questions; you guys don't have any authority."

Well that's when we educated her to the fact that we not only had authority, but we also had the right to take her rights away from her. So I ordered her bound and gagged, we dragged her out of the house, and put her in the back of the Humvee along with all the voodoo stuff we could get our hands on.

The local people were rather shocked to see that we actually came out unscathed and that we had all the voodoo stuff. I talked to them and tried to convince them that there was no power in any of this stuff and that it was all hocus pocus but they didn't really believe me.

We brought everything back to our compound, the statues, and the large vases, and all the other stuff we had found. After we turned the girl over to one of our interrogators, we decided to leave.

We had also arrested the guy who was coupling with "Detroit Dolly" and we brought him back to one of our interrogators whose nickname was "Herr Hess," as in Rudolf Hess, Hitler's deputy. This guy was very impressive in his trade craft of interrogations.

What Herr Hess did was take all the voodoo stuff we had captured and he made his own little house of horrors. He set it all up and covered Backa with Chemlite juice that glows an eerie green color in the dark and he had some other items in his house of horrors, the large cross and different things of that nature. Hess had arranged this all into a macabre setting, creating a really creepy environment. That was where he would do his interrogations and work his own brand of voodoo. The voodoo priest came in, took a look around, and knew that Herr Hess had more mojo than he did. The whole scene was designed to scare the living crap out of the suspects—which it did. The Lieutenant Colonel West story comes to mind again.

After a few days of interrogation, Herr Hess had gathered enough information to put the whole Zinlandu organization together and started looking for other members of the gang.

We captured a new guy from another operation who was extorting money by denying electricity. He cut off people's power and then he charged them an exorbitant fee to turn it back on. We came to find out that he was also involved in the voodoo ring and Herr Hess went to work and got some great information out of him as well.

Well, a week or so went by and we had made enough progress that Colonel Jones was so pleased we were told that we were going to go back down to Les Cayes again. That was the extent of the operation.

I found out some months later that they captured the high voodoo priest. They arrested him and they put him in jail. When the day came for him to go to trial before the local magistrate, they went to the cell and he was gone. The guard had no explanation. He had disappeared. The rumor out on the street was that he turned himself into a butterfly and escaped. To the best of my knowledge, they never caught him. He never returned to his home. There was no end to the creepiness of this whole episode.

Lesson Learned: We as Americans have a very tough time in comprehending all the nuances of a foreign culture, no matter how much we study it from afar. Reading about the power of voodoo priests over the people cannot convey the pervasive atmosphere of fear and foreboding that surrounds them. This palpable, very real to them, fear, is not easy for us to understand. It is also unreal to us that the Taliban in Afghanistan and the Baathists in Iraq still hold enormous power over a significant number of people. This power can be used to recruit suicide bombers and generally create hell for the coalition.

Let's recognize that power and identify its wellsprings. Let's use the natural antipathy that people have toward the latent fear that lies just below the surface and bring it out in the open and turn it to our advantage. Ignoring it and pretending that hellish forces will go away is not the answer. In fact, that is the road to hell.

Chapter Three

Broadcasting the War: Shock and Awe on Cable TV

Preparing for War—Behind the Scenes

In February 2003, the balloon was about to go up in Iraq for the second time in twelve years. Fox News pulled together a war group of all the regular talking heads along with some of the producers and graphics people to prepare for what came to be one of the most televised conflicts in the history of warfare—real-time reporting with embedded reporters. A lot of attention was given to the idea of embedding reporters and what a new and innovative idea this was. To be honest with you, it wasn't that new and innovative. It had actually been done before, as you have read, in Haiti.

There have been combat photographers and reporters since World War II, but not necessarily with the cameras rolling and the ability to send back home images via satellite. People could literally sit in their living rooms and eat popcorn, if they desired, and watch the conflict on TV.

While in general, I think that was a good thing for getting the media to understand the military and having the military understand and appreciate the media, I also think it really desensitizes warfare and turns it into another reality show—that becomes some kind of macabre theater. This is really the last thing we need if you think about it. Did we do this to satisfy our secret blood lust? God, I hope not.

If we remember anything, we should remember the devastating effect TV images from the battlefields in Vietnam had on the morale of the American public. In the Vietnam conflict during-and-after action videotape was televised days after the event, after having been routed through Saigon and Hawaii before arriving in New York. Just look at what the effect has been, on the whole world, from the images of the abused prisoners. Rest assured there will see more of these images over time and they will be worse.

In my opinion, we need to show more images of what the enemy has done to us. If they mutilate, burn, and desecrate the bodies of Americans, then we need to show that. We need to show the pictures of flag-draped coffins arriving at Dover. We need to repeatedly show pictures of Americans leaping from the burning World Trade Center towers—and what happened to them when they hit the ground. These are the images that need to be burned into the collective soul of America. If we don't do this and aggresively initiate a public relations war, the enemy will win the sympathy of the world for what they project as the suffering they are enduring under U.S. policy.

Don't get me wrong, I think the soldiers and commanders that allowed the abuses at Abu Ghraib Prison to happen should be punished to the fullest extent that justice allows. I also think that the damage inflicted on Americans and our allies needs the fullest exposure possible and that the perpetrators of these acts need to be rapidly and lethally dealt with. Let's keep everything in the proper perspective. War is hell and lots of bad things are going to happen on both sides. After the absolutely inhuman decapitation of an American contractor and the public display of the man's murder, no American should have any doubts about this.

The War Group

The Fox News Channel (FNC) War Group met on a weekly basis to discuss the maps that we needed for the conflict, having a general idea of how our forces were going to enter Iraq. We developed the graphics to support our commentary utilizing some really amazing technology. I'm talking about three-dimensional spin-arounds where you could see the weapons system like a B1 bomber or an F-16 and it had the nomenclature of the platform, the weapons system, it described the armament that was on it, how fast it could fly, its altitude, and different things of that nature.

The majority of the weapons systems that the graphics department prepared for belonged to the Air Force, and, as I sat through meeting after meeting and saw what had been done, it just amazed me that not one graphic depicted an Army ground warfare weapons system. I waited until they were done and I asked my question, "Okay, so where are the graphics for the weapons systems that are going to actually fight the war?"

Everybody just looked at me like I was some kind of military propeller head and I got a snicker from one of the guys across the table. I said, "You know, the M1 tanks, the Bradley fighting vehicles, the Humvees, the self-propelled M109SP Howitzers, where are they? That's what's actually gonna go in and liberate this country."

Still Telling It Like It Is!

This was where we encountered the ego and the self-righteousness of the United States Air Force, and, yes, I have a little bit of an axe to grind here. The Air Force was convinced that it could fight and win the nation's wars almost independently and unilaterally. The Air Force felt that through an aggressive bombing campaign and precise selection of targets that it would break the enemy's will to fight and force him to some type of surrender or peace accord and negotiation. Folks, I have to say this is a very flawed strategic view of warfare.

The Air Force was created to support ground forces as they engaged the enemy. I say to you today that nothing has changed. The Air Force still exists to support the ground forces as they carry out the main task of destroying the enemy's forces and occupying his territory.

We then addressed the common terminology that we were going to use, trying to get everybody on the same sheet of music. This is when the discussion of "Stay in Your Lane" came up.

Stay in Your Lane

One of the producers raised the issue. "You know we get a lot of e-mails from people that ask why a gentleman from the Air Force is commenting on Army ground tactics and why a Navy guy is commenting on Army ground tactics." We were told that we needed to stay in our lanes and stick to our area of expertise—it didn't work.

The responsibility for keeping everybody focused and on track does not so much belong to the individual that's being interviewed. Rather, it belongs to the news anchors, or whoever the talent is at the time that's doing the interview. They needed to realize that you probably shouldn't ask an Army major how a B1 bomber drops its payload and how joint direct attack munitions (JDAMs) work. That probably needs to go to an Air Force guy, and it's up to the talking head to say, "Well, you know, that's not my area of expertise. You may want to ask one of our Air Force representatives that question."

But it never ceased to amaze me to watch guys that had little to no expertise in an area go into a subject they've never seen, never touched, and never felt. I think this is really a disservice to the TV viewers by giving them an incorrect, unqualified perspective on things.

The other thing we discussed was getting a new war studio, a new look—something that was a little bit more advanced, a little bit more up-to-date. The war set that we had used for Afghanistan was very simplistic. We had a large map that showed the topography of the country and that was about it.

We didn't think Fox had the visual effects we wanted to illustrate, effects that allowed the viewer to see the campaign as it rolled out in Iraq. So a new studio was designed and it was like walking onto the set of *Star Trek*, like you were sitting on the bridge of the *Enterprise*. One of the things that, of course, we had to deal with was the screenwriter. For those of you who grew up in the video generation, using a screenwriter is fairly simple. It's the John Madden way of portraying warfare. In NFL broadcasts, commentators would move plays around on a football field or draw *X*'s and move lines and show you where a play just happened or how a runner had just gone down field and caught a pass. We did the same thing with the screenwriter.

Maps

For a talking head like me, maps were a challenge, because not only did I have to concentrate on answering the questions, but I had to lead the news anchor through a series of maps and show the disposition of forces. This was challenging because you really can't have some of the maps preprepared. In other words, you can't already have the lines drawn on them and the icons drawn on them unless you put a lot of prep time into it. I never liked using a map that already had everything laid out on it. I liked to put the icons in, drive around, and draw lines and indicate what forces were on the move, how indirect fire worked, how close air support worked, and how the enemy may or may not react to what we were doing. This, I believe, gave the viewer a much better feel for the dynamic flow of action and it just made for better television.

So I had all that going on while I had to answer questions and, in the back of my mind, as I looked up at the teleprompter, I knew that there were probably a million people watching everything I was doing. That can be intimidating if you dwell on it. It was like doing a jump out of a high-performance aircraft. If you took the time to think about what you were getting ready to do, throw your body out of an airplane moving at 135 knots at 800 feet off the ground, you would have second thoughts and tie your stomach up in knots. If you really stop and think about what you're doing, it bothers you and you would tend to get yourself spun up, allowing doubts and concerns to take over. I would try to block out the thought of what I was getting ready to do. That was the way I approached doing interviews, too. I never had any training in doing media work or anything of that nature, so I just relied on my past experiences.

I just blocked it out. Forget the fact that I had a million people watching. I just talked to the news anchor, answered their questions, tried to break it down in a simplistic manner, and avoid the use of acronyms—not easy; the military lives by them. The military has so many acronyms that if I got caught up in using military jargon and fired off a dozen acronyms, most people, I felt, would simply tune me out. If I couldn't grab them and portray warfare in a simplistic nature so that they could appreciate what was happening on the ground, I thought I would lose my audience.

One of the things that I always tried to do and continue to do is keep it simple.

We had the set established, we had our graphics done, and we had our maps and other associated materials prepped...we were ready for anything—at least that was what we thought. Then the government started the public relations campaign for the war. We had to get the American people ready for what was about to happen and tell the world why we were going to war. Fox was preparing to show the Americans how the military was going to take down Iraq, not an easy task, especially when we didn't know the plan.

The Night We Dropped the Big One

Sheppard Smith

I had an interview with Sheppard Smith on his 7:00 pm show. In my interrupt feedback device (IFB), which provides audio, Shep's producer started telling me that Shep was running over and my hit time was going to be reduced. Instead of having five minutes to tell the world how the war was going to begin, by using the screenwriter, I only had thirty seconds.

So I figured I would just get right down to what I thought the first target was going to be, and I remember saying this, "Sheppard, I think what's going to happen is that we are going to drop heavy ordnance on a suspected location of Saddam Hussein, his bunker, that we're probably gonna open up a hole using bunker busters and then fly a MOAB (21,000 pound Massive Ordnance Air Burst bomb—also known as "the Mother Of All Bombs") into the bunker and give Saddam Hussein the mother of all sunburns."

I had a lot of fun using the graphic and flew a MOAB into the bunker and then showed how the fireball would disperse and kill everybody in the bunker system.

Rant

I never really thought that I'd get called back to the studio two hours later to talk about exactly what had happened, which was what I had predicted. One of the things that I found interesting several months later was that all the leftist liberals that loved to just sit there and Monday morning quarterback everything that Fox News said had posted on several Web sites that Bevelacqua was a propagandist and had inaccurate analysis. They said I was wrong when I reported we were going to use a MOAB on Saddam's bunker and give him the mother of all sunburns, when in fact we didn't do that, we used bunker busters.

They didn't take the time to actually sit back and recognize that Bevelacqua called it right on the money, because the first target that he indicated would be hit would be a command and control facility that Saddam was in and that we would go after that first. That's exactly what happened, literally, two hours after I said it on TV. They couldn't see that, they were too busy shooting holes into Fox's coverage and the war wasn't even an hour old. They didn't want to give Fox the credit for having the ability to just call it like they see it—you know, fair and balanced.

Highway Turn Around

After I finished my Sheppard Smith hit, I was driving south down I-95 when my cell phone rang and some guy in the studio said, "Bob, the war started, can you come back?" So I turned around, drove back to the studio, and sat on the sidelines for about an hour or so until I got back on the air. I basically commented on what I had talked about with Sheppard Smith. They went after a regime command and control target and tried to take out Saddam Hussein.

As it happened, the intelligence reports were inaccurate. Saddam was not in the bunker, although this had been confirmed from a ground source, and that's why they carried out the leadership decapitation strike.

In My Never-Humble Opinion…

I have problems with the way they did the strike, and I talked with one of my buddies that was working that night in the National Military Command Center. My buddy had the same concern I did, that we weren't taking the gloves off. What we did was emphasize surgical strikes to the point where they became ineffective. What I mean by this is, if Saddam was in the bunker, and we knew he was in the bunker, had it confirmed with eyes-on target when we dropped the ordnance, that's one thing. But we didn't.

There was speculation and concern that Saddam was probably leaving the bunker when we dropped the ordnance, so in Bob Bevelacqua's book of strategy, I would have either taken out an entire grid square of that location or not hit the target at all. Yes, there would have been some collateral damage. But in the end result, we would have gotten Saddam

Hussein and quite possibly brought the war to a close that much faster. But we didn't do that. We just put a couple of bombs on target and left it at that. We accepted the risk that Saddam would get away in order to reduce civilian casualties, and he did get away for several months.

When the war started, I basically stayed at Fox that night and through the next morning. I'm not sure how many hits I did, it seemed like I was on the air probably every other hour. That next day, I got up and watched a little bit of the war on TV and then I went to work.

Shock and Awe "Hollywoodisms"

One of the things that was talked about a lot before the start of the Iraq offensive was the "Shock and Awe" operation and how the Air Force would blow everyone's socks off with their bombing campaign. I kept asking, "Okay, guys, what are you gonna bomb? How are you going to do three thousand sorties and drop all this ordnance and on what? What targets do you have right now that you can bomb; because you can't go after key infrastructure sites. We need those to rebuild the country. So what targets are you going to go after?" The term "Shock and Awe," by the way, was first used by Harlan Ullman, teacher at the National War College in his 1996 book, *Shock and Awe: Achieving Rapid Dominance.* This book became the theoretical bible for many pundits who used it to prophesy, incorrectly in my opinion, how the war would be won.

Likely targets, they told me, were buildings that belonged to the regime such as the Interior Ministry, the Ministry of Trade, and different organizations like that. Also to be destroyed were targets closely tied to the military, the headquarters of the Defense Ministry, Republican Guard locations, and things of that nature. Keep in mind the vast majority of these sites were not populated—so we were basically bombing concrete into submission.

I personally felt that there were limited targets that could be selected that would result in bringing the regime to its knees. We had to put boots on the ground. We had to get forces to roll into Baghdad in order to either engage the enemy or control the population. Either way I was convinced that a prolonged bombing campaign, as was the case in 1991, was definitely not the way to go. In fact, we didn't do that. We didn't have a prolonged bombing campaign. We launched our coalition Army and Marines into Iraq when the ground forces got into position. This is when the real war was fought, not from thirty thousand feet, but from six feet off the ground.

Keep Telling It Like It Is...

This leads me back to my comment about focusing on graphics of nothing but Air Force assets, because they really had limited use, in my opinion. The essence of victory during the ground maneuver war in Iraq was getting our soldiers engaged, getting them into built-up areas, either taking out the enemy or talking with the populace to get intelligence information.

Crock and Flaw

Some of the Army guys behind the scenes described Shock and Awe as "Crock and Flaw," because it just smacked of Hollywoodisms. The Army also had a bad habit, which I have a problem with, of using fancy terms and giving everything a sexy operational term such as "Ivy Serpent" (a 4th ID operation in July 2003) and code names of that nature. When you do that, I think you diminish the overall aspect of warfare and I think you tend to turn it into, once again, a reality show on TV. Everything has to have a fancy name, or you have to use some kind of sexy slogan or bumper-sticker catchphrase that describes what you're doing and how perfect you will do it—zero defects at it's worst. Typically when these missions don't turn out the way they were advertised—you don't catch or kill the bad guy, or you inflict massive collateral damage—the fancy code names and the manner in which we portray total dominance comes back to haunt us. These names and terms were, as I later found out, offensive to the Iraqi people. The people that lived in the area where Ivy Serpent was conducted thought the operation was referring to them as snakes—it's a cultural thing.

Air Force Strategy

Sometimes the military tends to describe its capabilities and the damage it can inflict on an enemy in a zero-defect environment. They say we will achieve total area dominance or that we have persistent dominance in the area of intelligence that will allow us to use our weapons systems in an overwhelming fashion, providing us with total battlefield dominance—what a load of bull. Actually, this was not, and continues not to be, the case in most combat situations. The Air Force was guilty of this more so than the Army, although the Army at times was almost as bad. I'd have to say that the Air Force was the leading offender of bragging and shooting off its collective mouth. I have seen interviews with Air Force generals on TV where they flat-out say that wars can absolutely be won by a massive air campaign. I think Operation Iraqi Freedom demonstrated the Air Force and the Army should lose the fancy terminology and stick to the basic principles of war.

March to Baghdad

After the annihilation of the Saddam bunker, the 3rd Infantry Division coming out of Kuwait began to prep the enemy side of the border with indirect fire. They used their artillery systems to soften up or prep the area so they could cross the border and begin their tactical advance.

Moving a Mechanized Task Force

When a tank remains at a high idle or tactical idle, even though it's not moving, it consumes a tremendous amount of fuel. An M1 tank, depending on how fast it's going, whether or not it's on tactical idle, may burn two gallons for every mile that it moves. It is imperative that fuel trucks stand by somewhere in the combat trains in order to refuel the assets.

We, the talking heads, weren't really sure what the objectives were for each unit. We weren't sure of the exact air and ground tactics that were going to be used, either. We knew that Baghdad was the center of gravity and, in order to topple the regime, they had to secure the capital. When you look at the distance on the map, five- to six-hundred-kilometer distances don't seem too far to drive a vehicle, but when you were moving in a mechanized task force, whether it was a column, a brigade wedge, or an echelon formation, you covered a lot of lateral distance. That means you have to have room to maneuver. On the logistics side of the house, you have to feed vehicles with an incredible amount of fuel, a mechanized vehicle like a Bradley fighting vehicle or an M1 tank burns more fuel in one day than your Chevy will consume in a month. Most military vehicles have the ability to drive almost five hundred kilometers without being refueled, but that metric is affected when you have time periods that you don't move, unless you're an M1 tank. The tank's turbine engine stays at high RPMs so that it can back up or move forward from *defilade*. This means that the front of the tank up to the turret can't be seen because it's behind either a wall or a berm.

So the logistics have to move with you, meaning soft-skin vehicles keeping up with heavily armored vehicles while your lead elements are engaging the enemy. This was but one of the challenges facing our forces.

Real-time Coverage

One of the truly amazing events was watching a news crew move with the 3rd Infantry Division. The film crew had their satellite phones and video cameras hooked up in their Humvees focused on the brigade commander's vehicle rolling across the desert—live in real time.

Typically, when you have something move on one of those videophones, it is very granular in clarity and you end up with a blurred image. So, what the guys did was very smart. They had their vehicles stay at the same speed as the vehicles they were filming and without moving the camera. This resulted in a pretty clear picture. The only thing that moved was the dust coming off the vehicle, providing a very good sense of speed. We could watch the task force roll across the desert in real time; that in itself was just an incredible thing, it really was. I actually got butterflies in my stomach watching it on TV because I knew what the guys were going through rolling across the desert. You got a sense of action like you were actually there. It's hard to describe action like this verbally, but the American public, for the first time, got the picture.

One of the things the viewer at home got was an appreciation for the long hours our forces had to endure while driving to Baghdad. Witnessing drivers and tank commanders staying awake night and day resonated in the pubs and restaurants across America—our troops were giving it their all. For every hour the task force drove, they remained awake. From what I understand, some individuals went as long as seventy-two hours without any sleep. I've only gone fifty-four hours without sleep—it isn't pretty. It's actually dangerous, because your ability to process information is severely degraded. Remember my Ranger school stories? Well, no one was shooting at us then. I think our guys did a magnificient job of managing that and this was evident in the limited amount of fratricide that occurred, or, as the press likes to call it, "friendly fire." It's all very unfriendly and lethal because bullets have no friends.

In true testimony to their training and the effectiveness of training centers like the National Training Center in the Mohave Desert, our soldiers displayed the ability to deal with the task at hand, whatever it was.

Calling the Shots While in a Studio

One of the things that I enjoyed doing was calling the shots as we watched engagements unfold in front of the camera. I wanted to describe to the audience what they were seeing. That included everything from an M113 A3 outfitted with rucksacks hanging off the sides of the track or the track commander (TC), positioned behind the 50-caliber machine gun inside the cupola. I tried to explain what each crew member was doing, how they all had sectors of responsibility and that they weren't merely along for the ride. I had a great time describing an M1 tank, its capabilities, what the bezel rack is used for, and what the guys inside do. I tried as best I could to get down to that level of "You're actually there. You're in the turret of the tank." I found this to be the most exciting part of covering the war, not so much the "Whad'ya think's gonna happen next?" and "Why did they do this and not that"—boring stuff to me. I just wanted to talk about what the camera showed and provide context and background for what people were seeing. I felt that if I could accurately · describe the environment our guys were dealing with, the American people would better appreciate what our guys were going through. Recognizing all the hype we give our professional football and basketball athletes, I wanted to do the same for our guys, who by the way get paid next to nothing compared to a pro athlete.

Into the Belly of the Beast—Entering Baghdad

It was truly amazing to see how fast our forces closed in on Baghdad and got into a position where they could charge into the city. One of the things that came up on the news was when the 3rd Infantry Division stopped just outside the city. Everyone asked the question, "Well, why this big pause, why aren't they continuing to move? Something must be wrong."

The Big Pause

Ranting Again...

You'd think at some point TV commentators and analysts would just give the military credit for having a tactical plan. Maybe they had actually built a pause into their plan in preparation for conducting movement into the city. Maybe they had intermediate march objectives or an operational rally point prior to entering the city, allowing them to marshal their forces, get final accountability, conduct final combat checks, and prepare to go downtown.

But the media and their analysts knew better. I watched armchair generals get on the air and say, "Obviously, we've lost the momentum and this pause is unexpected." Most of the on-air analysts, frankly, didn't have a clue as to what was happening on the ground. Instead of just giving the ground commanders credit for having possibly built this pause into the tactical plan, they had to pontificate as to why we weren't moving any more. Here, I have to single out General Wesley Clark's very negative comments about the operational pause on CNN. As a former supreme commander of NATO, he should have known better than to say what he did, to portray the pause as a serious delay caused by enemy action against our extended supply lines. I can only conclude that the political demon had already taken him over and he was pandering to CNN executives, all anti-Bush people, who liked that kind of negative analysis.

When I was asked that question, I said, "Well, the reason we've stopped is obvious. Before a butcher gets ready to carve up a piece of meat, he sharpens his knife." And that's exactly what it was. We were honing our systems and preparing to go in for the kill.

Thunder Run

Watching the lead elements of the 3rd Infantry Division go into Baghdad and conduct their Thunder Run was extremely exciting. It turned out that Fox News embedded reporter Greg Kellywas in one of the lead elements with his satellite camera rolling. This happened in the dark hours of the morning here in the States, but it was exciting to see the replays, to watch a mechanized task force roll down the freeway and drive into Baghdad streets was simply incredible. Off in the distance you could see some of the prominent icons of Baghdad; the large mosque, the radio signal tower, and some of the prominent hotels. When I was in the first Gulf War, we always talked about what it would be like to go into Baghdad. We have watched over the past twelve years since then the scenes from Baghdad—Saddam Hussein standing on his palace balcony, shooting his rifle into the air, the masses and crowds—and all of a sudden, here we were in downtown Baghdad. This leads me into discussing one of the most entertaining characters in the war—"Baghdad Bob."

New Sheriff in Town

Baghdad Bob was Saddam's minister of information, or dis-information. This guy would make Joseph Goebbels, Hitler's propaganda minister, blush. If there was any one guy in Saddam's regime that deserved to get a medal for his dedication to country, well, it was Baghdad Bob. He was the ultimate in spin and propaganda and I would've loved to have seen an interview between him and Bill O'Reilly. I'm sure it would have made for a good interview—of course neither one of them would have heard what the other was saying. This guy had the ability to flat-out deny that we were achieving any type of tactical success, that Saddam Hussein was no longer in power, and his interviews provided some comic relief. Everybody looked forward to seeing Baghdad Bob, and from what I understand, and what a couple of folks tell me from inside the White House, the president rarely watches TV, rarely watches the news, and didn't watch the constant coverage of the war. But whenever Baghdad Bob came on, his folks told him and he would come out to watch him. From what I understand, one of the reasons that Baghdad Bob was allowed to live and didn't make the deck of cards was because, really, he was a harmless mouthpiece. I think the level of dedication that he displayed, actually won him favor in the White House. So we just left him alone and I think a lot of that had to do with the president enjoying watching him so much. If you stop and think about it, network news biggies like Jennings, Rather, and Brokaw probably really admire the guy's ability not to let the truth interfere with a good story. It's really surprising that Ted Turner didn't hire him on CNN. Ted needs and appreciates that kind of loyalty and devotion.

The tactical stupidity displayed by the small bands of fighters, particularly the Fedayeen Saddam, never ceased to amaze me in the manner in which they attacked our forces. Some people referred to them as courageous. I disagree with that assessment. Courage is the controlling and overcoming of fear—not the absence of fear—they were stupid. I was amazed to watch a thin-skinned vehicle, like a truck or an SUV, drive toward an M1 tank and attempt to attack it. Probably the SUV was laden with explosives, and the M1 tank would just chew it up with its turret mounted 50-cal or coaxial 7.62 mm machine gun. Tactics like this didn't seem to make a lot of sense, but it did show you the level of dedication, or perhaps desperation, that some of these fighters had.

When our task force was faced with tanks from the Republican Guard, it was Desert Storm all over again. Our tank crews and our gunners were so far superior that the enemy didn't stand a chance. They were slaughtered in the streets as they sat in their vehicles. It became obvious to anyone who was a potential adversary of the United States of America that nobody engages our military on the open battlefield, weapons system against weapons system, and wins. You can't fight a conventional war with the United States of America. That, however, opened up an entirely new type of warfare and a whole new can of worms—unconventional warfare.

The Midnight Shift—Covering the War with a Full-time Job

By the end of the first week of the war, we were in a real battle rhythm at Fox News, and everybody pretty much knew what shift they were on.

Battle Rhythm

For whatever reason, I got the midnight shift and I got in at eleven PM and stayed until six in the morning and did coverage of the war. This slot was a great news time for Iraq, since they are eight hours ahead of the

U.S. East Coast, eight hours ahead and two centuries behind. Pulling this shift did provide for good coverage, but wore me down. Working the graveyard shift and fulfilling my other work requirements took its toll, at one point; I actually started to feel sorry for myself.

What Is Sacrifice?

Ranting and Telling It Like It Is...

What is sacrifice? What does it mean to put your life on hold in service to your country? When you look at the men and women in uniform, recognizing what they get paid, the amount of time they spend away from home, the benefits package they get, and then compare that to corporate America; there is no comparison.

Soldiers, sailors, airmen, and Marines continue to be underpaid. They are on duty a tremendous amount of time away from home and, really, get little in return. So why do they do it?

Where they get reward and appreciation is by the celebration of the people back home and the support of their government. When you have mass demonstrations that support the troops, when you have politicians uniting on TV, and have true bipartisanship, that helps the morale of the soldiers, because they know everyone's at home rooting for them. When there are yellow flags out, when the American flag is being flown, that's what supports the soldier who is sacrificing everything for his country.

What kills their morale are political agendas. What kills their morale are demonstrations by leftist liberals that say what we're doing is wrong, the military shouldn't be over there. In some cases they actually degrade the military by resurrecting the old terms of baby-killers and insensitive warmongers, and things of that nature. That adversely affects morale. When you see John Kerry on TV and denouncing the president, and denouncing the war in Iraq, and statements like, "I will get us out," that, too, directly affects troop morale. I submit to you that if John Kerry had truly served his country honorably, and had spent enough time in country in Vietnam, he would remember those negative statements and how they affected the morale of the Vietnam soldier. But he didn't spend enough time in country, only four months. He got his chest full of medals and he got out. Frankly, in most military circles, his service remains highly questionable. No—I'm not voting for Kerry.

Watching Saddam Fall

Three weeks into the war we were awed and entertained by an incredible spectacle. We watched the Marines use an M88 tank recovery vehicle to pull down a huge statue of Saddam Hussein that stood just behind the Sheraton and Palestine Hotels in downtown Baghdad. An Iraqi crowd attempted to pull it over with a rope and didn't have the ability to do it, so a couple of Marines volunteered to go in and pull it over for them. Prior to toppling it, we watched one of the Marines crawl up the boom of the M88 and take out an American flag and drape it over the face of Saddam Hussein.

Well, there was a tremendous amount of symbology in that act, both positive and negative. We have to recognize and remind ourselves that when we are on camera there is a worldwide audience watching our broadcasts, not just viewers in the United States of America.

Every Soldier Is an Ambassador

While most Americans stood up and clapped and cheered when they saw the American flag draped over the face of Saddam Hussein, the other audiences saw imperialism, occupation, and a political agenda. One of the things the soldiers have to understand is that everything they do is watched and evaluated. They are all, literally, ambassadors of the United States of America.

Flag Incident

Fortunately, a Marine was handed an Iraqi flag and he replaced the American flag with it. To me, that was a sign that our guys understood the implications of their actions. The crowd cheered and we won a couple of hearts and minds. That is what unconventional warfare is all about. That's what psychological operations are about. Not dropping five-hundred-pound bombs on people, but winning them over, getting them to support you. Soliciting a positive response from them allows you to accomplish your mission in a much more painless fashion. That's what that Marine did when he pulled out the Iraqi flag and draped it over the face of Saddam Hussein.

With the fall of the statues of Saddam Hussein, everyone had pretty much come to the conclusion that the regime was done, Saddam was on the run, soon to be caught, and other members of the famous deck of cards were being rounded up. So the war was winding down.

Well, that was not the case. That was where the accomplishments of the military, the speed in which they executed their plan, the brilliance of that plan all stopped. We entered a new type of warfare and a new phase of conflict. Frankly, we didn't have a plan. I know we didn't have a plan, because I sat in a briefing at the Pentagon where the secretary of defense (SECDEF) talked about the Coalition Provisional Authority (CPA), how it was going to work, and what it was going to do. I addressed two questions to Secretary of Defense Donald Rumsfeld. "What are you gonna do with the military when you have mass surrenders, and what are you gonna do with the police force? Are you gonna vet the police force and put them back out on the streets?" I got what I call the Polish salute, which is a shoulder shrug. They didn't know; there was no plan.

Looting in the Streets—"I Told You So"

There was a break in planning and communication between the military and the CPA. One of the worst things that we could have possibly done was not to enforce law and order on the streets of Baghdad after the fall of Saddam. People will tolerate almost anything except a total lack of personal security. How would you feel in a darkened city with millions of people absolutely unchecked by any kind of law enforcement? Consider, too, how many men had automatic weapons they took with them from the Army or the police and in Baghdad AK-47s were like cell phones in New York City—everybody had one.

I recall a reporter asking the secretary of defense about the looting, why they weren't stopping it. It was obvious to all that there was chaos on the streets and we had lost control. His answer was, "Well, you know, when you see a guy carrying a vase out of a store on TV, over and over and over and over again, if that's the evidence that we've lost control, then that's not a very accurate portrayal of the situation."

The secretary of defense was right, and the media does have a bad policy of doing that, showing the same footage which soon after gets rolled over and over again. Images like that get ingrained into the minds of the viewers and they think that this is happening on a continuous basis.

What Was the Plan?

But, looting was happening on a continual basis. Regime offices were cleaned and gutted, a museum lost artifacts, some of which were several thousand years old. (Most, thankfully, were found again.) We lost control of the streets and I attributed this to the fact that we didn't have an aggressive follow-on campaign that was unconventional in nature and recognized the fact that we had to transition from a war situation to an occupation and stability operation. We should have prepared for a backlash, prepared for an insurgency.

Re-ranting…

Lesson Learned: I was asked to comment on the situation of the looting and what was happening and I had a flashback immediately to Haiti and to the expression the Haitians used, *desucage,* which was the time of payback and retributions against those who had done things to them, had oppressed them over a long period of time. That's what was happening on the streets of Baghdad.

You have to have a plan for that. That is the key to maintaining law and order. That was a lesson we were learning over again, history doesn't repeat itself—we just keep making the same mistakes.

The CPA

So who's in charge? At this point, the Coalition Provisional Authority began moving and established an organization. That probably was one of the most difficult jobs on planet Earth.

I won't say it's an impossible mission, but it was pretty damn close to it.

The problem with the CPA was that it brought with it a bureaucracy that was associated with a large entrenched government here in the

United States of America. Let me tell you, in a wartime situation the last thing a commander in the field needs is bureaucracy. Having to go through red tape to get approval to use funds for programs in order to create a peaceful environment through prosperity and get people jobs is a recipe for guaranteed failure.

The best example of a commander who did it right was General Petraeus, commander of the 101st Airborne. Petraeus was a how-to study in unconventional warfare that probably should be institutionalized within the military. The way he engaged the tribal leaders in Mosul, the way he used Iraqis to help control his area, the way he negotiated opening the Syrian border in order to facilitate cross-border commerce, all of it was just incredible. What he did should be emulated throughout the other regions. A lot of people will say that's not really possible, because other regions didn't have the stability that they had in Mosul. Do you think maybe they had stability in Mosul because they actually went out and embraced the local population and used prominent leaders, the sheiks of the area, in order to create and facilitate a stable and peaceful environment? Did that have something to do with it?

Disbanding the Military and Police

One of the fundamental mistakes that the CPA made was the disbanding of the Iraqi military. That was the last thing they should have done. The other mistake—and this is still happening—was the segregation of former Baath Party members and former military members that held key positions in the military or in security organizations. The CPA stipulated that we would not do business with them. They couldn't be hired. This was a bad move. This action created a stable of recruits for the insurgency and demonstrated the CPA's inability to understand the environment in which they were operating.

Recently, the CPA, now the U.S. Embassy, was considering taking some measures to reverse that decision, but nothing happened. It would have made an immesurable impact if they reversed their decision, because a lot of damage has already been done. By the way, we didn't even attempt to dismantle the regime infrastructure of Nazi Germany or Japan after we occupied them in 1945. We realized then how dangerous and unproductive that would be, even though we had far better reasons. Why didn't we study our own past successes? Why do we keep making the same mistakes? I attribute this to one thing, the good old boy political system—Paul Bremer was the wrong man for the job.

Disenfranchised and Dangerous

Do you know the expression, "Keep your friends close; keep your enemies closer"? By disenfranchising all of the former regime people, the only choice we had given them for peace and prosperity was to fight against the coalition. They could get paid to do that. There was no money in it for them to embrace the United States, the government, the coalition forces, because they were not going to get paid.

The interim council and the interim Iraqi government had the same thoughts on the matter. So how were these people supposed to get jobs? Did we expect them to uproot and move from the area? If we had the same policy when the Berlin Wall came down and the former Soviet Union collapsed, the people would not have tossed out their corrupt leaders. It never would have happened. That we would not work with former party members of the Communist Party would have been a non-starter with the Soviet Union, with Russia. There's no way that we would have been able to get to some normalcy in relations.

The policy of freezing out former Baathist regime and military leaders was totally flawed. We were not studying our past successes. Interestingly, after World War II we had no objection to bringing a lot of German rocket scientists to the U.S. and putting them to work. It was Werner von Braun and his team that enabled us to reach the moon. The fact that they had been Nazis employing slave labor and working for one of history's most brutal regimes didn't matter.

Saddam's Palaces

One of the other things the CPA did that I completely disagreed with, and that really bothered the Iraqi people, was that they moved into Saddam's palaces, into the prime palace in downtown Baghdad. Now, think about this for a minute. You have a palace that is the symbol of a dictatorship. You move in and set up your seat of power in a symbol of torture, murder, and rape. Then you start to dictate terms to the people of that country, in a dictatorial manner. It doesn't take long before you begin to look a lot like the former tenant of the building. A lot of Iraqis asked me, "Why does Bremer [head of the CPA] reside in Saddam's palace? Why have they surrounded themselves with twenty-foot slabs of concrete? Why do they never leave the palace? It appears that they have become the new dictators of our country." I can't say that I had an effective or convincing reply for them. This same type of logic persists with the use of facilities like Abu Ghraib Prison. A lot of Iraqis told the Americans that since so many bad things happened there under Saddam that we shouldn't use it. It identified us with the former regime and its oppression. But we did it anyway.

From a symbolic standpoint, they were absolutely right. That's the way it looked in the Middle East. That's the way it looked to a foreigner. Appearances are everything in that part of the world.

Iraqi Interim Council

The members of the Iraqi Interim Council were invited to come to the palace to meet with the CPA to discuss plans for the new state of Iraq. One of the stories that came out really blew me away. I learned that the members of the Iraqi Interim Council were strip-searched, their cars were searched, and their bodies were searched every time they went to visit the CPA in Saddam's palace. Talk about irony!

But fifteen feet away, you could watch a former Gurkha soldier who was working as a private security contractor walk right through the gate because he had a plastic ID badge. South Africans that were contractors walked right through the gate because they had plastic ID badges. But not the Iraqis that were identified as the new leaders of their country, who had the responsibility of putting together a constitution, they weren't allowed to do that. *They weren't trusted. They* had to be searched and scrutinized because we "felt like" they were going to try to do us harm. Come to think of it, we probably are not even treated as bad as this going through security at a U.S. airport—so much for winning hearts and minds.

Big Rant...

This, ladies and gentlemen, is not how you build rapport with the locals. This creates fractures and problems between the cultures.

So members of the Iraqi Interim Council expressed great discontent at having to go through this, to be subjected to this. So we came up with another solution. We had bomb dogs sniff them. Now for those of you who aren't familiar with the Middle East, dogs are not treated like they are here in our country. They are not pets. They are especially not welcome in the home and they're seen as scavengers, almost like rats or buzzards. Think about your Old Testament dogs and the story of Jezebel. So when you have a dog that's considered to be a filthy animal sniff you, it doesn't go over well, especially when they sniff the bag that you have your bible in, the Koran. When a dog is allowed to sniff the Koran, it is a slap in the face of Islam. We're not talking Islamic extremists here. We're talking about moderate Muslims that support what we're doing in their country. The members of the interim council supported what we were doing in their country. I won't take the time here to go into it, but three interim council members were women, and the idea of nonbelievers or dogs touching them is horrific.

This incident, while large in the Middle East, wasn't carried that much in the press over here. It created another fracture in the already strained relationships between the United States and the Muslim world. These are the mistakes we cannot afford to make, and it's only because we don't take the time to learn the history of the people that we're trying to help. We're trying to help these people; we need to be their best friends, not their worst enemies.

We have a certain level of arrogance that lends credence to the term, the ugly American. I will tell you that the CPA, at that point in time, was making us truly ugly Americans.

I don't want to give the impression that everyone that worked in the CPA didn't know what they were doing, because there were some real heroes in the CPA. There were some extremely hard-working people. I met a chief warrant officer, Paul Holton, whose good deeds I will describe later, and he served as an example of dedication and devotion to mankind.

There are other individuals in the CPA that put their lives on the line because of their beliefs; they knew what they were doing was just. I never want to take anything away from them. The problem was their leadership.

I had a problem with the key leadership within the CPA. Some of the people they surrounded themselves with were twenty-five-year-old kids with college degrees from Georgetown. These kids held key positions. While I was visiting the CPA, I was surprised to see how many unqualified people there were running the show. I've forgotten more about unconventional warfare and stability operations than these kids could ever have learned. But, there was no limit to the level of arrogance they displayed. I heard this time and time again from officers that had dealings with the CPA. As I heard one officer put it, "I have met the enemy and he is us."

I Still Tell It Like It Is...

What I saw there was the good old boy system at its worst. This is why I get upset when I see people just flatly support one party because it's their party. Look, we all make mistakes, we're human, right? If you're a member of the Republican Party, and you make mistakes, you have to do a self-assessment, a correction, and then move forward. You can't just accept everything that's done because, well, that's my party. The Democrats are just as guilty. But I find a lot of fault with a lot of the right-wing, heavy-handed conservative pundits that do nothing but bash the Democrats and praise the Republicans over and over again. We were making some serious mistakes. The Republican Party made a serious mistake with the appointment of Paul Bremer as the head of the CPA and he made some serious mistakes with the appointments of some of the individuals he brought with him—some of them, not all.

Contracting

After the CPA was established, the discussion of bringing in contractors began to percolate in the news. Then, immediately everybody had to attack the fact that Halliburton got a multi-billion dollar contract to basically rebuild Iraq's broken and dysfunctional infrastructure.

Halliburton

According to the critics, the only reason that Halliburton received the contract was because of its ties to Dick Cheney. He had been president and CEO of that company before running as Bush's vice president. Let me submit this to those who leveled that charge at Cheney. Name five companies other than Halliburton or Bechtel that can do this type of work, at this level, and that have the history, a proven resume, of doing this work. This list is very short. What people also have to realize is that

Halliburton had existing contracts that were already in place to do this type of work. This allowed the modification of an existing contract, thus, permitting additional funding to be put on that same contract so they could get to work rapidly. A key concern at that point in time was getting to work right away. If you went through an extensive bidding process and writing proposals, months could go by before a contract was awarded unless the company was willing to operate at risk and burn its own overhead money—not likely. Lack of rapid progress meant suffering for the Iraqi people. The lack of water, the lack of electricity would never have been addressed, because we would have been too busy going through our bureaucratic red tape. That's why Halliburton was awarded the contract. They had already done an impressive job in rebuilding Kosovo after that war. They had plenty of experience in security issues in an unstable area. You can't just put an unproven minority contractor from Topeka into a situation like that. You can do anything you want with your historically underutilized business bidding (HUB) points but, political correctness aside, it would be murder.

That said; Halliburton also has some internal problems of its own. One of the things that Halliburton did that I completely disagreed with was using subcontractors from outside Iraq. How could we possibly justify using South African contractors, people from Nepal, Germans, French, or anybody else to come in and do work in Iraq and make money, before we consider using Iraqi companies or Iraqi people? This, to me, was and continues to be a travesty. The people that should be making the money off the reconstruction effort within Iraq are the Iraqis. The majority of the subcontractors hired by Halliburton should have been Iraqi companies. Now, they have hired a good number of Iraqi companies to be subs. I give them credit for that. But not the majority.

People say, well, the Iraqis don't have the ability to do some of those jobs. They don't understand the infrastructure requirements. They don't have access to the technology. They don't have the mental capacity. This couldn't be further from the truth. There is an ancient saying in the Middle East. The Egyptians write books, the Lebanese print the books, and the Iraqis read the books. There is an incredible amount of talent and education and experience within the country of Iraq.

I Am Telling You...

There are Iraqi entrepreneurs. There are Iraqi businessmen that are quite familiar with doing large construction projects, whether it was a hydroelectric power plant, stringing power lines, or rebuilding a water system. All of that experience resides within the Iraqi professional community. The problem was, the CPA didn't want to leave the protected confines of the Green Zone and go out into the hinterlands and find these individuals, because it was dangerous. So they did the easiest thing and the safest thing possible. They hired one prime contractor to go out and hire subs from overseas because they didn't want to go out into the boonies and meet the Iraqis that would have the ability to do this type of work.

Bechtel

The opposite example of Halliburton would be Bechtel. Bechtel was awarded a contract from the U.S. Agency for International Development (USAID) and it had to fight for that. They had to bid for that contract, write proposals for that contract, justify, show, and demonstrate how they had the appropriate expertise to execute that work. Then Bechtel turned around and hired a majority of Iraqi subcontractors. This was exactly what needed to happen. They demonstrated the ability to think in an unconventional manner with a rapid response to satisfy a requirement, and they did an excellent job.

Bechtel had some faults of their own, too, no one's perfect. A lot of their subs got away with skimming off the top of projects and the quality of work that was done was not what was specified in the statement of work or in the task order.

To give you a specific example, there were a number of schools identified as needing fifty thousand dollars worth of reconstruction work. Buildings were to be painted, new plumbing installed, new desks, new chalkboards, chairs, and things of that nature. There were a great number of schools that only received a paint job; about five thousand dollars worth of work. The rest had been skimmed away. This wasn't necessarily reported, because Bechtel had somehow managed to do their own quality assurance and quality control, which I believe is in direct defiance of the Federal Acquisition Regulation, the FAR. Somehow, Bechtel managed to get away with this. I got this information from an inside source within the

CPA that was disgusted with the fact that Bechtel managed to avoid being audited or held accountable.

What's the repercussion? Well, here's the repercussion. When the Iraqi people see that the schools weren't rebuilt and refurbished as agreed, they don't blame the Iraqi subcontractors that skimmed the money. They blame the prime company that was chartered to do the work, received the funds to do this work, and then the work did not get done. All of this falls on the head of Bechtel for depriving the schools of the money and work they should have received.

As contracts were awarded, the CPA took hold, and the military had established its bases of operations, George Bush flew onto an aircraft carrier and declared an end to the war in one of the most gaudy publicity stunts that I've seen from any president. Frankly, it was pretty shameless, and whoever advised the president to do this should have been fired. The problem was he announced the war was over, but nobody bothered to tell the bad guys that the war was over, because the war was just beginning. At that point we had probably killed less than 20 percent of the bad guys. They had all gone to ground. This was exactly what happened in Haiti, except times ten thousand.

The Truth Rant...

So you can't declare an end to hostilities until you have a recognized form of government that surrenders and you either have the capitulation of all armed forces whose commanders must come in and surrender their arms or their apparatus. That hasn't occurred, yet we called an end to hostilities. The war as we planned it was over—we simply wished it away.

Insurgency

A new kind of war has begun a kind of war that the United States typically has a hard time understanding. The catch phrase in corporate management these days is "Think outside the box," but most people don't really do that. One of the most dangerous forms of warfare is unconventional warfare. Why do you think Spartacus was so successful? That is exactly what we are seeing in the insurgency.

The insurgency was our own creation. We got rid of the old regime and we were trying to cobble up a replacement government. This was an insurgency that began, as most do, with subversive acts of sabotage against the coalition forces and against key government and economic targets like the Basra oil terminal.

The only way you fight these bands of resisters or guerillas is with a paramilitary force or your own guerilla force, which we commonly refer to in the Special Forces, as a G-Force. You must have G's. If you don't have G's, you can't fight the bad guys effectively.

Going Native

It takes an Arab to understand another Arab. It takes an Iraqi to identify who's good and who's bad on the streets, and I've seen this. It's incredible to see their ability to identify the outsiders. To say that guy's from Jordan, that guy's from Lebanon, that guy's from Syria, that guy's an Iranian; they have the ability to do this rapidly and from the other side of the street. The clothes, the accent, the way they walk, all of these are clues, and we tend to be clueless.

White Boys from Arkansas

Spot identification in the Middle East is something that, frankly, a white guy from Arkansas just can't do. One area that was fighting the insurgency quite well was Mosul. The 101st Airborne had embraced the local people, including them in a lot of their efforts, and were using key and influential tribal leaders to provide advice and participate in operations. This was not being done so much in a unilateral fashion, but more in the way of having the Iraqis involved in policing themselves. This is the key to success in fighting an insurgency. I said this in one of my Fox hits, but it wasn't until two months later that I heard someone in uniform use the term "guerillas" and state we were in a guerilla war. I just couldn't believe that it took that long for somebody to realize what was going on in country.

Hey, I'm a former Army major, this isn't rocket science. We tend to avoid admitting the obvious. We want to say everything's going great, we have total mission dominance, we have perfect intelligence, and these were terms that were thrown around loosely in the Pentagon. This mindset is extremely dangerous, especially in unconventional warfare. We will never have perfect intelligence, nor will we have the ability to get into the enemy's decision-making process unless we embrace the enemy himself. That means using the locals to break up these organizations, infiltrate them, and provide information. The bad news is this takes time; it is not a short-term fix. Cultivation of this kind of cooperation takes time, money, and patience and it requires a certain skill set that most people in the military never learn. The practitioners of this art reside within a small community: the U.S. Army Special Forces, the Green Berets. Counterinsurgency, guerilla and unconventional warfare are taught at Fort Bragg, North Carolina. But, trying to get conventional commanders to understand that and insert them where they can do some good is very difficult. During the standoff at Fallujah, where were the Green Berets when we needed them? Where was our foreign internal defense (FID) mission that is the key to the success of a counterinsurgency?

Putting an Arab Face On It

General Petraeus truly grasped that concept early on. Once again, his methodology and the way that he conducted his operations in Mosul must be institutionalized within the United States Army. It needs to be taught throughout the major institutions in the Army, it needs to be taught at the War College. It needs to be taught at the Command and General Staff College. It also needs to be taught at the Combined Arms and Services Staff School; but at this point, I am pushing a wet noodle up a hill.

What the 101st managed to do was put an Arab face on the occupation. This was a term that started to get accepted in the later months of the war. It became obvious that we needed to put an Arab face on this operation.

We didn't do it, and I will tell you to a certain extent we still aren't doing it.

In the month that I spent in Iraq, one of the things that I did was watch television every night, I had satellite TV. The majority of the channels I got were Middle Eastern channels, go figure, and I was impressed with the amount of news coverage available. I was also impressed with the professional way these organizations ran their news bureaus. You may not like Al Jazeera, you may not like some of the messages and tones that they use; but, it is a professionally run organization that really did some incredible investigating and very professional reporting—I am not evaluating content, merely presentation. I was making these observations not as an American, rather as an operator that wanted to leverage existing media platforms to our advantage. Yes, I would tell you, Al Jazeera was and still is in cahoots with the bad guys. They have been at locations where there have been attacks that unfolded in front of their cameras, because they had a network of sources that western journalists would never have, so why not use this to our advantage? Should Al Jazeera be shut down? *NO!* It shouldn't be shut down. Al Jazeera should be embraced and exploited by U.S. forces through a positive PR campaign. I watched every night fearful of how bad we looked in the eyes of the Arab world.

On several different channels, LBC out of Lebanon, Al Arabia out of Dubai, and Al Jazeera out of Qatar, I watched them show the occupation in the West Bank and Gaza, Israeli soldiers going house-to-house demolishing homes, and then they would seamlessly transition into scenes of our soldiers going into an Iraqi home, kicking in the door, and bringing out Iraqis, some of them women and children with their hands up in the air, with guns pointed at them.

The message was crystal clear. I got it. I knew exactly what they were doing and so did the Arab people. The Israelis and the Americans are waging war against the Arabs.

Other than the new American-funded Arabic language TV channel, Al Hurra (the Free One), we have absolutely no countercampaign to this. Frankly, this is a travesty, because we do have the ability to promote master themes and messages, to counter the propaganda campaign that is being fought against us overseas. We talk about winning hearts and minds and providing information from a different perspective, we will never get there unless we step up to the plate. We'll never be able to close down the Wahabis in Saudi Arabia, we'll never be able to affect organizations like al Queda that have the ability to recruit from an incredible mass of people. There are 1.6 billion Muslims in the world. We have to convince them that we are not the crusaders that they think we are; that we're not the bad guys. You don't do that by dropping five-hundred-pound bombs on everybody. You do that through information, which means getting the word out. We have yet to figure out how to do that. I would love to see a commercial effort that stood up a true Middle East TV station that waged war against Al Jazeera and its management team in Qatar.

Live from Baghdad

I became increasingly uncomfortable commenting on the war without actually having been in country, so when I got the opportunity in October of 2003, I went to Baghdad and actually lived as an Iraqi. I lived on the local economy away from the military, away from the CPA, and I experienced what was going on from an Iraqi perspective.

In May 2003, I received a phone call from a friend of mine, Dave Bossie. Dave is a conservative political operative who does a lot of interviews on the media circuit, including Fox News, CNN, and MSNBC. Many of his articles have been published in newspapers and magazines in support of the Bush administration. His main target was the leftist-liberal agenda in politics, in the media, and in the culture. Dave was also responsible for rallying over twenty thousand Americans on the Washington Mall during a rally supporting our troops—a real patriot.

Dave called me to ask if I had any interest in doing security projects in the Middle East, and I told him, "Yes, I do, who wants to know?" He said there was a business associate of his living in Lebanon that he has known for quite some time, who was interested in doing commercial projects in Iraq. This man, an American citizen of Lebanese descent, wanted to make use of his close ties with prominent Iraqis. No deals could be made without security being negotiated with the Americans and the CPA.

I told Dave I was interested and we could talk about it.

By way of background, the first civilian authority in Iraq after the fall of Saddam in April 2003 was headed by retired General Jay Garner. He was soon replaced in May of that year by Ambassador L. Paul Bremer. Bremer's CPA office in July appointed an Iraqi Interim Governing Council composed of a mixture of religious and ethnic groups representing different regions of the country. This council, among other things, was charged with drafting a new national constitution and eventually preparing the country for democratic elections. It was this CPA that I wanted to engage.

After about a month went by, I ran the idea by my business partner, Bill Cowan, who seemed to be very interested. Bill had experience working in Lebanon in the darker days, in the 1980s when the civil war in

Lebanon was going on in full force. This was when the Marine barracks and the American Embassy were bombed. Bill was running the streets of Beirut undercover doing a number of different special ops activities, BLACK OPS.

So Bill was very interested because he liked the Lebanese; he knew they had a great reputation and Lebanon really was the gateway to the Middle East. You don't see that until you get there, but Lebanon is unlike any other country in the Middle East. It truly has a westernized culture with a heavy Mediterranean influence, very much like Italy.

There is a Muslim presence, but not quite as prominent as it is in other Middle Eastern countries. This is due to its large Christian population.

Beirut is a beautiful city, having re-rebuilt itself since the war and regaining its reputation as the Paris of the Middle East. There are sections of the city with great outdoor cafes—very cosmopolitan, very chic. I would describe it as Monterey, California, with pieces of Miami and New York City thrown in.

We spoke with our new friend from Lebanon, Charles Chidiac. Charles was a businessman and construction developer. He had worked in Hawaii for many years and did many multi-million-dollar construction projects. He had a close friend in Iraq, Dr. Hameed al Gaood, who was a son of the head sheik of the al Anbar region. The Al Anbar region accounts for one third of the land mass of Iraq and includes hot spots like al Ramadi and Fallujah. His father is Baziq al Gaood. Hameed is fluent in English and was a successful businessman during the Saddam regime because he had the ability to import goods into Iraq even though there was an embargo. He imported construction-type equipment like Caterpillar earth movers, vital for construction of Saddam's palaces among other things.

Hameed expressed concerns because his father was trying to get information out of his region, the Al Anbar, and was experiencing frustration in the way that the Americans were handling the situation. He felt that the people were supportive of the Americans, but that would only last for a month or two and then he wouldn't be able to control them. He wanted to get a message out to the CPA and to the world that Iraqis were not all evil; that they did support the American goals. "We Iraqis want more input; we have our own ideas and strategy on how we can improve and better the situation." That was his message.

Then the story changed, we weren't trying to do security contracts; we were, in fact, trying to get information to the CPA before they had a real problem on their hands. Our mission was to get exposure for the sheiks of the Al Anbar and help them vent their frustrations on the way post-Saddam Iraq was being handled by the CPA. A vital opportunity in preserving a reservoir of goodwill was at stake here. If the population remained supportive, American lives and those of innocent Iraqis would be spared.

First we decided we'd meet in Lebanon with some representatives from the tribes (there are fifty-five different tribes in Al Anbar). I arrived in Lebanon in mid-July, a little concerned because Lebanon is a Syrian-controlled state. It was Syria and Iran that supported Hezbollah (Party of God), the terrorist organization responsible for so many bloody acts in Israel. So Lebanon, while thriving and prosperous, still has its dark side—I had my reservations.

I grew a beard to soften my American look a little bit! In Lebanon, the people speak English, French, and Arabic. Most everyone speaks one or more of these languages fluently so I figured I could get by with French to lessen my American profile.

We flew from Dulles Airport to Charles de Gaulle in Paris. We then boarded a Middle East Airlines Airbus and flew to Beirut, which was about another four-hour flight. In all, we were in the air probably twelve to thirteen hours.

We arrived at Beirut International Airport, which is a fairly good-sized airport with reasonably decent accommodations, especially the duty-free section. There I enjoyed a huge walk-in cigar humidor with the finest selection of cigars—yes, I have my vices, too many to number.

We arrived and were received by our host, who had a couple of expediter personnel move us through the passport section. It became obvious to me that Charles was a very well-connected man, because Charles didn't wait in line and everybody knew him. We moved right through the immigration customs checkpoint, got our stamps, picked up our luggage, stepped into a couple of Mercedes-Benz sedans, and were whisked away. If you want to know who's got status in a third-world country, check and see if they have professional drivers, with guns and a fleet of mulit-colored Mercedes. That's a great clue right there.

We stayed at a hotel that I would have to say rivaled most three- and four-star hotels in the United States. It was located on the northern end of the city on a cliff overlooking the Mediterranean, just a beautiful, beautiful location. The hotel was huge, but there really weren't all that many people in it. It had four different restaurants, each restaurant had a different cuisine—Lebanese, Chinese, French, and American fast-food—and the quality of the food was unbelievable.

This was when I had my first exposure to the Lebanese, the way they eat and the way they socialize. They really had made an art of socializing while eating; they had that down to perfection. Their food was of superb quality, typical Mediterranean cuisine, and they had some traditional dishes that they eat at every meal. Of course, lamb was always present, but the food came in waves. It's not like in America where you sit down and you have a couple of plates of mashed potatoes and chicken or steak and some kind of vegetable. It's not like that. It comes in two or three different servings of food. The end result is the table is completely loaded with food—finger food, things for dipping, different types of salad, vegetables, lamb, chicken, fish—and then once you're done with that, they clean the table or they pick you up and move you to a new table filled with nothing but fruit; pears, apples, oranges, bananas, papayas, kiwi, pomegranates. It's all grown in the Bekaa Valley, which has been the breadbasket of the Middle East for ages. This was true even during the time of the Roman Empire. This is one of the reasons why there are dramatic Roman ruins in the city of Baalbak, which is located in the northern portion of the Bekaa Valley, not far from the Syrian border.

We settled into our hotel and prepared for our meeting with the sheiks.

Two of the sheiks drove in from the al Anbar region, a third sheik, Sheik Hameed, was already living in Lebanon, basically in exile. The two sheiks from the al Anbar region drove from their town of Ramadi, which is about thirty kilometers west of Baghdad, through the desert into Jordan, through Syria, and then into Beirut. Now that makes for a full-day. I believe it was a fourteen-hour car ride, accomplished without them having papers or passports, because they just don't need them in Iraq. They had never really left their area, their country. They were prominent men, everybody knew them and their family lineage so there had never been a reason for them to have paperwork. They simply called the Jordanian and Syrian governments and had it cleared so they could get through. This was the way they arrived for our meeting.

Lesson Learned: The trappings and outward appearances of power are very important in the Middle East. Power, however, is not conferred or even signified by a piece of paper, much less an election. Power is based on family relationships and is recognized instantly and is immediately respected. Governmental power in the Middle East is not as important as the unofficial power of the sheiks who rule the tribes and clans. Everybody knows this in the Middle East. I begin to wonder why our policy makers and their administrators didn't make better use of this fact. It's like we are trying to establish and administer power using our frame of reference, not theirs. That's why what we are trying to do in the Middle East is having so many problems in winning the support of the real power brokers.

I walked into our meeting room and, of course, it had the typical Arabian flair; gold-leaf trim, an Italian marble floor, and gorgeous crown molding encased the room giving it a royal chamber appearance. There is something about a flowing white robe with black and gold trim and the ceremonial headdress, or *kuffia,* that the sheiks wear, it just commands respect. You know these guys are to be taken seriously. Their skin is dark from the sun, leathery, definitely weathered over the years of exposure, pitch-black eyebrows, dark mustaches, and large, pronounced, strong noses and bone structures, and a staring glance with their eyes, very penetrating. I met both of them, shook their hands, and used what little Arabic I had in a traditional greeting, "May peace be upon you, *asalam-aliekum.*"

I received a very cold reception. This didn't bother me too much. I figured we were either going to get along or we weren't. So we all sat down, Dr. Hameed at the head of the table and the two sheiks on either side. I was at the other end of the table. Charles and my business partner, Alex, were there. Alex was a Marine, a Vietnam veteran, who later turned businessman, financier, and mortgage banker. Alex can structure a deal with just about anybody, and was excellent at putting together joint ventures and sniffing out opportunities as well as sensing a potential minefield. He was the gray-haired representation for our company, the wvc3 group, and I was the younger guy who had experience in doing security and connections with the media. Since my experiences were a little bit more recent than Alex's, I felt together we made a good team. I felt pretty comfortable sitting at the table knowing Alex was next to me.

We started into the discussion. First, we thanked the sheiks for driving the distance and coming out to see us, and then we let them do all the talking.

Their message was this: "We appreciate being liberated. We're glad Saddam Hussein is gone. But now that he has passed, there are certain things that are being done that we find intolerable. The number one problem is we cannot allow the random searching of our homes in the middle of the night, rousting our families out of bed, our women, our children walking downstairs with their hands held high as the house gets searched because someone gave information that we had a weapons cache, that we were Saddam loyalists."

The other problems the sheiks took issue with were having to pass through constant checkpoints, having to get out of their cars, having their cars searched, and worse, having themselves searched while their townspeople watched. The sheiks presented themselves to the military in the area, they told them who they were, and they were given a pass to carry guns to protect themselves. But still they were constantly searched. Not having an ID that said who they were added to the problem.

When this constant harassment happened in front of their townspeople a wedge was driven between the American forces and the people of Iraq. How would it be if Rudy Giuliani got searched every time he went across the Brooklyn Bridge, in front of his own police and in front of his own staff? This would become very uncomfortable and he would lose face. Again, their power was unknown and not respected by the American forces. The sheiks refused to stand by and allow their honor and prestige to be degraded and diminished in front of their people. The sheiks specifically expressed concern that in their region they could only contain their people for a couple of months, after that they would have problems. Two cities were mentioned by name—Ramadi and Falluja.

Another issue was the confiscation of large amounts of money and gold. The way they expressed it, the U.S. Army assumed because they had gold and large amounts of money that they were Saddam loyalists, this was Saddam's money in U.S. eyes.

One of the things they made known was that they were prominent businessmen that operated in the Al Anbar area. A lot of them had wealth from a number of different resources and it was quite common to have large amounts of cash and gold in a country where the banks aren't stable, especially given the fact that they were getting ready to go to war.

> **Lesson Learned:** You cannot expect business and financial transactions to take place in the Middle East like they do in America or in Europe. For example, Islamic banks ruled by Islamic law forbid the charging of interest on loans. For Arabs, banking is done on an entirely different basis than in the West. Cash is a much more widely used commodity and people have it on hand in many forms, including gold and diamonds—we're talking about a diamond worth $25 million. We assume that the most important thing in restoring economic health in a country is getting the banks up and running. This must be done in the Arab way or it won't work.

They aired their concerns and they vowed to support and assist the coalition forces. But, they said, there had to be a change.

They wanted to provide their own security and they wanted to promote prosperity by creating jobs for people. For example, there was a cement plant in Fallujah that had been abandoned. This plant was state-owned. They wanted to buy it, they wanted to employ Iraqis, and they wanted to produce cement for the country, because, at the time, and to this day, cement gets imported. If you can, imagine bulk cement being imported into Iraq. This was insane. The whole country, the majority of the construction in the country, is reinforced concrete—cement and rebar. To import a product like that which can be produced in-country and create jobs and foster peace through prosperity is just ludicrous.

So that was one of their ideas, to create a cement factory or to buy a cement factory and then create jobs in the area, especially in a town like Fallujah.

They said they would receive us openly and we looked forward to visiting them and their brethren. We told them we would come to Iraq and visit them in their villages on their terms and try to get the CPA and Army to listen to their concerns. Our intent was to hold a large meeting with the sheiks of the al Anbar and invite the CPA. They could air their concerns, and then, we would try and get this covered by the media. With our connections at Fox News and some of the other news outlets, we figured we'd be able to do that for them.

We had some free time while we were in-country, so we decided to go to Baalbak in the Bekaa Valley and see the Roman ruins.

We drove through very high, twisting mountain passes and roads that brought us to an elevation of about ten thousand feet. Finally, we crested the mountain and started down the other side. The view of the Bekaa Valley was gorgeous. One of the things that impressed me was the Lebanese ability to build structures on the side of mountains, and I mean major apartment high-rises and complexes, small towns and villas outside of the built-up area of Beirut that were built on elevations ofsix-, seven-, or eightthousand feet.

It was about a two-hour car ride on not the best roads in the world, and, of course, everyone in the Middle East drives a car like it's their last day on earth. Their driving was very aggressive and very dangerous. There were four of us in the Mercedes, the driver, my business partner, Alex, and his son, Alex Jr.

Whoever hauled the concrete up there, mixed it, and poured it did a fine job and obviously wasn't suffering from a fear of heights.

When we came down the mountain pass, we started to encounter checkpoints. These checkpoints were either run by the Lebanese or by Syrians. Imagine if you can, inside your own country, having to drive through a checkpoint that was run by Canadians, by Mexicans, or by Guatemalans. These guys had the ability to pull you over, fine you, or worse, throw you in jail. So the Lebanese are truly an occupied state.

> **Lesson Learned:** We totally lost credibility in 1982, under President Reagan, when the embassy was blown up along with the Marine barracks, and we pulled out. We really hurt the Lebanese when we allowed the Syrians to occupy their country. This Syrian model of occupation (keep in mind what's going on in Iraq) that was effective in taking over Lebanon is being used in Iraq and being employed effectively. Granted, there are more soldiers in Iraq than there were in Lebanon, but the ability exists for insurgents to create instability and to disrupt the rebuilding of Iraq. Their ability to disrupt the handover of power was made evident when the CPA pulled an early morning transfer of power and got out of dodge. Disruptive activities are being funded and run by both Syria

and Iran. Once again, we failed to study past history and learn from it.

We passed through different checkpoints and experienced a little uneasiness as we drove into one of the cities on the way to Baalbak that displayed yellow Hezbollah flags flying in the streets. The Hezbollah flag has the symbol of a city with an AK-47 over it; very distinctive and hard to miss. The streets were basically lined with Hezbollah flags sticking off every telephone pole and every shop, and I noticed people were walking around in more traditional garments and the Westernized look of modern Beirut was all but gone. The area was rather impoverished, the towns didn't have the infrastructure that we saw in Beirut, and the quality of life seemed to be reduced dramatically.

We went past a couple of checkpoints that were run by Syrians and the most formidable equipment I saw was a couple of M113s, which were U.S. armored personnel carries from the 1960s. Other than that, I'd have to say the Syrians probably had the worst trucks I've ever seen in my life. It amazed me that they actually had the ability to move them. They had to be from the '30s, '40s, or '50s. But, they were beaten up and one thing that we saw constantly was these trucks broken down on the side of the road, waiting for repairs.

I think it was safe to say that kicking Syria out of Lebanon would probably take the United States about a day and a half. That was if the Syrians didn't flee the country as soon as they found out we were coming. Liberating Lebanon would be rather easy on our military. Politically, it may actually gain us some favor. I would tell you that one of the reasons that we continued to have problems in the Middle East was because we've let Syria get away with murder, we allowed Iran get away with murder, not to mention the taking of fifty-two American hostages for 444 days.

Lesson Learned: The Carter presidency fell largely because of the Iranian hostage crisis. Don't imagine for a minute that events in the Middle East can't change dramatically overnight and that these events can't have huge effects here in the U.S. We can no longer afford the luxury of turning our back on the turmoil and inhumanity practiced by dictatorial regimes. If we do ignore the Middle East and its problems and imagine that we can remain aloof and immune from problems there, then these problems will come crashing into our cities with devastating effect. The Democratic Party today wants to ignore this lesson and pretend like we live in the pure and unsullied era of pre-9/11 where our alabaster cities gleamed undimmed by human tears. Those days are gone for the rest of our lifetime. We forget this lesson at our peril.

We drove through the Bekaa Valley, which was just laden with orchards, crops, and fruit stands. It is unbelievable how much agriculture was contained in this valley. We passed an area where there were streams coming out of mountains and running through hotel outdoor cafes. It was 90 degrees on that day and the mountains were so high they had snowcapped peaks and really highlighted the edges of the valley—really beautiful. One stream in particular that came out of a mountain had restaurants built around it, and casinos. Having lunch next to the stream was a must on a hot day. One of the restaurants had set up a cooling system that worked by trapping the water, forcing it through a series of pipes, and creating a cool mist—similar to a tiki bar in the Florida Keys.

The one thing that I didn't see or hear of in the Bekaa Valley was all the Iranian terrorists that were supposedly running around in this heavily fortified valley concealing Saddam's weapons of mass destruction. Hah! You know, it was kind of funny when I got home and I heard that intelligence report. I just had to chuckle.

It's amazing the difference between the impression you get from people who have been on the ground and people that study overhead photographs and listen to the sources that they've paid money for information who have never been on the ground. Yes, I'm talking about the CIA; and, yes, I'm talking about the FBI; and, yes, I'm talking about the NSA. Some of these guys, not all, live in steel tubes and conduct their analyses in cubes located in basements of buildings. They have very little time on the ground, if any, and when they do get on the ground, all they do is walk around with their briefcases filled with money and try to recruit sources. Now in fairness to the true operators that are working the streets, doing a superb job of collecting information in a less than hospitable environment, I salute you and thank you for your service.

Lesson Learned: Relying on satellite imagery, reconnaissance photos, or electronic snooping is a bad way of getting intelligence, and to anyone who might argue that with me, I would tell you to go to New York and study the skyline. It's changed for a reason. Our intelligence community is broken and needs an overhaul. Ollie North on Fox had a great way of putting it: "We can read license plates from a hundred miles up in space with our satellite technology. This is really great if we are about to be attacked by a license plate. Who's driving the car and what his intentions are, nobody knows."

We arrived at the Roman ruins and I expected a couple of columns, maybe a few foundations, and what I saw was, well, I was blown away. I had never seen anything quite like this outside Rome. A large amphitheater made out of huge blocks of stone. I think they said one of the largest stones in the world was discovered at this site. One of the stones was 111 tons, fifty feet long, twenty-eight feet wide, twelve feet deep—a huge rock. This block was moved from a sand pit or a rock quarry some two or three kilometers away, dragged by an estimated fifteen slaves—holy back ache.

There were large Parthenon-type buildings displaying plaques from Kaiser Wilhelm's day when he visited the area prior to World War I, just incredible, all laid out, right there in the middle of the Bekaa Valley. This was truly an incredible sight. Our tour guide spoke pretty good English, and had an impressive depth of knowledge of the ruins. It took us about an hour to walk through the site.

After that, we drove back to Beirut, which was really kind of an adventure unto itself, but well worth the experience.

Charles had us over for dinner prior to our departure and invited over numerous other guests.

In the Middle East, they don't conduct business like we do, specifically I'm talking in terms of the Lebanese. They don't go to the office at eight in the morning and sit and watch the clock until five at night and then go home. They might get into work around ten oreleven, work for a couple of hours, talk to a few folks, take an hour-and-a-half lunch break, go back to work, and maybe work until five, six, or seven that night. When they get home, they prepare their meal. They typically sit down to eat very late, nine or ten at night, but they have all their business associates come over. They sit down over dinner, they talk pleasantries, and they also talk business. You would see several sidebar conversations away from the head table that would manifest into groups and they would talk business for hours. You didn't necessarily ink a deal at that point, but a handshake was probably the closest you could get to putting ink on paper with the Lebanese.

We had that environment going that night with several different people coming in talking about construction jobs and security efforts; they were interested in working in Iraq. I remember meeting Charles's cousin who was a palm reader and this guy was actually pretty good. I've never had much faith in palmistry. But one of the things he boasted about was being an excellent shot with a pistol. I remember Charles coming over and saying, "My cousin can outshoot anyone in Lebanon."

I could not leave this challenge unanswered and I said, "Charles, if I can beat your cousin does that mean I am the best shot in Lebanon?" Charles laughed and said I could never outshoot his cousin.

We went into the basement of his home, which was 250 years old. Charles's great-grandfather's grandfather had bought this home and it's been in the family ever since. Not too many Americans live in a 250-year-old family home. It was a very large structure that sat on the edge of a cliff overlooking Beirut. It had been damaged during the civil war and repaired over time.

The basement of Charles's home used to be a dungeon a couple of hundred years ago. The room was shaped like a Quonset hut. It was cluttered with posters, paper, boxes, and things of that nature. We walked into the room, turned around, and faced the doorway we'd just come through. I saw the marks on the wall, bullet holes. His cousin and servants came down carrying a couple of pistols, a 9 mm and a .45, and Charles said, "Well, choose your pistol."

I grabbed the 9 mm, stainless steel Colt, a nice pistol, and we squared off and faced the wall. We shot at the wall that had the door in it and on the other side of the door was the dinner party. Ha! Ha! So! I looked at Charles like, *Was this a good idea?*

He said, "Oh, Bohb, I do this all the time. Eee's okay."

I asked Charles, "That stone there, what's your house made out of?"

He says, "Sandstone."

I said, "Okay...so the bullets don't ricochet?"

He said, "No, they more or less clump up on the wall, knock off a chunk, and fall to the ground."

"All right, Charles, let's do it."

So they put three targets on the wall and we drew three rounds for each target. I put one round just high and to the right of the bull's-eye and my two other rounds placed dead center in the bull's-eye. His cousin stepped up, his first round went high and to the right, his second round went low and to the left, his third round was not even on the wall. The guy couldn't shoot a barn if he was in it.

Then Charles stepped up, shot one time, and we couldn't find his bullet hole, either. Hahaha! Granted it was two in the morning and we'd all been drinking. Guns and alcohol do not mix! I guess I was just lucky.

As we walked out, he patted me on the back for being the best shot in Lebanon. His cousin said I cheated because I used two hands. I told him I used two hands because I was trained to shoot people, not walls. There was just no beating this guy. He refused to admit he wasn't that good of a shot. Needless to say, we had another shooting competition later on that fall in October when I came back over to finish our work in Baghdad.

Back in the States I used my connections with Fox News to get them to cover our meeting with the al Anbar sheiks. We set it up to take place in Ramadi. The idea was to get the story out so we could get some exposure for the sheiks with the CPA. We wanted to see if we could cause some type of effect, some type of change in this area that would lead to greater prosperity for the people and generally better relations with the Americans.

I departed the States for my return visit to the Middle East on October 16, 2003. Alex, my business partner, was again my companion. We arrived in Beirut on the seventh and had a series of meetings to discuss how we were going to enter Iraq. The scheme was to go to Jordan via airplane from Beirut International Airport, arrive in Amman, do an overnighter there, meet Sheik Baziq al Ghaood, who was in Amman doing business, and have preliminary discussions with him there. We'd never met him before. From Amman, we would get in a couple of vehicles and drive into Iraq. We had to coordinate several moving pieces.

We departed Lebanon on October 21, 2003. When we got into Amman, I came down with some kind of stomach virus. I drank bad water or ate something I shouldn't have and was pretty much down for the count. I mean, it really wiped me out, so I was struggling through that.

We met the sheik that night. I also met one of his sons, another doctor—a very well educated family, and we discussed having a meeting with the sheiks of the al Anbar region. The location of the meeting and the logistics were planned as well as the media coverage.

His son made transportation arrangements for us. The next morning, we got up at 05:00 hours. Two Suburbans met us and the five of us loaded up. At that time, I had a Lebanese bodyguard with me who had been part of the Muslim militia during the civil war, and who I will refer to as Lucca Brazzi. It's the name that was used in the movie, *The Godfather,* the large hit man who sleeps with the fishes. That's what this gentleman looked like, not quite as heavyset, but a slimmed-down version, tough as nails. He had been captured and tortured for sixty-two days by the Hezbollah back in the mid-80s, and bears the scars of it. Needless to say, there's no love lost between him and the Hezbollah.

We left around 06:30 hours. We drove out of Amman and headed west on the highway that links Iraq with Jordan. This was pretty much a very long, straight road, with nothing but sand, some rocks, and mild elevation off in the distance. But for the most part, it was relatively flat and there was just a whole lot of nothing to look at. Talk about a place that could use a few Texaco stations, they were few and far between. For those of you who haven't been in the Middle East, the majority of the refueling done in a country like Iraq is accomplished by roadside fuel points, where there are literally kids with five-gallon cans, Pepsi bottles, two-liter bottles filled with gasoline, and that's how you get your gas.

If I were going to do a reconstruction effort in remote areas, I would put in large gas station-store complexes along that road from Jordan to Iraq, and the main thing I would put in would be clean restrooms. I mean, you want to talk about a scene from the *Texas Chainsaw Massacre,* walk into a public restroom in Iraq, for that matter, in most places in the Middle East, but especially in Iraq. It looks like somebody cleaned and gutted an elephant in there. It's unbelievable; the stench will just knock you off your feet. There is absolutely no concept of hygiene or sanitation.

I would put in these mega-gas stations with clean facilities, I'd employ the local people, and I'd have management that was very familiar with the service industry and give them classes on hygiene and the proper use of disinfectant. There's a growth industry for you.

It took us about four and a half hours to get to the Iraq-Jordan border and we had to go through a series of checkpoints and get our vehicles inspected. We got our passports stamped, which didn't take very long. It took half an hour to get through the entry process and then we were inside Iraq. The roads here were actually in better condition than they were in Jordan. The road that we took from Jordan to Iraq was only a two-lane highway, whereas when we got into Iraq, it split off and there were two two-lane highways. The road was in good condition, the cement and tar were also in good condition. We made great time getting to the outskirts of Baghdad. It was not surprising that when we drove past Fallujah we were greeted by a Bradley fighting vehicle sitting in the middle of the road with a couple of troops around it. On our side of the road, we had to skirt around it and get over to the other side of the highway and then we passed a Humvee with troops dismounted along a berm, actually firing into a small built-up area and that was Fallujah.

That was the first time I'd seen American soldiers in Iraq and I couldn't resist the temptation to roll down a window and yell out a greeting and a cry of support. Of course they realized immediately that I was an American and that I had been in the military, because of the manner in which I greeted them. They responded with large smiles and thumbs up. I have so much respect and appreciation for these guys who had been in country for eight months, and knew that they were there for a year and in some cases more. Some of them actually came out of a rotation from Afghanistan, some of them had served in Bosnia—no rest for the weary. The Army was not like it used to be. It deploys constantly and it was frustrating to me because I have to listen to politicians who polish a seat with their butt, continually saying the Army's not too small, we're not spread too thin.

> **Rant:** BS! We are way too small, the Army's been cut in half since Desert Storm. We had to activate hundreds of thousands of reservists over a year for a two-year period in order to augment the active component that had been spread entirely too thin and all we did was we make the soldiers suffer because the politicians didn't have the backbone and the general officer corps in the Army didn't have the backbone to say, "We're too g*ddamned small, we need a bigger force or you need to use us less."

We reached the outskirts of Baghdad and I saw some of the prominent architectural features, for example, the extremely large mosque that was on the northwest side of the city, the largest mosque in the world. It's a shame Saddam didn't spend that money on building hospitals and schools.

As we got into town, I noticed that the city was extremely busy; there was a lot of hustle and bustle with thousands of cars on the streets. It was the land of the forgotten Peugeots. There were taxicabs everywhere. Taxicabs were white cars with their fenders painted orange. Some of the taxicabs were Suburbans. The storefronts were just loaded with merchandise. Keep in mind, due to the embargo, nothing was getting in, with the exception of black market items and the stores couldn't hold their merchandise inside, they were busting at the seams. So they dumped it out on the streets and you could see refrigerators, air conditioners, washers and dryers, satellite dishes out the wazoo. I've never seen so many satellite dishes in my life, all out on the streets for sale.

After we weaved our way through the city, we headed toward our compound, which was in an area called ad Doura. This was located in the southern portion of the city just south of the bend in the Tigris River, two kilometers south of the double-decker bridge. We were staying at a business associate's ranch. He probably had a fifty-acre ranch that was filled with date palms, pomegranate trees, lemon trees, pear trees, wild turkeys, and a fish pond. It was really a nice location surrounded by a large ten-foot-high cement wall with a huge iron gate, complete with guards carrying AK-47s. To my surprise, everyone in Iraq seemed to be able to carry an AK-47. You were allowed to have an AK-47 in your house for personal protection. A lot of people had applied for weapons cards from the CPA. The U.S. Army also issued weapons cards authorizing them to carry the weapons with them in their car while they were out on the street. It made you wonder how they could possibly secure the area if everyone's toting an AK.

Of course, the Iraqi dinar was also a problem. At that time, 250 dinars was worth about 12 cents. So when you exchanged a twenty dollar bill, you literally got three or four inches of money. I soon developed an appreciation of how much money you had by how thick the stack was, because the most common denomination on the street was 250 dinars. The new 10,000 dinar bill has helped solve that problem. But it was incredible. I mean, you had to push around a wheelbarrow of cash if you were buying any significant item—this was why many prominent Iraqis used gold. Keep in mind that some of this was offset by the items that we would typically pay a lot of money for, but were cheap in Iraq. For example, gasoline. You could fill up a Suburban with gasoline in Iraq and it would cost you about two dollars and twenty cents, because gasoline was around eighteen cents to twenty cents a gallon. So it's pretty affordable.

The house in the compound was very nice, tiled throughout, with the latest fixtures, set up extremely well, and, to my surprise, very clean. It was a two-story home with three bedrooms, a nice sitting room, a dining room, and a good-sized kitchen. We had a maid that would cook and clean for us, and we had four or five guards who were supplied by the gentleman who had been living in the house prior to us. This was the same guy that was being paid by the United States Army to conduct security operations in and around Baghdad. I will refer to him here as Jabba, and that's just like Jabba the Hut out of *Star Wars*. Well, Jabba had done a pretty good job of winning the hearts and minds of the local military and convinced them that he was an advocate for the regime change, but I saw things and my business partners heard things that led us to believe that his intentions might not have been the best for the coalition forces.

The first night after we arrived, we were greeted by a car bomb at the front gate of our compound. The car bomb didn't go off. Jabba and his security men had gotten intelligence that there was going to be a car bombing at the gate.

His guys headed it off at the pass, more or less, and notified the local police and the military, which came in and made an arrest as soon as the car stopped in front of our gate. They took the car, dragged it out in the middle of the road, and arrested the individual who, rumor has it, was Syrian, and blew up the car. It had about 120 pounds of Italian-made TNT in it.

Either our compound was being targeted because Jabba had been living there or the compound was being targeted because we were living there. Or maybe the compound had been targeted because of my business partner who owned the compound. It could have been a combination of any of those three; but, needless to say, during our first night in Baghdad, we realized that either ourselves or the people we were staying with were on somebody's hit list.

Jabba was very cordial, he invited us to have dinner with him on several occasions, and his wife did the cooking. He was a good host, actually. We met him in my business partner's offices, which I used, and I was impressed to see the number of people coming to visit him on a daily basis. He would hold court in his office and receive people coming to him for different needs and requirements, wanting assistance, to get in and talk to the CPA or look for a loan for a business opportunity, things of that nature.

All the while, his office was surrounded by at least a half a dozen guys, armed with AK-47s, G3s, MP5s, and other types of weapons, so there was always a formidable armed presence in front of the office.

One night in late in October, after Ramadan had started, we were invited to a party given by a relative of Jabba at his house. We went there, and after dinner we were sitting on couches and I watched Jabba slide down on the couch lower and lower, all the while checking his watch two or three times with every passing minute. All of a sudden, we heard a loud *BOOOM,* which violently shook the house. Evidently someone had launched a rocket that hit the Baghdad University only five hundred meters away. As I watched Jabba's reaction to events that occurred that night, I had the uneasy feeling that he had prior knowledge of the incident. I watched his mannerisms, eye language, body language, and it was the first time I suspected our gracious host was up to no good.

My suspicions were confirmed later that evening when we sat down and had an after dinner discussion over a few drinks. He talked to my business partners in Arabic. I know very little Arabic, but I could tell by the tone of the discussion and some of the words being thrown around, that it was pretty heated.

After that I got into an argument with his business partner, the Palestinian, whom I will call "Splinter," because he looks like Splinter the rat from *The Teenage Mutant Ninja Turtles.* We were discussing the Hamas, he believed they were freedom fighters and I, of course, said they were terrorists. His point was that Hamas was actually a freedom fighter organization and he didn't understand why we were labeling them as terrorists. I said, "Well, you can't blow up a bus full of women and kids and not be a terrorist. I'm sorry. There's nothing heroic, honorable, or just about it—they are terrorists."

We went back and forth on that topic for ten to fifteen minutes, and he was obviously upset. I observed the eye language between him and Jabba when my business partner, Charles, would speak. Jabba and Splinter would roll their eyes, or nudge each other under the table, making it obvious that they had a problem with our position on certain topics.

After we left that evening, we drove back to the compound and Charles told me that he suspected Jabba was not on our side. I asked what made him feel that way. He said, "Well, the conversation we had led down the road of me making a recommendation that the Americans should leave Iraq, that we should just turn it back over to the Iraqis. Then Jabba says, "No, no, no, we want the Americans here, because we want to teach them a lesson. We want to teach them a lesson for the 'accountability act' that was being placed on Syria and for their treatment of Iran over the past ten years."

That hit us all right between the eyes. Charles's other business partner, who was traveling with us, was Kassem Khalil. Kassem was a very soft-spoken man who spent most of his time listening and processing information. Kassem's advice was simple—let's not piss this guy off—let's keep him happy and keep an eye on the bastard.

We did not expect this opinion from someone that was working for the U.S. government, who was an advocate for the U.S. government, and the coalition forces. Why, all of a sudden, would an ally of the coalition express an interest in wanting to teach them a lesson?

Then I was introduced to the fact that he was the publisher of a newspaper, a newspaper that was filled with anti-American rhetoric. It was inciting a violent reaction from the Iraqis against the coalition forces. This newspaper, I later found out, was printed in Lebanon by a Lebanese firm known as al Shark. One of the leading heads of al Shark was a gentleman by the name of al Kaki, who was supposedly a known Syrian agent. The paper was distributed in Syria and in Iraq. It's one of the few newspapers in the Middle East that you have to pay for—Jabba was making money hand over fist.

After our argument over dinner and some of the events that followed, I became bothered by the information I was being exposed to, and I felt compelled to bring it to the attention of the U.S. military and the Coalition Provision Authority. I didn't want to go to the U.S. military because Jabba's guys were driving us everywhere we went and I didn't want them saying, "The Americans requested to be driven to a military compound today."

I began the laborious process of making phone calls to get into the CPA—not an easy task. The CPA had insulated itself so well from car

143

bombs that they also insulated themselves from people trying to get information to them.

I actually had to go through a point of contact in the Press Release Office in the Pentagon for the secretary of defense to get a phone number for someone that worked for Ambassador Bremer. Without this contact I never would have gotten in. I brought in all my information and a map showing where I was located. I told them what I had seen and I was received very well by the CPA. Once I got into my briefing, they brought in a couple of their security personnel that provide personal protection for Mr. Bremer and I was asked if I wanted to speak with representatives from other governmental agencies (OGA), and I said, "No, I don't want to speak with anyone from the CIA."

I'm really uncomfortable working with that organization, because the methods and tradecraft they insist on using would have resulted in me having to turn over all my sources and run the chance of getting burned along with my partners, so I avoided them like the plague.

After that visit with the CPA, I went back to my villa. The bombings had been stepped up; we'd had a couple of mortar attacks very close to our compound. They were being launched close to our villa. In fact, one night I was out walking with Charles up by the front gate of the compound. It was about nine at night, and I heard a very distinctive *thunk thunk, thunk, thunk*. I looked at Charles and he looked at me and he said, "It's not a rifle, it's a shotgun. They're shooting birds."

I said, "Well, it's late at night, not good for hunting birds. Didn't sound like a rifle, I hope it's not a mortar."

About twenty seconds later, a mortar round impacted pretty close to our location.

But what concerned me was how close the mortar was when it was fired. I believe it was a small caliber mortar, something around 80 mm and it was either fired inside our compound or just outside the compound wall. Night after night, these mortars were going off, extremely close to our compound. I knew they were being fired just outside the compound wall.

I kept this information in mind and would try to revisit the CPA and give them an update on what was going on.

On my second or third trip to the CPA, I was introduced to Chief Warrant Officer CW4 Holton, who was doing a number of different things, one of which was collecting information from Iraqi sources. He was also working with the schools in Iraq and collecting toys for them. He had a Web site by the name of Chief Wiggles, a blog Web site and I was surprised to find out how well-known he was in the United States when I got back. He would collect toys for the Iraqi kids and then deliver them. They were literally getting tons of toys. Thousands of dollars worth of toys were being sent to support his effort. It was refreshing to see something like that. When you see an American who's in a billet, in a position to do something that is combat-related, but in his free time takes it upon himself and his men to volunteer to do this, to do something noble for the children of Iraq, it is very moving.

That was the kind of message that needed to get out to the Iraqi people, that there were Americans like this that really cared. It's also the kind of message that needs to get on ABC, MSNBC, CNN, and Fox News, that this was what's going on inside of Iraq, rather than about the constant body counts, which, by the way, really aren't that high.

On the one hand, we had focused reporting with what I would call horse blinders on; and, on the other hand, we had reporting that was spun to the point of disinformation or lying. This was nothing new. This has been happening ever since JFK was killed by one bullet. Or should I say, since JFK was killed by one shooter.

I remember telling my bodyguard, Lucca, that if we had truly upset Jabba one of the indicators would be losing our transportation. Lo and behold, a couple of days later, his head of security showed up and said, "We need the car. We have a mission; we have to run up to Mosul."

We said, "Okay, what do we do for transportation?"

They said, "Well, you'll have to arrange that for yourselves, but we need the car."

So we lost our car.

Then, of course, I looked at my bodyguard, who looked at me, we gave each other a glance like, *Okay, here we go.* I remember him asking, "Whadda ya think's going to happen next?"

I said, "The next thing that we can expect is to lose our guns."

Jabba had given us an MP5 for personal protection and he'd also given us his weapons card for the MP5 and a G-3. A couple of days went by; his head of security showed up and said, "We need the MP5."

I said, "Okay, no problem."

We handed over the MP5. I looked at my bodyguard, he looked at me. After the head of Jabba's security left, my bodyguard said to me, "Okay, now what's the next thing that's gonna happen?"

I said, "We're gonna lose the guards."

A couple of days went by and one of the guards got into an argument with the maid. It was not a long-standing argument. Next thing I knew the head of security showed up and said, "We're taking all the guards."

And I said, "Okay, now why are you taking all the guards?"

"We're taking the guards because they don't get along with your maid."

I said, "Ah, now let me get this straight. You're stripping away our security for personal protection because they don't get along with our maid."

"That's correct."

"Okay, alright, that's good. I understand. I just want to make sure I understand what you're doing and why."

He left and I looked at my bodyguard and he said, "Okay, what's next?" He couldn't believe that I had predicted all these things before they happened, but he wasn't as surprised as I was. It seemed so obvious that these were the next steps that were going to happen, I couldn't believe how blatantly obvious his motives were. I knew for certain Jabba had it in for us and I believed the next event that would happen was an attack against our party. Jabba wasn't the sharpest knife in the drawer, but he was cunning.

A lot of the guys running around Iraq, setting off explosions, and attacking American columns weren't the sharpest knives in the drawer, but they were cunning. They do possess a level of tradecraft that we, as Americans, really do not understand, because we've never operated or lived in these types of environments.

I replied to Lucca by saying, "We're gonna get attacked."

Now that raised the eyebrows of my two business partners. They had been skeptical of my assessment of Jabba; that he was actually a bad guy, even though initially, they had told me they felt he was a Syrian spy. Now they were getting a little skeptical of my predictions. I insisted that we were in danger of being attacked.

A few days went by and our phone started to act up. It was on again, off again, and then we could hear another person on the line with us, which is not all that untypical because the phones of Iraq had bad connections. In fact, the rumor was that the CPA wouldn't repair the phones because they thought the terrorists would use them to coordinate attacks. I found this kind of laughable. There were a lot of things that the phones could be used for that were very positive. For example, reporting information, reacting to an incident, calling for emergency vehicles, and things of that nature, that people could use to help fight these attacks. But from what I understand, the phones weren't being repaired because they thought the bad guys would abuse them.

A couple of days went by and we were into what was going to be my last week. I had spent the morning at the office typing up some reports, and couple of letters that I wanted to get to the CPA. I left the office and headed back to the villa. We were going to have Fox News over to the villa that night, some of the crew guys and some of the CPA folks, kind of our last party before I left town. My partners and I were discussing the success of the trip, the fact we had been able to have a meeting with the sheiks of the Al Anbar and to get an interview for Baziq al Ghaood.

Around six, Fox called saying they couldn't make it because they had something come up. Our guests from the CPA showed up and around six thirty. One of the guys who worked for my business partner, Hameed, drove up in his vehicle and starting talking to Charles. In my limited Arabic, I picked up two words. One was *infijaar,* "explosion," and the other one was *maktab,* "office." This was followed by a lot of fast talking and mannerisms that displayed concern. I knew what happened before Charles told me.

But I asked him what happened anyway and he confirmed they'd blown up our office.

Oh brother, I thought. *How unoriginal this guy Jabba was.* He was trying to build the case that the attacks were against him. That he was being targeted the whole time, because he was working with the Americans and he truly was a good guy. They tried to blow up his house. They did blow up his office, and they tried to kill him because of the work he was doing with the Americans. However, the fact that none of his guards were killed, (because they had, all at the same time and just minutes before the explosion, gone to a location in the office which was safe from the explosion) led me to believe that there was still enough suspicious activity here for him to be definitely a person of interest. We decided we were definitely going to leave that week. If they were targeting us, if they were trying to send us a message, we didn't have enough support on the ground to react appropriately.

One of the things that had occurred was that my business partner told Jabba he was no longer welcome in the office, or in the house, and that he needed to move from both locations, because we felt we were putting ourselves at risk by being associated with him.

I reported all this information to the CPA along with some other information that I had collected from another source.

One of the incidents that occurred on the last night I was in Baghdad was that I had listened to two mortars fire on a couple of locations inside the city. Both of the mortars were in close proximity to the ranch. I called the CPA to see if they could get some kind of quick reactionary force to respond to the mortar attack, or if they could get birds up to try and spot them. The insurgents got off at least thirty rounds. One mortar was large, one mortar was small, one could've been anywhere from 100–120 mm, the other was somewhere between 60–80 mm, but they fired in a staccato fashion, which means one fires while the other one's being moved. Once that one gets done firing, he'll pick up and move, while he's moving, the other one starts to shoot.

This happened for an hour and a half and I watched a couple of Little Birds come in. These were, I believe, OH-58 Echos, which is an observation helicopter that's been outfitted with 2.75" rockets. I watched them fly around and try and pick these guys up. When you fire a mortar, it has a muzzle blast that you can see, if you happen to be looking at the right area at the time. But you have to be focused on that area. It's not like it's a large explosion, although a mortar does make a large sound when you're near it, you don't get a tremendous flash out of the barrel, but you do get something that's large enough to see at night.

There was also an AC-130 that was put up in the air; it was circling overhead, so I figured that they would probably nab these guys. My concern was that because we were so close to the area from where the mortars were shooting, we might actually get caught up in some of the return fire from the Americans.

But nothing happened. The insurgents fired for an hour and a half and evidently they didn't pinpoint them.

I heard a couple of vehicles driving around extremely fast in front of our compound, up and down that road. I believe at least one of them was involved in doing a hip shoot, which is basically you step out of the car, you set your tube up, drop a couple of rounds, get back in your car, and take off. While you're moving, the other guy starts to fire. The other gun, which was larger, I believe, was being kept inside a personal residence or a garage, an overhanging area, and was brought out into the open, fired, and then taken back inside. This type of operation is very hard to detect and very hard to do anything against, unless the Iraqi people have the ability to get on the telephone and call the authorities and say this is what's going on.

How to Bring Prosperity, Peace, and Democracy to Iraq (in That Order)

During the month I was in Iraq waiting for things to happen, I was able to meet with some of the members of the interim Iraqi Governing Council including Dr. Achmed Chalabi and Dr. Ayad Alawi, who was the chairman of the council's Security Committee. I also met with his cousin, another Dr. Saabah Alawi, who was regarded, more or less, as the senior consigliere to the Alawi family. I was able to get a lot of insight from them regarding issues and challenges facing the CPA.

After spending a couple of hours with both Alawis I came to realize that the solutions to the most serious problems didn't require a lot of intelligence gathering and analysis and didn't require an extensive background in nation building or even in security operations. What they required was a little bit of humility and the recognition of a culture that we really don't seem to understand. Nor did we seem to want to understand it and that was the culture of the Middle East.

For example, by dismissing the military and disbanding the police force and other security that existed under Saddam Hussein we cut ourselves off from a large number of people that had the training to conduct military operations similar to counterinsurgency and also had the weapons and the know-how to use them. Finally, the outcast security people were the only ones in country who had all the connections in place to create one hell of an intelligence network to foment an insurgency. This last item was bound to be the case once these men were outcasts without jobs and nowhere to go for money or protection—talk about a fertile recruiting ground for the bad guys.

Without a doubt, the largest mistake that the CPA committed after the war ended was the release of the military, the police force, and intelligence people that were in the security organizations. That was what I call nothing but stupidity on the part of the leadership of the men that were put in charge of the CPA, namely, Ambassador Bremer and his principal deputy, Walter Slocum. If they had only listened to the advice of our own military commanders and security professionals, as well as to sympathetic Iraqis, this mistake wouldn't have happened.

Telling it like it is tends to be unpopular with the Bush administration, but here it is: They were narrow-minded egotists and didn't want to hear suggestions from the outside, being too smart for their own good. We now had over half a million disenfranchised and disaffected people that were willing to be recruited by the enemies of the coalition to commit acts of terrorism against our forces and innocent Iraqis. At the same time, we were losing face with the Iraqi people, a fact which is now being realized. We were now reversing our decision by trying to create an indigenous military and bring some of the old army's officers and men back into active service.

The most powerful statement that I heard from the Iraqis was, "We need jobs. You want peace? You get peace through prosperity." Let me spell this out very carefully; the Iraqi people have to be able to go out and earn a living and put food on their tables and take care of their families. Without this fundamental capability in place we would be sitting on an active volcano of hatred and revenge. There were enough satellite dishes throughout Iraq, especially in Baghdad, for many Iraqis to be aware of what's going on in the outside world. They watch our news and were fully aware of how we viewed their problems. They saw the wealth and affluence of the West and wanted it for themselves. They expected us to put a plan in place to see that they got a decent living and security. How could it be otherwise?

Under Saddam Hussein, there was no encouragement of entrepreneurship. There was no safety net or belief among the people that their country would take care of them in their old age or if they became ill or disabled. Now, they wanted systems in place so they could retire and reap the benefits of their national oil wealth and their economy. A feeling of personal security never existed under Saddam. To imagine that all of a sudden there would be millions of jobs with health and retirement benefits because the Americans liberated Iraq was unrealistic. Yet, unrealistic or not, that's the way they see it.

The people that had jobs under the old regime and lost them were not receiving pensions and that still remains to be fixed. One of the suggestions that I made to one of the members of the CPA was that stability is created in unstable regions by employing a large population of people through a specific project. Within that project you embed security personnel that monitor the day-to-day security posture of the local area and the project that is underway. I specified transparent security, which means that not everyone having a security function walks around in uniform.

For example, there was a cement plant in Fallujah. Under my model, we would get a local sheik that had money to purchase the cement plant from the Iraqi Interim Council. Once the cement plant had been purchased it would employ many people, not just to get the plant up and running, but to manufacture cement. Cement is currently being imported into Iraq from Lebanon and Jordan. Imagine the total dollars of U.S. and donor aid being pledged for reconstruction of Iraq. Be aware of how little of this money actually stayed in the Iraqi economy because local people were not being hired.

Once the cement was being produced and the plant was up and running, you could place people who collect information within the labor force that actually work at the plant. These sources come from the local area and work right alongside the people within the plant. This way you head off problems before they come to the surface because nine times out of ten, there are two to three degrees of separation within the Iraqi people. Everyone knows that supposedly there are only six degrees of separation between any two individuals on earth. Iraqi families are large and cohesive and they are stretched across the countryside. So I would guarantee if you hired eight hundred people from Fallujah, the majority of those people would either know each other or know someone that was a relative of the guy standing next to them. The rumor mill in Iraq is probably one of the most developed and advanced grapevine networks I've ever seen and I think that's because of the oppression of Saddam Hussein over a thirty-five-year period.

The word would get out if there was going to be an attack. This would give enough warning so threats could be headed off by passing information either to an Iraqi security force, the CPA, or to the American military.

But we have to create peace through prosperity. We have to create jobs. Once the people have a vested interest in keeping their cement plant open and running, because it's their life blood, it's their umbilical cord, they will defend it. They were not going to want anyone to attack it and they were not going to allow anyone to attack it. I think setting up operations like this in the most volatile areas would send a message. Once we flip the proverbial middle finger to the bad guys and we demonstrate our ability to grab the bull by the horns, we will get the stability we need to turn things over to the Iraqis. Letting an Iraqi buy the cement plant and permitting his employees to share ownership in the cement plant, and by paying them wages of $250 to $300 a month we insure dependency on the security forces, the Iraqis who patrol the streets and keep terrorism from happening.

We also would create a sense of entrepreneurship and a true sense of a democracy. This is what capitalism is all about. Once ownership took hold, it would be infectious, because other Iraqis would see the quality of life that these people were experiencing and they'll want to get a piece of that for themselves and their families, but this must all be executed under the umbrella of Islam and not a government institution.

This was the most common suggestion that I received from the Alawis, and from regular Iraqis that I spent time with, including my security guards and farmers that worked on the ranch.

They must have jobs. They were very happy Saddam Hussein was gone. But, when it comes down to it, if you're not making money, you're miserable. That was one reason why fanatical Islam had spread so much in the Middle East, because of the disparity in wealth between the different classes. You had a small portion of the country that was mega-rich, and a large portion of the country that lived at the poverty level. Folks, we're not talking poverty as we know it in the United States, we are talking two to three echelons below that.

I attended a meeting at the Pentagon in late 2003, and it was in the secretary of defense's conference room with the man himself present. In the briefing presented by an Army colonel, he talked about five different groups that they believed were conducting guerilla-type activities in Iraq. He listed foreign fighters, al Queda, criminal elements within Iraq, former Saddam loyalists, and new and emerging terrorist groups. The one category that wasn't mentioned was, I think, probably the largest category of them all; disillusioned, disenfranchised Iraqis, just plain old regular Iraqis. These coalition enemies were people that really have not seen their lives improved by being "freed," quite the opposite. Now they saw an occupation force in their country committing acts that violate their culture and traditions. So, they felt a need to respond in some way. There were people sitting on the fence who saw the occupation force of the United States as the enemy. They don't have jobs, so when they were approached by someone with a handful of money, offering to pay them five thousand dollars to create their own little cell to go out and kill Americans, or kill contractors, or kill foreigners, that's quite the proposition. They were being recruited by the bad guys. So we didn't necessarily have to contemplate what the next attack was and how to protect sites, what we had to do was out-recruit the bad guys. We needed to out-recruit them in the same manner that businesses in corporate America out-recruit one another in retaining the best and brightest people that are coming out of college or are part of the American labor force. That's the key to success in Iraq.

People argued that the tactics that we used needed to be changed, and that we were approaching our warfare in Iraq with too conventional a mind-set; we probably are. But at this point, I think arguing about the techniques and tactics being used is really a moot point, because, truthfully, we shouldn't be doing any of it anymore. The Iraqis should have a paramilitary force that conducts convoys and relief operations, border security, intelligence gathering, the movement of money from one point to another point, from one bank to another bank. So when a convoy gets ambushed by a bunch of bad guys supposedly dressed as Fedayeen Saddam, we could count on Iraqi security having a vested interest in killing them. After all, it could be their payroll or that of their cousins being hijacked. In that way we could create animosity within the local Iraqi community against the bad guys because they inevitably would kill their neighbors or threaten their livelihood.

Iraqis protecting Iraqis, this is what we need. We didn't want Americans being ambushed and accidentally killing Iraqi civilians. We want the Iraqis to do that. Just like we see in Saudi Arabia now, with the Saudis fighting their own Islamic fundamentalists, it is Saudi against Saudi. So when a fundamentalist killed a Saudi, they brought down the wrath of the family of the people that were killed, which meant tribal influence.

They brought down the wrath of the religious community of the people that were killed, which meant a clerical influence and the issuing of a *fatwa*, or religious decree, against the extremists.

It's this model of pacification that will allow the Americans to back away from the situation and essentially work themselves out of the responsibility. This is what the Special Forces do best. You train, assist, and advise the local indigenous security forces to solve their own problems and you work yourself out of a job, which means you work yourself out of the country, out of the theater, and you just provide enough support so they can accomplish their mission, which is peace, stability, and economic prosperity. Once that's done, we've accomplished our mission.

> **Lesson Learned:** You can't run a country and gain the respect and loyalty of the general population unless you can demonstrate beyond a doubt that your presence there is a guarantee of their personal safety and prosperity. If we strip them of basic needs in life while at the same time demonstrating our contempt for their culture, they will be hostile to us. If we are not protecting and feeding them, they will rely on the insurgents for their protection and food. It is in these simple ways that we are failing to win many Iraqis over to the side of democracy and freedom. Their economic prosperity and livelihood are just as important as their physical security. What is a man worth who can't support his family and have respect for himself by holding down a job? It was a big mistake for the CPA to have ignored that basic fact of life and not put it on the front burner where it belonged. The art of unconventional war was as foreign to the CPA as the Middle Eastern society that they attempted to control.

Photo Gallery

Figure 1.

Me standing outside my tent in our tactical assembly area just south of the Iraq-Kuwait border, Desert Storm.

Figure 2.

Photo taken just before Desert Storm when I caught a quick
catnap in my Humvee.

Figure 3.

An ammo crate being pulled off an Iraqi BMP—most of their ammo was supplied by Jordan.

Figure 4.

Me (left) and my driver, Specialist Rome, standing next to our camouflaged Humvee in Iraq a couple of days after the war ended.

Figure 5.

Me with my MP-5 standing next to the bombed-out car in front of our compound, Baghdad, November 2003.

Figure 6.

In-flight air refueling with KC-130 en route to Haiti, photo taken from door gunner position of my bird.

Figure 7.

Me (right) and Pat with confiscated weapons from the
lieutenants' apartment, photo was taken on the day that Don
Halstead was shot.

Figure 8.

Me (right) and Vince in the voodoo house of horrors
standing next to Backa.

Figure 9.

Mike McInerney standing at Secretary of Defense Rumsfeld's right. Picture taken in early September 2003 in Gardez, Afghanistan, at his firebase. He had just returned from his last combat operation and was packing up to return to Bagram to fly back to the U.S.

Figure 10.

Mike on the road to Kandahar, September 2003.

Figure 11.

Bob and friend "Dave," Baghdad, August 2004.

Chapter Four

Corporate Security: What Can We Do?

After dedicating a decade to force protection and physical security, I ventured into the corporate security field and here are my lessons learned. What do business leaders need to know in order to protect their infrastructure from penetration and attack?

Security Professionals

In September 1999, I was approached by a friend of mine to see if I was interested in doing security assessments for a private investigation company out of Maryland, Maxwell Security Management. Maxwell had just received a contract with a large telecommunications company to assess the physical security of their key communications nodes and facilities.

I had experience in doing this type of work, specifically site assessments for U.S. embassies overseas, and I felt very comfortable in talking to anyone about the issues involved with physical security. I signed on to the project fully confident in my ability to help.

The client had several facilities located up and down the eastern seaboard and was headquartered in northern Virginia. Our plan, initially, was to conduct probing operations and attempt to penetrate their different facilities by finding weaknesses and vulnerabilities. Once inside we would then exploit the break-in.

The key to a successful probe was basically just walking in like you owned the joint. Fitting in, assimilating with their people, and just looking like everyone else was the technique we used.

Because most people are not security minded, it was easy to use company employees to help penetrate security defenses. A method I liked using was called tailgating. What I mean by tailgating is you walk right behind people who have a badge and are cleared for access to the facility. They open the gate with their badge and then they hold the door open for you—being polite has its drawbacks. This becomes difficult in a turnstile-type environment where you needed a key card that you have to swipe through a reader to get through a gate, but there was always a way to bypass that. I found that back door and side door entrances to buildings sometimes aren't well safeguarded and are easy to get through. Better yet, find a back or side door that someone has propped open while they smoke a quick cigarette. You'd be surprised how often that happens.

Where there's a will, there's a way when it comes to the penetration of a "secure" facility.

American Society for Industrial Security

Prior to 9/11, there were several established security organizations that were very reputable, consisting of successful security professionals. The American Society for Industrial Security had several thousand, if not tens of thousands, of members nationwide that dedicated their lives and their careers to improving security.

National Cargo Security Council

The National Cargo Security Council is a group of several hundred professional business, commercial, and government personnel that are dedicated to thwarting cargo theft; the counterfeiting of false bills of lading, invoices, and the overall cargo theft area. While most of their work dealt with shipping and trucking, when you look at the seaport issue, you realize that within the cargo crime area there exists a huge potential for terrorism to thrive.

The fact is that cargo crime in the United States totals about $15 billion annually—quite the growth industry. This showed the level of involvement that criminals had in the cargo and shipping industry. This type of crime was not going away, which is why terrorism will never go away. Crime can't be stopped and terrorism is a form of crime, therefore, it, too, would never go away. The best we could work toward was the mitigation and negation of crime, which I believe facilitates terrorism.

Coming Out of the Closet after 9/11

One of the things that truly amazed me was, immediately following the 9/11 attacks, how many security professionals there were, and how many companies became security companies on September 12.

The amount of people that came out of the closet, if you will, was staggering. It wasn't because they had the credentials or their patriotic duty compelled them to get involved in the war on terror. They were looking for the big cash payout. They wanted to make a ton of money and everyone immediately assumed that there were billions upon billions of dollars about to be dumped into security. It was assumed that everybody would need a security assessment. Everybody would want to have proper training in risk analysis; how to handle a national level event or terrorist attack within their area; developing a first responder's kit and things of that nature.

Not true. Not true at all.

If you think about it, that jumping on the bandwagon, or gravy-train, was similar to what happened in the run-up to the year 2000. Then it had been the "Y2K" problem, where all the computers were supposed to crash and the lights would go out because computer software had never been updated to handle year digits that didn't begin with 1-9. Billions were spent quite unnecessarily on this boondoggle and it was natural to believe that the post-9/11 security panic would bring a similar or even bigger windfall to anyone who could pose as a counterterrorism or security "expert."

Security Was Never a Priority

Corporate funding for security efforts was minimal, at best, and the faucet for large government contracts was running at a trickle. So there was no large cash cow that immediately appeared. Some of the security companies that appeared on September 12 have died on the vine since then because there simply wasn't any funding for them and they lacked the big corporate traction of the super firms like Halliburton, Bechtel, Raytheon, etc.

I attended conferences for the National Cargo Security Council and the American Society of Industrial Security after 9/11 and noticed the turnout was incredible. Normally, some of these events I'd gone to in the past would have maybe twenty or thirty booths set up at the conference, allowing companies to demonstrate their products. A year or so after 9/11 there were literally hundreds of booths and the turnout had increased tenfold.

I also found it amusing to see and hear some of the guest speakers that were on the agenda for the security forums. Ha! There were people that really had no business being on the podium, let alone trying to talk about security issues. They possessed none of the requisite skills.

Stereotyping Security Personnel

Security personnel have suffered from being stereotyped over the past fifteen to twenty years. When you talk to someone about security and you tell them you're in the security profession, they assume that you have a closet filled with blue uniforms that say Atlas Security on a shoulder patch. That stereotype, I believe, has been slowly chipped away and that paradigm of the security industry has been broken since 9/11, because people have come to understand the massive implications of poor security and the amount of training required in order to be a good, effective security manager.

Most security personnel were thought of as $6.95-an-hour employees that sat at a desk for twelve hours watching TV, drinking coffee, or just standing out by the loading dock and smoking a cigarette. Unfortunately, in some cases, that description was and still is true and that is why we have so many problems with security in this country. That attitude was the prerequisite to New York's skyline being redesigned. This lackadaisical attitude crept into government organizations, in some cases, up to the highest levels.

Funding

Security really had never been a priority. I say this because the way I gauge it, if something is a priority it would be appropriately funded. If you look at our foreign policy you can see that Africa had never really been funded until recently with the president's AIDS initiative—therefore, I would argue that supporting Africa was never a priority. Look at most of your large corporate entities and assess the amount of money that was allocated toward security. Compare that to the different initiatives within the company where funds were allocated and you will see that most companies, specifically prior to 9/11, never really looked at security, outside of access control. As more and more companies began to develop an Internet presence, some funding was generated for security in the cyber realm, but even that was woefully inadequate.

Some firms have good counseling programs and monitoring programs for domestic violence in the workplace, because this is actually a large concern, and, if you look at the statistics on most women who are accosted physically, mentally, or sexually, it happened in the workplace. There were a number of companies that did allocate resources and funding to prevent domestic violence in the workplace, but this piecemeal approach to security only buys temporary solace.

An example of a lack of security funding was evident when I was conducting a security assessment for a telecommunications company in Virginia. After meeting their corporate "security" manager, it became quite obvious that security wasn't a priority and the gentleman's security background was limited, at best. The company's overall losses due to improper equipment accountability were staggering—large amounts of property were walking out the front door on a weekly basis. The lack of emphasis or seriousness in which security was addressed was blatantly obvious.

I recall conducting surveillance one night, sitting out behind a building just two kilometers south of Washington's Dulles Airport. I was in a vehicle with a night-vision camera and was observing the back of the building by the loading dock area—a lot of things tend to happen by the loading docks—and I witnessed a construction worker come out of the building carrying a laptop computer hidden beneath a newspaper. He put it in the trunk of his car, just as brazen as can be, with no reservations about it at all, and then he went back inside the building.

To give you an idea of the professionalism of the security guards that this telecommunications company had hired, we watched a prostitute come in one night, in a very tacky leopard-skin outfit I might add. She slid under the security guard's desk and serviced him right there at the check-in point going into the building. Something tells me this type of action was not covered in his guard instruction manual—the problem was that the prostitute earned more money than the security guard did. Proper training and adequate salaries can help alleviate situations like that.

Where the Security Manager Plugs into the Corporate Ladder

A key indicator of a lack of proper security policies and procedures within a company is when the security manager plugs into the hierarchy of the corporate leadership. If you have a security manager that doesn't speak directly to and work directly with the chief financial officer, the CEO, or one of the VPs, then security will never be a priority. The security flaws identified by the security manager and his recommendations on how to remedy them, followed up by his funding proposals, will never carry any real weight, because he never has access to the right people.

> **Lesson Learned:** Tie your security manager to your hip, know what he knows and provide adequate resources for him to protect your most valuable assets—your people.

In my experience after looking at several corporations, the security manager was normally off to the side, or on the bottom rung of the organization chart. Frankly, because he didn't generate revenue for the company he was considered a profit sponge. Because of this paradigm people looked at security with the attitude of, well, that's why we have insurance. And, well, you're right. That's why we do have insurance, but when you look at the potential for loss through a significant event, your insurance won't help you, not to mention the loss of life and the possibility of lawsuits that would ensue. Companies tend to get buried in litigation for extended periods of time and this is why many firms are now self underwriting their insurance—talk about risk management.

Reactive, Never Proactive

Companies that are in desperate need of proactive versus reactive security measures are the organizations that deal with large volumes of goods. They are the ones that move stocks of supplies and consumables from Point A to Point B. This can be from a main distribution warehouse out to retail centers or from an international port of origin to the continental United States.

For example, if you look at the trucking community, America's warehouses are on the highways. Because of just-in-time logistics and just-in-time manufacturing, the days of having million-square-foot warehouses stocked full of goods and supplies no longer exist. Manufacturers produce items within seventy-two to ninety-six hours of the item being requested from a store or from a distributor that anticipates being at zero-balance within the next twenty-four to forty-eight hours. So, as goods are manufactured and shipped just in time to get to the stores, the critical element becomes throughput, not security. The shipping industry has never placed security at the forefront of their operations—terrorists aren't stupid. That's why our seaports have the vulnerability problems that they have. They were built to maximize throughput; the passing through of the most amount of supplies and materials physically possible in a selected time period with a minimum amount of human labor involved.

Once these goods are injected into our intermodal system, they're moved rapidly from Point A to Point B. Just drive down a freeway and take a look at most of the tractor-trailers that are on the road right now and look at the double-locking bars on the back of the tractor-trailer. You'll notice that most of these trucks are secured with a padlock and a prayer. People may ask, well, what does that have to do with terrorism? I would tell you, a lot. So would the FBI. In fact, massive shipments of cigarettes are typically hijacked from the Carolinas and then moved to the northern region around Detroit where they're sold at a much higher price. This is done by organizations that have actually been traced back to the Middle East, terrorist-type organizations. The FBI has many examples that clearly demonstrate that the proceeds from the cargo theft industry are going into the hands of terrorists.

Continuing to look at the trucking community, let's talk about tankers. A fuel tanker laden down with thousands of pounds of fuel typically moves from a fuel distribution point just outside a city and has direct access to the city without having to go through a weighing station. The majority of these fuel trucks have no security other than the driver. Some of them have onboard systems similar to OnStar™ or that of a tracking system provided by a firm like QualComm, but the vast majority of the trucks have absolutely nothing. I know this because I've worked with large fuel companies and their security professionals in trying to develop ways of thwarting attacks against their vehicles. They feel the threat isn't high enough to justify allocating the amount of money necessary to secure their fleets. In the final analysis, it all boils down to one basic way of thinking—the government doesn't make it mandatory so why should we?

Next time you see a fuel truck, regard it as a very large bomb that can be delivered just about anywhere. All you need is a little motivation, a knife or a pistol to hijack the driver, and you own the truck. In fact, I would tell you at this point, putting money into airline security and ignoring the trucking industry is asking for another disaster. We are leaving open a tremendous vulnerability within the United States of America. Our roads are wide open to terrorists and allowing them to deliver either weapons of mass destruction or poisoned food supplies to citizens of this great country because nobody wants to get off the dime and allocate some funds toward solving the problem is ridiculous. Remember the severe damage caused by a twenty-foot Ryder truck packed with diesel fuel-soaked fertilizer? The bomb detonated by Timothy McVeigh in front of the Murrah Federal Office Building in Oklahoma City in 1995 killed 168 people—compare that to a fuel truck going off. The energy contained in that explosion was just a small fraction of what would be involved in an explosion of a tanker truck load of liquefied natural gas (LNG).

This is where the proactive versus reactive posture comes in. If we were proactive in the manner in which we safeguarded our assets overseas, the Marine barracks in Beirut, the embassies in Africa, the World Trade Center towers, and the USS *Cole* would not have been attacked. If we were proactive and had actually looked at the security assessments that were conducted on each one of those targets and we had put proper countermeasures in place to deny access to those targets, we probably would have a lot of people who wouldn't be dead right now, but we didn't do that. We tend to sit on our butts until something blows up or someone flys an airplane into a building before we say, "Gee, yeah, we could've done something to prevent this." Remember, we are always looking at ways to prevent the last attack, not the next one. We placed a lot of emphasis on airline security after 9/11 and have done little to protect our trucks or our seaports. You can bet that the terrorists will do their own assessments of our security flaws and will devise plans to exploit even small vulnerabilities to the utmost.

> **Lesson Learned:** We must safeguard transportation assets that move goods throughout the nation or they will be moving something far more sinister. The trucking community must secure its loads and track its drivers providing them with the latest in anti-hijacking technology—time is running out…

Security Assessments and Risk Management

So how do you prevent an attack? What can you do to prevent a terrorist incident? What can you do to prevent thievery? What can you do to prevent sabotage and acts of subversion? You can do a security assessment and you can practice good risk management techniques all day long, but if you don't train your people you are throwing your money away.

Risk management, is a term that is commonly abused and misused within a number of different communities, including the security profession.

What Is Risk?

Risk is when you put $150.00 on Black 22 and you roll the dice and you come up busted. That's risk. Risk is also when your security manager is standing in front of your desk and he says, "Sir, if we don't fix our access control system, we could have some serious problems. We could have people in our building who don't need to be here. We could have a loss of life. We could have property stolen from our facility."

And the executive who's sitting behind his desk half listening to his security manager and checking his stock portfolio on his laptop looks up and says, "Fred, ah, you do the best you can. We don't have enough money right now to throw into the, uh, equation. So let's just manage it as best we can. Thanks for your time."

That, my friends, is risk. That's where the rubber meets the road.

The way you manage risk is by funding appropriate countermeasures in order to negate or mitigate the effects of an incident. That can be the effects of a natural act of God, be it flood, fire, electricity, earthquake, or it can be countermeasures in order to prevent somebody from sneaking over your wall at night, kicking in a basement window, and sabotaging your main switching system, which provides services to about twenty-five thousand cell phones. That's risk management—reducing your chance of loss by spending a few bucks or losing a few man hours to training.

Can Risk Be Managed?

How do you actually manage risk? Well, you don't actually manage risk. You control the effects of it or you reduce the effects of it. You can try and put a system in place that provides a level of security, a level of protection, a blanket, an insulator. But you don't manage risk. You manage assets. You lead people while managing assets in order to reduce your risk. But you don't manage risk. You can't manage an act of God. You can't manage somebody breaking into your building late at night and stealing corporate information; you can only prevent it or minimize its impact.

Conducting Assessments

Personnel, Procedural, Physical, Information

The best way to provide security for your company, its information, your personnel, and your property is to conduct a security assessment, identify the shortfalls, and then train your personnel.

Security assessments should look at personnel, procedures, physical, and information. Those are the four areas of a security assessment.

Security assessments are conducted in order to identify two things: vulnerability and threat. They are both heavily dependent upon each other. One can cancel the other one out. What I mean by this is if you have no vulnerability, you don't have to worry about security. If you have no *threat,* you don't have to worry about security. I cannot think of a single organization that has no vulnerability and no threat. The first thing we should all do is recognize what constitutes a threat.

Threat Assessment—Internal and External

A threat is an event that when it's launched against a specific target, can either cause damage, loss of property, loss of information, loss of output, or loss of life. Threats can be carried out by a number of different means.

1. Act of God

2. Low-level crime

3. Terrorism

4. Corporate espionage

5. Domestic violence

I further break these threats into two categories. There are really only two kinds of threats: an internal threat and an external threat. The hardest threat to protect your company against is an internal threat. Why? Because you've already granted them access.

Internal Threats

Remember, some of the greatest espionage escapades—such as Robert Hansen at the FBI and Aldrich Aimes at the CIA—were carried out by people that had security clearances, that already had access, and they were co-opted into providing information to outside agencies by the almighty and ever-powerful dollar bill. Well, that holds true today in security. The most dangerous threat is the internal threat. Somebody that has a clearance, people that are trusted agents that have access, these are the ones who can do the greatest damage.

In order to keep an honest man honest, what can you do to help provide security checks and balances against internal threats?

First and foremost, trust no one. This may go against some of your beliefs if you think that all people are good until they prove otherwise. But in the security profession, that's what can get you killed.

No one person in your company should have complete and total access to everything—NO ONE…

Information within the company should be compartmentalized and only people who are on a need-to-know basis should have access to that information. Information or equipment that is very sensitive in nature should be monitored by surveillance devices, access control, or other types of auditing systems that will show who had access, when, and the last individuals to either take something out, access something, or simply walk into a room. If you choose not to do this you are accepting risk—by the way, this is not a form of risk management.

And lastly, the key word here to help limit an internal threat is leadership. This is directly tied to an action called supervision. You must supervise your employees. You must lead them. Not manage them, you manage assets. You lead people. This means constant communication, supervision, mentoring, and training.

External Threats

The next form of threat is an external threat. What are external threats? They are acts of God, terrorist organizations, low-level crime, vandalism, counterfeiting, domestic violence, hostile actions by your domestic and foreign business associates, just to name a few.

How do you safeguard yourself against an external threat? Most people typically envision a castle with a moat as being secure against outside forces. And I would tell you that this holds true today. The castle and moat theory is alive and well for protecting personnel, physical property, and information—a firewall for IT systems is a modern-day moat. Employing a variety of firewalls, whether physical or cyber, that protect your facilities, personnel, or systems against attack from external sources are standard and, if updated regularly, provide ample protection.

Developing perimeter security, a fence or a wall, gates, Jersey barriers (concrete median blocks), an access control system that prevents unauthorized access into your building and into specific key areas, while providing much protection may or may not be necessary depending on your threat level. But the best thing, the absolute best thing you can do to negate or mitigate an external threat is to train your company employees in the policies and procedures that should exist within your company that deal with security. Training is the key to success and it is very cheap.

Lesson Learned: Most of the companies I conducted assessments on did not have a standard operating procedure that included training for company personnel and some firms didn't have a security standard operatiing procedure (SOP) at all. The firms that did have training plans rarely enforced them.

When conducting a threat assessment, you must assess company personnel, procedures, physical security, and informational security as a whole; you can't dismiss a category or focus on one area without considering the impact of the other categories.

The only true way to accurately assess your threat is by getting a snapshot of what I refer to as your "threat posture." The way you get a snapshot of your threat posture is by conducting surveillance or an assessment of the threat categories that are applicable to your firm: acts of God, corporate espionage, internal and external employees, people or companies you're doing business with. Acts of God and threats that you can not physically observe require a detailed historical analysis or trend line analysis. Threats that fall into the category of being perpetrated by personnel require active surveillance. The best way, and I would submit the only accurate way, to do this is through observation and gathering information, similar in fashion to a law enforcement or military operation. This means you need to have eyes on your facility, you need to be able to monitor your environment, both internal and external, and you need to be able to watch people that may be watching you. It's almost like doing counter-reconnaissance.

This is conducted with trained security personnel and by training your corporate personnel—they need to know what to look for. There are different indicators that your people are being worked for information, commonly referred to as "social engineering." You can also watch for signs of people observing your building or conducting "waste engineering," which is Dumpster diving, going through your trash in an attempt to find corporate or personal information.

Lesson Learned: Train your employees not to be polite to strangers; don't hold the door open for people without proper badges or identification. When asked a question by a stranger respond with a question—who are you and why do you want to know? This may seem like a simple "no brainer" solution, but you would be surprised at the impact it will have.

A lot can be learned by just observing a site and by looking for people that are watching your site—trust me—someone is watching you. I can cite different instances where we've observed people taking photographs and videotaping bridges and key infrastructure sites in the U.S. Following 9/11 there were several incidents where people were stopped and their cameras were confiscated because they were filming a nuclear power plant —safe to say they weren't admiring the architectural beauty of the structure.

There is only one way to get a true snapshot of your threat posture, and that's through human beings gathering information.

Lesson Learned: If your firm has three hundred employees then you have three hundred sets of eyes and ears at your disposal for your security operations—train them and use them.

Cost-benefit Analysis

Potential Loss Versus Prevention, Historical Analysis and Trend-Line Analysis

Security booths and store shelves are filled with the latest in automation software boasting their ability to conduct threat and vulnerability assessments—danger Will Robinson! While these programs do provide a great deal of added value they do not replace a well-trained security expert; they enhance his capabilities, they don't replace them. Recognizing the value added of a software program and the reason it was created must be taken into account prior to spending money on the heavy price tag that most of these programs are tagged with. If you are going to be conducting numerous assessments on a regular basis, I encourage you to look at an automation security assessment program.

Software programs that use algorithms to assign a numerical value or ranking to your threat posture, your vulnerability, or the probability that you may actually experience an attack, I must say, are very questionable. The only way you can determine your real threat posture is by conducting random assessments through active and passive observation and surveillance missions. Your security manager must conduct an actual hands-on assessment of your threat in order to determine who's watching you, if anyone is actually attempting to get into your facility, if there have been hacker attacks against your Web site, or if you've noticed suspicious activities on or around your site. Once you gather information and determine that you do have a threat, a specific threat that you've identified, you can take appropriate measures to mitigate or negate that threat through the implementation of countermeasures and training.

Automation programs that simply crunch preprogrammed information and spit out a value telling you your potential for loss or what your threat level may be without considering real world observations, to me, are a waste of time and money.

If after conducting several months of random surveillance of your compound, building, boat, whatever it may be, you haven't noticed any activity and there doesn't appear to be any threat against you, then you need to conduct a historical analysis of incidents within your area. Assess areas such as low-level crime, vandalism, and acts of God—the last time there was a flood, things of that nature. This will enable you to determine from a historical perspective the likelihood of experiencing one of those events. This is where automation programs that have up-to-date databases of incidents in certain areas come into play—they will reduce your hours and days of research into literally seconds. Then you can apply the appropriate countermeasures to mitigate or negate the effects of a possible event.

Another critical piece of a security assessment is determining your vulnerabilities. A vulnerability assessment is assessing weaknesses that exist, permitting attackers or natural events to harm your organization's facilities, people, or information.

Vulnerability Assessments

The first thing you need to do when conducting a vulnerability assessment is to identify the key assets that your company has. The military uses the acronym MEVA: mission essential vulnerable area. The key assets that you have within your company can be discovered very simply by determining which systems, if lost, would compromise your ability to conduct your mission, and if you were still able to conduct your mission, how severely degraded would it be?

As an example of a key asset, let us look at a hydroelectric power plant. Hydroelectric power plants capture the energy released by water falling through a vertical distance, and transform this energy into useful electricity. In general, falling water is channeled through a turbine which converts the water's energy into mechanical power. The rotation of the water turbines is transferred to a generator which produces electricity. For the purpose of this study, I will discuss a high head hydro plant. High head power plants are the most common and generally utilize a dam to store water at an increased elevation. The use of a dam to impound water also provides the capability of storing water during rainy periods and releasing it during dry periods. It is the design of this type of plant that an attacker can use to his benefit.

A hydroelectric plant has several key components that allow it to provide electricity. Some of the key components of a hydroelectric plant are its dam, turbines, step-up and step-down transformers, main switch, back up or auxiliary power generators, and water induction shoots, just to name a few. If a hydroelectric plant lost any of these key assets or systems, it would cease to function or it would function on a severely degraded basis. Keep in mind that each one of the key assets has mission-essential components that perform a critical function for the key asset. A high head dam that traps water in order to feed the water intake chutes has several components that when interrupted will result in the plant shutting down. Some of these key components can be destroyed, interrupted, or rendered ineffective by using unconventional attack techniques. The point here is that taking out a single component of a key asset does not require a five-hundred-pound car bomb; it may only require dumping a gallon of water on a main switch or terminal control system. The end result is that the power plant or one of its mission essential components is vulnerable to attack, it may only be water, but its effect would be devastating—think like the attacker—not the defender.

> **Lesson Learned:** A vulnerability assessment has to be conducted through the eyes of the attacker. The Special Forces have a course at Fort Bragg that teaches how to protect targets against attack, they do this by attacking the site as the bad guy would and then reverse engineer the countermeasures to negate or mitigate the target's vulnerability. The key isn't the countermeasures; it is the uniqueness and accuracy of the attack scenarios.

What type of effect is the threat trying to achieve? Do they want to shut the hydro plant down? Or, do they just want to affect its operations? If they want to shut the plant down, then they may hit the dam, the turbines, or the transformers in a fashion that will totally remove the ability of the plant to function. If they just want to interrupt operations, slow operations down, then all they need to do is cause some type of effect that creates a problem within the plant's internal infrastructure that affects the ability to generate or distribute power. Recognize that a plant can generate power all day long, but if it can't push that power into a main grid it is useless.

This type of security assessment is referred to as an effects based assessment. What type of effect is the attacker striving for? In an airport scenario, a good example of creating a desired effect would be a passenger with a weapon simply passing through a security checkpoint. This kind of security breach would cause the entire terminal to be shut down for hours while the area was being thoroughly searched. While this search was being conducted the attacker may take advantage of the effect created and use that to facilitate a larger attack.

This type of reaction happened at the Atlanta airport when an innocent individual ran down an up escalator past security to retrieve a lost bag. Even though no weapon was involved, this incident basically paralyzed the whole airport for hours. If this were an actual attack the reaction of the security force could have been exploited—I don't want to go into scenarios for security reasons, but you can use your imagination.

Probes

Once you've identified your key assets and their mission-essential components, you then need to conduct a series of probes or attack scenarios. Probes are attacks launched against your key assets in order to determine the vulnerabilities that exist and the types of effects that can be created and then exploited. The security manager for an airport should ask the same questions his potential adversary would ask. How can I get access to the runway? How can I get access to the terminal? How can I get access to the control tower? How can I affect operations without taking the chance of being compromised?

Probes should not be a staged, or what I refer to as a canned, event. Probes are not something that you rehearse. They are not something of which people are aware. A probe is an actual attack that takes place against the target without the knowledge of the guard force that's in place or the employees. Only the senior leadership within the company should be aware that a probe is underway.

The probe team should carry some type of identification or document that states their purpose and their mission and a number to call in order to verify who they are. This is done in the event of the probe team being compromised.

I've conducted probes against military installations, power generation plants, railroad stations, seaports, personal residences, State Department targets, and in all the probes I've conducted, well over a hundred, I have never been compromised. The reason I was never compromised wasn't because I was so good, it's because the security was so bad.

The key to success during a probe is assimilation—this is what the attackers strive for. The technique of admitting nothing, denying everything, and making counteraccusations works in most cases of confrontation during a probe. Don't wait for the security guard to approach you, you approach the security guard.

One of my favorite techniques is to loiter outside a building in my vehicle with a digital camera and take pictures of people coming in and out of the building trying to get a close-up picture of an identification badge. Typically personnel are instructed to wear their badges above their waist in a visible position; this really helps out the attackers. I then go on to that company's Web site and try and identify logos from the Web site that were present on the badges; next, I cut and paste the logos and create my own badge. This wasn't for scanning purposes at a gate or card reader, this was in order to facilitate tailgating or social engineering.

The best groups of people to exploit within corporate America are smokers. Smokers, in general, are not allowed to smoke within the confines of most buildings. Typically, most smokers will smoke just outside the building, because the company refuses to pay for the construction of a smoking room. I simply walk up to a group of smokers, wearing my fake badge, normally backward or upside down so they couldn't read it, mixed in with other badges, and I'd light up. Smokers bond quite well within their community, so I make small talk, monitor their conversations, and then as they walked back into the building, I follow them right in. Once inside the building, I tail people around, making my way up to the top of the building, then I work from the top of the building down to the basement, using the side stairwell. I either carry tape or paper clips and jimmy each one of the side stairwell doors open so they can't lock. I typically do this from the top floor all the way down to the bottom floor allowing me total access to a side stairwell and all the floors in between. This is especially critical if you are probing a building that uses a key control device on the elevator. This technique of stairwell hopping allows an attacker excellent access to the building.

I then hang out in a bathroom until after hours, waiting for the building to empty. Once everyone is gone, I use the side stairwell that I opened earlier and gain access to each floor.

Once you've gotten inside the building there are few security measures to prevent an attacker from moving around. This is because most access control measures are designed to simply keep people out of a building; exploiting the probe once inside is easy.

In one instance when I did a probe in Washington DC, I actually had the late-night security guard escort me around and show me the inside of the building because I was a new out-of-town manager officially arriving at the building the next day, and I wanted to know my way around without being embarrassed when I met my boss.

The cover story was simple and he bought it.

Movement inside the building, even under secure means, is simple. Most secured rooms in corporate high-rises have a false ceiling or ceiling tiles. A simple chair up against the wall, going through the ceiling tile, over the wall, into the secured room provides easy access to legal documents, personnel files, telecommunications, and computer passwords, and due to the penetration being nonintrusive in nature no one knows they have been violated.

> **Lesson Learned:** It is the most natural thing in the world for people to want to be helpful. Ordinarily, people have to be trained to meet challenges. If something isn't quite right, the normal thing is to ignore it, don't cause a problem or get involved. Hanna Arendt taught us about the banality and ordinariness of evil. Evil people doing very ordinary things to create their havoc are the most dangerous threats in the world. Remember, the devil's greatest trick was convincing us he didn't exist.

The tools I normally use in probes as training devices for the security force and for the security manager are concealed cameras, notebook cameras, or a small personal camera carried on our body that has a button lens and a recording pack no bigger than a cigarette case. I use these to film the probe. Filming the guards opening the doors and capturing examples of tailgating proved to be invaluable training tools for the guard force. I also film interaction with employees in the company that gave me information or held doors open for me. I go through the trash holding up documents for the camera that were, in some cases, stamped classified. The end result of filming probes is assisting the guard force, enhancing training for company employees, and providing situational awareness for corporate leadership. Training to perform probes like this does not require a lot of time, it's not resource intensive, it's not manpower intensive, and it is fairly inexpensive compared to extensive security assessments offered by security firms.

I've defeated multi-million dollar countermeasure systems, access-control systems, and biometric systems, through social engineering, waste engineering, and good old Yankee ingenuity. So it really doesn't matter what type of system you have in place, because the breakdown within the system always occurs at the user level and that's because we tend to put an untrained person behind the monitor and an untrained person at the gate. Security personnel must understand the nature of the threat and the potential capabilities of an actual threat that is posed against them. In every case, I got access. I was never kept out of a compound or a building.

CARVER Matrix

One of the tools that I used from the Special Forces in conducting a vulnerability assessment is called a CARVER Matrix. It's an acronym:

Criticality
Access
Recoverability or Recuperability
Vulnerability
Effects
Recognizability

Using a matrix that outlines each one of these critical areas in order to identify the specific vulnerabilities that exist for key assets is very helpful in conducting probe operations and evaluating the countermeasures necessary to defend against an attack. This form of reverse engineering proves to be effective in determining appropriate countermeasures, but probe scenarios must be realistic in order to have effective countermeasures.

I can't overstate the importance of filming your probes, because the one thing you need from the corporate leadership is buy-in. And the best way to demonstrate that is by showing them a short film of you opening the company up like a can of peaches, getting access to the key critical areas, getting access to important documents, and showing the ease with which it was conducted. I found this to be very effective in dealing with the telecommunications company that I did the assessment for.

One of their key assets was a switching facility providing coverage for several thousand cell phones. When you take out a cell phone switch, the burden on the system is felt by several thousand users. I think this was demonstrated ten times over during the World Trade Center disaster when they lost the connectivity that was provided by the antenna on Tower Two. Verizon's communications were crippled over a wide area when that tower went down. This communication breakdown also affected the first responders when their equipment became quickly overloaded and there were no effective backups.

When you demonstrate the potential for loss to the CEO or CFO of a company, in the form of an actual filmed attack they tend to understand the gravity of the situation. The documentation of a probe and the assessment of vulnerabilities should be followed up with a cost-benefit analysis. This prerequisite event sets the stage for risk analysis—it's all about the money.

Cost-benefit Analysis

Most security professionals will tell you that the most difficult thing in conducting a security assessment is not the probe or the threat assessment. It's convincing the approving authority that they need to allocate funding toward countermeasures in order to secure their corporation or its operations.

Now in some companies where they've already experienced a loss, it's not that difficult. But my experience with both the government and corporate America has shown me that the managers don't want to spend that much money in protecting their assets or their people. This continues to amaze me.

You have to look at the nature of the company you're dealing with; expensive countermeasures are as much of a burden as loss due to an attack. Dealing with an industry that operates on a small marginal profit, like most trucking companies, typically results in limited to no security. If a trucking company is operating efficiently they may make a profit of a penny to a penny and a half for each mile their drivers log. They simply don't have the funds available to spend to protect each truck or each driver on the road, so they're willing to operate at risk; unfortunately that puts the rest of us at risk as well.

That's why most trucking companies are self-insured.

Potential Loss Versus Prevention

The key to a good cost-benefit analysis is articulating the potential for loss versus the cost of loss prevention.

If securing a truckload of computers worth half a million dollars requires only a ten dollar padlock, I can just about guarantee you'll buy the ten dollar padlock.

If securing a truckload of computers worth half a million dollars requires a detailed tracking and interdiction system that costs thousands of dollars, and in some cases, an additional thirty or forty dollars a month in tracking fees, most firms will not purchase the system. Instead they will go with the padlock and a prayer option.

When conducting a cost-benefit analysis, you have to provide realistic countermeasures and I would tell you the first countermeasures recommended should be security training. If training is not on the list of countermeasures being presented, I would tell the briefer to pack up his presentation and leave. Most security companies roll out the heavy merchandise and skip right over training because there is no money in it for them. You can never train your employees enough. The benefits, both direct and indirect, of training your people to be efficient and effective security managers and security-minded employees are endless. The best way to show or depict the return on investment for a good security training program is the overall reduction in loss or drop in security-related incidents.

If you have five hundred employees in your company, you have five hundred sets of eyes and ears to conduct social engineering, counter-solicitation, information collection, area observation, and point and target observation. This all results in a positive impact on loss prevention and it costs almost nothing.

I've also found that most employees enjoy receiving classes on some of these techniques. Most people enjoy feeling like they're taking part in the security of their company, especially if the company has experienced a domestic violence incident, or had a fire, or they were close to the Pentagon or the trade center during the 9/11 attacks.

The training program is a direct reflection of the leadership and skill sets of the security manager and his security force. If your training program sucks, take it from me, it's probably because your security management team and your security personnel suck.

Companies that outsource their security people need to have short performance contracts that can be turned off at a moment's notice. Having a one-year or longer security contract that's negotiated every year and is not performance-based is the kiss of death. You get what you pay for.

I've been asked to evaluate security assessment reports from corporations and I usually flip directly to the cost-benefit analysis and then back my way through the assessment. I always scrutinize what the recommendations are, what countermeasures are being recommended, and if training is anywhere in the package. I review with a very critical eye all the systems they're recommending. I look at the vulnerabilities that were identified, and the threats that were identified. In most cases, I can tear apart a security assessment within a half hour, determine whether or not it is valid, and whether or not the company that conducted the assessment is just trying to make some money off the countermeasures.

The security assessment firm you hire to conduct the assessment should not be responsible for providing the recommended countermeasures. If that's the case, then there is a serious conflict of interest.

Once the security assessment team has made its recommendations concerning countermeasures and provided the cost-benefit analysis, it may be asked to assist with the implementation of some of the countermeasures, depending on what they are, especially if training is recommended as the best countermeasure. I say this because by the time the security company completes the assessment of your firm they possess valuable knowledge that can be integrated into a training program. I have provided training to clients based on their requirements and needs following the delivery of the assessment report. I've also found that sometimes conducting in-progress reviews throughout the assessment resulted in me doing hip-pocket training. If I had identified a vulnerability that was gross neglect, providing an on-the-spot correction at no cost to the customer was standard practice. If this is not done then you continue to leave that company wide open and vulnerable, which really defeats the purpose of what you're doing anyway, and most companies seem to appreciate a courtesy on-the-spot correction. If you are dealing with a security professional this should be pro forma.

If security is taken seriously within a corporation, if it is a priority, and they have a trained professional security manager, most security violations or incidents can be prevented. An ounce of prevention is worth a pound of cure.

The individual responsible for threat countermeasures is the security manager. He has to have security as his full-time job. In most corporations I have worked with, the security manager actually had a job within the firm that had nothing to do with security and security was given to him as an additional duty. This is not a good way to run a railroad.

Rant: The Coast Guard was hosting a public forum on the issues dealing with maritime security, specifically international maritime security. I attended that conference a month or so after 9/11. I had been intimately involved with the initial Senate bill that was going before the House and Senate on port security and I had experience with security assessments for seaports, so I was very familiar with some of the talking points associated with maritime security. Beyond that, I had commanded a SCUBA team in the Special Forces and was familiar with maritime military operations and the security problems associated with ports and harbors.

One of the things I felt compelled to speak about was the issue of having a security officer on a ship. We're talking a Merchant Marine vessel or a commercial vessel that needed an additional officer on board responsible for security of the vessel. My point was actually very well received by the committee and their initial assessment of security being treated as an additional duty was revised. I have dedicated the better part of my life to security, along with thousands of other security professionals. It's not an additional duty. If you're going to have security, then you need to have a security expert, which means there needs to be a dedicated individual on that ship, whose job is to ensure security of the vessel and the security of the crew.

It can't be treated as an additional duty. It has to be that individual's job.

In summary, when I look at corporate America, I would have to say that we remain highly unsecured; our railways, seaports, highways, and airports continue to be extremely vulnerable. The threat is real. It exists on a daily basis.

With the exception of airports, there's been little to no movement on the protection of any of our sites. In some cases, like power generation plants, especially nuclear power generation plants, security has actually taken a step backward.

The driving factor in all this stagnation after 9/11 is, of course, money. No one wants to allocate the funds to fix the problems. We continue to conduct expensive assessments and analyses in order to determine where threats and vulnerabilities exist. We lack the initiative to fix the problems. We're not putting realistic countermeasures in place. If the truth be known, the reason the attacks on 9/11 were successful was because of a lack of corporate security and a security ethos within the airline industry, both in the airport itself and on the aircraft. If anybody wants to point fingers and find the individuals that were responsible for the attacks on 9/11, that's the first place we should look. It's the first place we fixed, so naturally, that's the first place the blame should fall, but we don't do that. We don't hold people or organizations accountable for their mistakes, for their foul-ups. We tend to just cover things up. We get therapy, we get past it. Sadly, we go for instant gratification and moving on.

When you combine the blunders of the airlines and you blend them with the incompetence of our intelligence agencies, you get what happened on 9/11. You get a series of individuals that should not have been in the country, that have the ability to get onto aircraft, albeit with limited, unconventional weapons, take control of four aircraft—simultaneously—occupy the cockpits, hold the aircraft, and drive them to the destinations. The fourth hijacked aircraft, Flight 93, went down in Somerset, Pennsylvania en route to Washington, possibly the Capitol. It's just a series of blunders that led to the collapse of the Twin Towers.

I sat and watched the 9/11 Commission's meetings and what happened and who was held accountable on whether or not the past administration had done anything or the Bush administration had done anything. My question here is, "Where's the finger that's pointing at corporate America? Where's the finger that's holding the airlines accountable for their inaction?"

Once again, Washington has fallen prey to the blame game and the process Nazis have taken over. It's all about politics. It's all about who's going to be in the presidential office next. It's about getting rid of Bush and putting in the Democrats, because that's what's good for the nation. No, that's what's good for the Democratic Party. It has nothing to do with what's good for the nation. If it's what's good for the nation, we'd have some stability in the White House. We'd aggressively pursue the war on terror and we would build coalitions. Instead, we have partisanship tearing everything apart. Cooperation is what's good for this country. Not politics! And, unless we see our way out of this mess, that's what will kill this country.

Chapter Five

Unconventional Warfare:
War without Weapons

War wasn't created by modern man. Ever since tribes realized the importance of land, cattle, and women, they have fought over such assets.

It doesn't take a rocket scientist to figure out that he who carries the biggest club is probably going to win and he who has the most panzer divisions is probably going to win.

However, in today's age of unconventional warfare, the use of the tactics we now call "terrorism" is defined by the walking thesauruses in the Pentagon as an asymmetric threat. We find ourselves in a position where possessing massive combat power, having more planes, more tanks, more ships, more bombs, and the ability to see at night, is not necessarily—no, is decidedly NOT—effective against this type of threat.

This is what I refer to as unconventional warfare. You can label it whatever you want to label it. If you want to call the resistance fighters in Iraq "terrorists," fine, call them terrorists. If you want to, call Usama bin Laden a terrorist, or Hamas, or any other group that uses tactics to exploit very vulnerable areas, specifically soft targets. Call them terrorists. It's all unconventional warfare when you boil it down and in the final analysis, if you don't have the ability to think in an unconventional manner, and go after the enemy in an unconventional way, you will end up losing the conflict. I will tell you that if we continue on the current course in Iraq, we will lose in the long run.

What is the long run? The long run is expressed as a word called "vision," and it exists at the strategic level of warfare.

According to Army doctrine, there are three levels of warfare. One is the tactical level, which basically happens at the maneuver, battalion, company, and platoon levels. Two is the operational level, which typically happens at brigade and division levels. The third, or strategic level, includes corps assets and above. A corps typically consists of two to three divisions and may have ad hoc units assigned to mission-specific tasks.

In my opinion, the third level, the strategic level, isn't actually the responsibility of the military. I think strategic warfare happens at political levels within the State Department, within the policy-making agencies of whatever the ruling faction is—dictator, Baath Party, pick a name. That's where real strategy is made, that's where the real vision happens. Clausewitz connected the dots between warfare and politics in his famous book *On War* published over a hundred and fifty years ago: "Warfare is merely the continuation of state policy by other means." There is a reason why he and another famous strategist, Sun-Tzu, are coming back in vogue in the military as well as in corporate boardrooms, judging from the spate of books lately devoted to their theories. The reason is they were right and truth is timeless. I digress here a little bit, but, as somebody once said of Bill Clinton, "It's tough keeping track of the truth."

One of the reasons we've been so unsuccessful in the Middle East is because our strategy, our vision, has always been very inept. In essence, it's broken. Most of our policy makers lack any experience at all in the Middle East, and when they do, it comes from a very myopic view, typically from the rarefied atmosphere of an Ivy League university like Harvard or Yale. How many State Department, Department of Defense, or White House staffers do we have who speak Arabic, Farsi, Turkish, Hebrew, or any of a host of other Middle East and southwest Asian languages?

Until 9/11, our policy-making agencies were almost entirely Euro-centric, with some emphasis on Japan and China, but that was about it. By the time the Cold War started winding down in the early 1990s, lots of Soviet experts were no longer needed, so much of the resources in the analyst functions were cast overboard, in a drastic reduction in the size of our intelligence services. Not only did we reduce our capacity to accumulate intelligence and analyze it, the capacity we had was tilted drastically away from the threat that so abruptly emerged from Islamo-Fascism.

So when you have a flawed and weakened foundation for strategy, for strategic thinking, for long-term vision, regardless of what combat power you possess, you are at a severe disadvantage. We have enormous power to force production capabilities, force entry capabilities, to conduct distributed operations in multiple theaters, all nearly simultaneously. But, regardless of all those great military capabilities, if our long-term strategic vision is inadequate, we cannot be a success.

In terms of unconventional warfare, strategic power consists of a nation's ability to influence other nations to come to a settlement or a compromise on whatever problems exist between the conflicting parties. It's the nation's ability to leverage relationships and associations in order to solve problems. To me, this is the strategic level of unconventional war.

The operational level of an unconventional war is the ability to win the hearts and minds of the local population at the operational level. We must be able to recruit large groups of guerillas or paramilitary forces in order to conduct military operations. We must be able to develop a robust auxiliary, an underground network, within the theater in order to support paramilitary operations. In short, the operational level is concerned with the infrastructure of supporting a theater-wide conflict by making the maximum use of indigenous assets. These assets can be overt or covert sympathizers or they can be "useful idiots," that is, people who are manipulated to help your cause without being aware of it. This can happen most obviously in the case of foreign politicians, media, and journalist types.

At the tactical level of an unconventional war we see combat operations, subversive-sabotage attacks, and the measures taken to counter these attacks. For example, to conduct a successful counter insurgency you have to build local intelligence information networks in order to get into the enemy's "decision cycle." Cellular organizations will carry out subversive acts, sabotage, in order to take away the legitimacy of the government that's in place or enhance the legitimacy and authority of the insurgency that's been created. For example, in Iraq, the modus operandi of the insurgent cells is to demonstrate the coalition forces' inability, not only to control the situation, but to understand the situation and to show that they really don't know what they're doing. Their goal is to make the people believe the coalition doesn't understand the challenges of dealing with people in the Middle East. They continually try to drive a wedge in between the people that may be sitting on the fence for supporting coalition forces and the people that are not real sure whether or not they want to support the insurgency.

So how do you wage a war without weapons? Can you technically call it a war if you don't physically use a weapon? If you don't physically harm somebody or kill somebody, can you call it war? Time and time again, I've heard the saying, "a war of words," and I would tell you, that there exists today an ability to wage war without physically hurting anyone. There are different levels of conflict, and the Army will tell you that a low-intensity conflict (LIC), Grenada, for example, was a conflict in which light forces were used, either to overthrow a government or as part of a resistance in an attempt to overthrow a government.

Then, there are gradients of warfare engagement and intensity. As you might imagine, the ultimate strategic level of warfare is nuclear war.

Desert Storm is a good example of mid-level warfare, with a heavy-mechanized force and over a hundred thousand troops operating within the borders of one country.

So where does unconventional warfare fit in? Is it a low-intensity conflict? Is it a mid-level conflict? Is it a high-intensity conflict?

Unconventional warfare resides within each one of those levels and has the ability to change from one level to the other quite rapidly. It just depends on the number of people within the area that are sucked into supporting whatever movement has been created or whatever conflict currently exists.

I would submit that we are at a mid- to high-level of intensity today simply because we are disliked by so many people within the Islamic community, within the Arab world, within the Middle East, and someone right now has their hands on a nuke. If you look at the current war on terror from a war of words perspective, not from directly dropping bombs on amorphous targets, we are in about as high-intensity a level of conflict as you can get without another nation actively taking up arms against you or enforcing an oil embargo. That would be the highest level.

I'm saying this not because I've read books or I'm scholarly and I've been educated on these things through universities and through formal institutions of learning. I say this because I've spent time actually on the ground in the Middle East, in Lebanon, Jordan, Iraq, Saudi Arabia, and Kuwait. I have seen the heightened frustration with the United States and our foreign policy. The resentment against us resonates in every conversation. The bottom line of the majority of conversation is, "Why does the United States continue to support Israel in such open, unconditional manner and why have you taken sides with them, why do you position yourself against the rest of the Arab world?" That's point number one. I intend to address this legitimate issue as fully as I can and I will do so in the final chapter of this book.

Point number two for most of the people who seem to have an axe to grind with the United States of America, if you remove Israel from the equation, is their perspective of the United States from what they see on television and movies. This is, let's face it, their only real exposure to American culture and values. If you take a step back and you watch American television on a satellite dish, widely available throughout the Middle East and now even Iraq, we look pretty much like modern-day Sodom and Gomorrah. This is true whether it's from a news angle or from watching Hollywood movies or some of the sitcoms. We have crime in our streets, we have extreme racism problems, and these manifest themselves on television to a higher degree than the reality within the country.

No matter, that's the perspective that they see. You have to understand, perception is reality. We do not have a counter-public relations campaign within the Middle East. What I am talking about now is the heart of unconventional warfare, and that is winning the hearts and minds of the people. If we had an aggressive public relations campaign, a counter-information campaign that we waged in the Middle East to get the word out, to get the truth out, to show the American perspective of what real Americans are, what they look like, what their concerns and family values are, it would greatly improve our public relations problem.

The case in point to support this argument is, if you watch Al Jazeera Arabic television and you have a chance to see that what they are showing on Al Jazeera is a seamless transition between the occupation by Israel in Gaza and the West Bank to our guys kicking in doors in Ramadi and Fallujah. It looks like it's all about occupation by the infidels, by us, and by the Zionists. From an Iraqi perspective, from a Middle East perspective when they see these images, their beliefs are justified because, to them, pictures tell the story better than a thousand words, they don't lie. We don't do anything at all to try and change that point of view. In fact, instead of engaging Al Jazeera, instead of engaging Al Arabia, LBC out of Lebanon, and these other foreign channels, we ignore them, because, oh, well, they lie. They spin their point of view. Well, you know what else they do? They also allow other individuals to get on their channels and present their point of view. I know that for a fact because I've seen it and I've been there when the bad guys have been on camera. If we would embrace these news channels and use them to our advantage, and leverage the coverage they have within the Middle East, we could begin to start to change Middle Eastern perceptions of the United States of America. Another idea is to fund a joint venture between American investors and Arab investors to establish a moderate Middle Eastern news station whose goal is the destruction of Al Jazeera and the rich sheiks who fund it out of Qatar.

I shouldn't mention it, but these media conduits could also provide additional sources of information that, when corroborated, may actually be turned against our enemies. Al Jazeera has to be getting its bin Laden and al Zarqawi tapes from somebody. One of the hostages recently captured by the insurgents was going to be beheaded, a Pakistani. He related a truly hair-raising story about how one of the bad guys picked up a phone and within an hour had an Al Jazeera reporter coming in the door with a camcorder ready to tape the deed. He escaped after an American raid nearby scared off his captors.

I appreciate stories like this because I currently have a friend in Iraq who's advising a high-level Army commnader on cultural, political, and military issues. I had a conversation with him the other day and he was saying that while the Fallujah operation was underway, he had gone back to his room on a break. He was watching Al Jazeera TV, and Al Jazeera supposedly had a reporter with the Marines covering the war. He had found out that, in fact, he wasn't a reporter. He was a decoy and Al Jazeera had another person reporting, covering the action within Fallujah. The real reporter was truly behind the scenes and no one knew about him. He was doing separate reporting directly to Al Jazeera and the other networks weren't picking it up. This guy was right in there, embedded with the insurgent elements, with the guys from Syria, with the guys from Iran, and with the former Baath Party members, and this guy had incredible access. I remember asking my counterpart that works for a government organization, "Well, are the guys in the intelligence section watching this? Are you guys talking about it?"

He said, "No, they don't watch Al Jazeera because it's bad reporting and you can't believe anything they say, it's all propaganda."

In other words, it's not what anybody wants to hear, so therefore we're not gonna watch it. This is the worst possible thing to do.

Another mistake we continually make is that if you're going to negotiate with a foreign country and try and reach some point of compromise, we don't send over somebody that has the ability to speak their language, and looks like them, and can commiserate with them, even if that commiseration isn't genuine. In other words, we should at least try to be perceived as genuine.

What I mean by this, and I'll just be as frank as possible, if you're gonna try and negotiate with the Harlem Warlords, you probably should send somebody that used to be a Harlem Warlord himself. Keep in mind unconventional warfare means you use unconventional thinking—if your idea is unique and most people say it won't work—use it!

Getting to the point, when we negotiate with Arabs, we should send an Arab. Can you image that? What a concept!

We should actually send somebody that can communicate on their level, has the same religious beliefs, and can talk with them about common issues of concern, and completely understands where these people are coming from. We don't do that. Why? Because the government is occupied by a bunch of old, rich, white men from the same university graduate schools. That's why.

This holds true for the Clinton administration, the Bush administration, or just pick an administration. Somebody show me where we've had a special envoy to the Middle East or a State Department member that was an envoy to the Middle East that was an Arab. Please. Somebody show me that.

These are the types of tactics that have to be used in unconventional warfare at the strategic level. You have to win the hearts and minds of people, which means you have to communicate at their level. The only way to win over the hearts and minds of people is for them to be convinced that you truly care, that you're gonna make a difference, and that you're gonna improve the situation, or that you're gonna at least attempt to satisfy whatever itch they have, whatever is bothering them. Most people don't go to war just because they want to kill; they are driven by an ideology. The people who do go to war strictly because they want to kill are truly sick and need to be wiped from the face of the earth.

You know, it's funny. I get such a kick about how we demonize people immediately and turn them into Lucifer, the devil incarnate. At one point in time, Usama bin Laden was a friend of the United States. His organization, the infamous mujahedeen that had been created in Afghanistan was a by-product of the United States of America's war against the Soviet occupation of that country. How many people know that we dumped $25 million a month into a place called Waziristan in northwest Pakistan? Anybody familiar with that? Well, you should be familiar with it, because we just had a huge operation there earlier this year, because of the incredible amount of mujahedeen that had retired there. They retired there because the United States had set them up quite nicely.

The 5th Special Forces Group and the CIA manned, equipped, and trained an organization that had later become the Taliban and al Queda, which was led by that individual named Usama bin Laden. It's all incestuous, because our long-term vision in the Middle East has always been flawed. We supported Islamic extremists in order to fight the Soviets, but we lacked the strategic vision required to determine the impact of our actions ten years down the road. We don't have the ability to see past the end of our nose, and typically, in the political arena, the length of the nose is four years, which is the normal length of one presidential term. That's also the length of our long-term strategic vision.

And that type of short-term, near-term thinking is what puts us in a bind continually. That's why we support people like Saddam Hussein, and have to turn back around and demonize him fifteen years later and say he needs to be removed from power. The people that were involved in that process of propping him up and giving him the arms that he needed are the same people that turned around a decade later and demonized him.

The irony of the whole thing, to me, is just incredible. I can't believe that most people can't sit back and recognize this, and when they do, they're labeled, they're thrown off into a corner, and they are shunned.

Frankly, we are in a battle within Iraq to hire people from the pool of unemployed individuals. If that pool of unemployed individuals is full of Baath Party members, then we've been told—and we have been told—that you will not hire former Baath Party members, where do you think they're all gonna go? Who do you think will hire them? It's not a trick question!

The bad guys with briefcases full of money are flowing in from Iran and Syria, remember the Lebanese model of occupation? The Iranian situation should be controlled at the strategic level of unconventional warfare, but it's not, because we are too inept in our policies. We don't even recognize that, nor do we know how to deal with them. In our minds, the best way to deal with them is by dropping GBUs or smart bombs. Once again, when you have flaws at the strategic level, they directly affect the short-term level of warfare, be it at operational or tactical level. Basically, because we have a flawed strategic-level warfare policy, we have fighters coming in from Syria funded from Iran, as well as insurgent fighters coming in from Iran.

The country of Iraq is a boat that is taking on water. The only thing the military is authorized to do in this boat that's taking on water is to bail, and the way in which they bail is by trying to kill the fighters, the insurgents within the country. The military is not authorized to plug the holes. The holes that exist are the nations of Syria and Iran that continually fund insurgent activities within Iraq.

Because the military's not authorized to plug those holes, this boat will continue to take on water and we will bail for as long as we're there. As fast as we kill these guys, others will be sent into the country and literally they will be reproduced. It's a sausage grinder. That's all this is, and because of inept strategy, we don't have the ability to plug the holes and the boat will take on water for life. In some ways, the situation is a bit like Vietnam. There, the enemy fighters had sanctuaries in Cambodia and other places that were hands-off to us. We also couldn't penetrate the north on the ground. You show me a war where the enemy has untouchable sanctuaries and we have soldiers dying on the ground because we can't get at the enemy's source of supplies and personnel, and I will show you a war that we will lose. Let me repeat, if we don't shut down the sanctuaries in Syria, Iran, and, yes, Saudi Arabia then WE WILL LOSE. Got it? Good, you heard it here first!

These are the points I want to make on TV, but I can't, because I always have to discuss everything in the weeds. People want to know what we can do to stop this and what you do to stop it isn't at the operational and tactical levels of warfare. It's at the strategic level of warfare. You've gotta cut the problem off where it exists. There's always a cause and effect. The majority of the problems that exist in the Middle East are being perpetrated and carried out mainly by three countries: Syria, Iran, and Saudi Arabia. What we're seeing right now in Iraq is the same occupation model used by Syria in Lebanon.

We could have very easily prevented the occupation of Lebanon by Syria, but we didn't. In essence, we handed Lebanon over to Syria.

I don't think we're going to do the same thing with Iraq, but until we recognize the fact that Syria and Iran are actively involved in the destabilization of Iraq, that problem will not go away. Let me say it again, there's nothing the military can do within the borders of Iraq to solve that problem.

These have all been examples of lessons that we can learn from that are associated with foreign policy, unconventional warfare at the strategic level.

Unconventional Warfare at the Operational Level

Examples of Fairness and Success

In order to recruit paramilitary forces or bands of guerillas to fight an insurgency or counterinsurgency, you have to know the lay of the land. You have to know what groups currently exist within the country that would be sympathetic and would provide a good recruiting base. This means you have to have in-country contacts. In order to have in-country contacts, you have to tap into a number of different resources that exist.

Some of these resources may exist within the CIA or other intelligence agencies, some of these resources may exist within the State Department, the country embassy team, and some of these resources may exist within commercial entities, with businessmen that have relationships with other businessmen in country. They can provide a great deal of information on the current status within the country. Journalists, too, can be used in this way, perhaps without their knowledge. Peter Arnett's broadcasts from Baghdad during the run-up to our invasion revealed important information about Iraqi readiness and resolve to fight.

Using these different sources to get information within the nation prior to hostility, or even the anticipation of hostilities, is a key element to our overall ability to recruit people and establish a support movement within the country rapidly. Unfortunately, we typically don't do this well.

An example of us doing a good job of this was in Afghanistan. The ability to access and support the Northern Alliance and use them in order to overthrow the Taliban allowed us to go into the country with minimal forces. We deployed Special Forces to train, assist, and advise the already existing insurgent forces, if you will, the Northern Alliance, and other tribal-organized militia, into assisting us in overthrowing the Taliban.

That campaign is a great example of a way to leverage resistance groups within country.

A poor example of it is not recognizing the need to do this or recognizing it too late to be able to execute it properly. This would be what we did, or didn't do, in the war in Iraq, Operation Iraqi Freedom. The Iraqis and most of the people in the Middle East refer to this war as the capitalist occupation of Iraq. Actually, come to think of it, most Democrats say almost the same thing. After all, didn't the Bush family's oil interests and Cheney's ties with Halliburton dictate that we take down Saddam Hussein? Folks, we have a severe problem in our country when the major political opposition party and our blood-sworn enemies, the terrorists, those who believe beheading is an Olympic sport, start speaking the same language.

In the early 1990s, following the first Gulf War, Operation Desert Storm, there was an uprising in the southern portion of Iraq, which is predominantly Shia. That uprising was against Saddam Hussein because of the oppression that he had placed upon the Shia and the uprising was going to be supported by the CIA, through funds and weaponry, and things of that nature. When the uprising began, we basically pulled a Bay of Pigs, didn't support them and they lost tens of thousands of people at the hands of the Republican Guard, Saddam's SS.

Now that group of people represents a very deep well or base that we can draw from in order to recruit people that will assist with the overthrow of a government in order to create an insurgency. In fact, that's what we tried in Iraq, to create an insurgency. But, we didn't do it right. So, when we overthrew the government, the blowback against us was a counterinsurgency.

Instead of embracing this movement and identifying resistance cells within Iraq, we simply recruited 150–190 Iraqis that were residing in the United States and put together the Iraqi Freedom Force and had them go in with one of the military units, the 101st Airborne as an example. We disbanded them a few months later. That was the big unconventional warfare play, as far as pulling together a resistance force within Iraq. I'd have to say, it's almost laughable. I mean, why even bother?

What should have been done was to identify resistance cells existing within Iraq, which means putting guys in country that are Arab-Americans or co-opting other Arabs to gain information for us. Or, use pre-existing business relationships within the country in order to get information. Now, some of this goes against the typical operating procedures. The techniques and tactics used by the CIA won't allow this to ever happen. It's either their way or the highway. With them, you know who is always right. If you don't know, they will tell you. This is why we have a new skyline in New York City.

I know this from first-hand experience, because on the three different occasions that I've dealt with the agency, none of the three occasions worked out. The agency continually displayed, and this is from a time period of over ten years, the our-way-or-the-highway method of dealing with people. Frankly, it's impossible to build rapport and I know agents right now who sit overseas and won't leave their embassy, because they don't want to take a chance on getting popped, identified, or compromised in the area in which they're operating. They are a bunch of white guys, and if you're in the Middle East and you don't have an agent who can go out and run sources and collect information, if he doesn't speak the language and doesn't look like the local people—it's not gonna happen.

These are the same problems that plagued us in the beginning of conflict in Iraq and continue to plague us today. This is why most agents are only doing a ninety-day rotation and getting out of the country. How can you possibly build a robust intelligence network and run effective sources and case manage those sources if you spend only ninety days in country? It's totally unrealistic. The 9/11 Commission has reported in full about the screwups in the CIA. But, you don't need to sift through mountains of evidence to know this. Just look at the mess in Iraq today.

At the operational level of war in Iraq, for an unconventional war, we should have immediately recruited and embraced former Baath Party members (I know Paul Bremer's probably having a heart attack right now if he's reading this) we should have embraced former military leaders, whether they were from the Special Services, intelligence, or Republican Guard. We should have brought these guys in immediately and started the process of co-opting them and vetting them to use them in the establishment of a new Iraqi paramilitary force that would participate in the stabilization of the country in a locking down of its borders.

But we didn't do that. We fired everyone. Thank you very much, Paul Bremer. This was the worst decision made in the campaign of Iraq. Why? Because there was no plan, because there was no campaign, because nobody in the top positions in the hierarchy of the CPA has an understanding of the nature of the paramilitary threat or understood unconventional warfare. Therefore, they were on, and continue to be on, a guided discovery. By the way, after his final trip home after the handing over of sovereignty to Iraq, Bremer appeared on *Fox News Sunday.* He told Chris Wallace he stood by his decision to disband the Iraqi Army and all security forces because, "we couldn't trust them, we didn't know who was still loyal to Saddam." Ah, hah! It was much better wasn't it to let lawlessness loose in the streets for months, to totally erode the people's belief and trust in the coalition's ability to provide security. It was better to let the Iranians and al Queda come in with bags of money and recruit military and Baathist Party people who were completely cut off from society and totally disenfranchised. Paul, from me to you, how did you think this was a good idea?

People ask me, "Do we need to send more troops to Iraq? Are we short? How many troops are we short in Iraq?"

The answer that I give them is that we're about four hundred thousand short. They look at me like I've got an eyeball growing out of the middle of my forehead.

"Well, our Army's not that big. How could we be four hundred thousand short?"

Look, the size of our Army is not germane to the situation in a conflict that dictates the amount of troops that you need. The size of our Army shouldn't figure into the equation at all. The fact of the matter is, we don't have enough troops in Iraq and the four hundred thousand we're short is the size of the Iraqi military that was essentially fired and sent home. They should be there to act in the same capacity as the National Guard would be here in the United States for domestic violence. That's the way these cells need to be looked at, as creating domestic violence situations within Iraq, within the different communities and they need to be squashed. The best way to squash them is with a paramilitary force that has the ability to act freely. What is needed is an Islamic, Iraqi, Middle Eastern force, so when it slaughters these sons of bitches in the streets, it doesn't get the same type of upheaval and disgust that we currently get from the Middle Eastern world, and from a good portion of the rest of the world.

At the operational level of war you never come out and make statements that disenfranchise a large portion of the society which you are trying to control or influence. You never come out and say, "If you're a former Baath Party member, you have no future in Iraq."

Because people joined the Baath Party in the same manner that people joined the Republican Party, that people joined the NRA, or that people joined the Democratic Party. It doesn't necessarily mean that they're all out lynching folks. Being a Baath Party member doesn't mean that you went out and committed atrocities. It's a party. It was a political party! So when you tell the hundreds of thousands of members of the Baath Party that they have no future in this country, what do you expect them to do? Pick up and move and go to another country? "Well, I guess I've got no future here in Iraq. I guess I might as well leave." That doesn't work. That's not how you win the hearts and minds of people. That's not how you influence people. That's not how you stabilize a situation. That is how you *destabilize* a situation. You separate people from yourself, you lose their support, they go to the other side, because they know that they have no future here, there's no prosperity for them. They're not going to be able to get a job, so they're co-opted by the other side. I remember being told an interesting story by an Iraqi general about pushing people over to the other side. He said there was a janitor that worked in the presidential palace. Every night this janitor would mop the main entrance to the palace and one night he accidently knocked a picture of the president off the wall. He was immediately grabbed by security who accused him of being a member of the insurgency. He denied it and said it was an accident, the guards didn't believe him so they beat him to near death. After the janitor was released from the hospital from the wounds he received from the guards, he joined the insurgency.

One of the other lessons learned that should come out of Operation Iraqi Freedom, at the operational level of warfare, was our inability to embrace and co-opt the sheiks at a national level. Now there were some units that did this in remote sectors, and a good example of that would be the 101st Airborne operating out of Mosul. While not a perfect solution, and still experiencing some problems and losses, they did approach the sheiks; they did leverage the influence of the sheiks in making decisions. This was also done by the 101st when they came up through Najaf in their use of Iraqi Freedom Force members to destabilize the situation at the Holy Alli Mosque. You may recall from seeing the footage on TV when our guys took a knee right in the middle of the street in front of that holy shrine. That whole situation was decompressed, was averted. That was basically done because there was a former Iraqi freedom fighter, Kadhim Al Waeli, tugging on the shirtsleeves of a senior military official, saying, "Look, sir, you can't do this. This is what needs to happen right now and your guys need to do exactly what I'm saying." That whole situation was averted. Kadhim saved hundreds of lives on both sides—this is what happens when you go native.

What happened at Najaf is an excellent example of unconventional warfare at the operational level. Embracing the locals and learning from them and getting advice from them led to a favorable resolution of a crisis which undoubtedly would have cost many Americans and Iraqis their lives. I'm not talking about intelligence. I'm talking about how to operate with people in the Middle East, in Iraq, about what works and what doesn't work. I say this incident was at the operational level because if the situation went bad it would have impacted the entire country—not just Najaf.

Another example where the military did a great job of doing things unconventionally was in engaging local council members and political organizations that existed within communities to help get information from them. We got recommendations from them on how to solve problems, especially in areas where there was not a lot of resistance. There has been some progress in these areas and there are some projects that are ongoing, civil affairs projects to rebuild the country, to refurbish schools, get hospitals back up and running. This goes a very long way and works very well and, frankly, we probably don't see enough of it on the news, because we're too busy talking about the one mortar round that was fired at the Sheraton hotel—God, we play into their hands some times. Shots like this really warrant no discussion at all other than the fact that they happened in front of the journalists, so naturally it's a huge story.

Lessons Learned on Not Co-opting the Sheiks

One area that the sheiks should have been engaged more so than any other was the al Anbar region. The al Anbar accounts for one third of the land mass of Iraq, contains about two million people, predominantly Sunni, and just happens to have some of the more volatile towns of the Sunni Triangle. Ramadi, Fallujah, and this all exist within the al Anbar region just outside of Baghdad.

The al Anbar region has a tribal system with fifty-five different tribes that date back several thousand years. One of the leaders of these tribes is a gentleman by the name of Baziq al Gaood, whom I've met on two different occasions. As you read in Chapter Three, the month I spent in Iraq, I basically spent it under his protection.

By engaging Baziq and the other fifty-four sheiks of the tribes of the al Anbar, we could have the ability to use their influence over their people and their power to create a stable and secure environment, to identify people within the area that don't need to be there and that aren't from there. They are Syrians that came across that are operating under direction from Damascus. Using locals, we would be able to pinpoint the chop shops that are being used to pack cars with explosives, preparing vehicles to ram into a compound. Locals could help us identify places that are storing large caches of weapons and those who are building improvised explosive devices (IEDs), the roadside bombs so deadly to our convoys.

The sheiks operate under the same type of system that you would see in Sicily or here in the American mafia under the title of "Godfather." A sheik is a godfather for his family. Not only does he provide advice to them, he also helps them out during financially troubled times or when there are feuds within the tribe or between other tribes. The sheiks get together and they take care of the problem.

By not embracing them, by ignoring the Sunnis, by disbanding the military, and alienating former Baath Party members, which predominantly came from the Sunni Triangle, we have created, once again, a large pool of talent from which the insurgents can recruit. The bad guys are willing and able to pay them money so they can create subversive-type activities. Their buddies dance over the bodies of the Americans once they are burned out in the middle of the streets, and that's what's happened.

On my trip in November of 2003, I remember the sheiks from the al Anbar telling me that they could only control the situation for a month or two and that after that, they couldn't control it anymore. That they were willing to weigh in at that point in time was incredibly good fortune for us. But, now here we are, several months later, in 2004, and we still haven't embraced the sheiks. It's quite obvious that Fallujah and Ramadi have spun out of control, so what the sheiks said was going to happen, basically did happen. Bremer's Coalition Provisional Authority (CPA) didn't have the time to listen to the locals, understand their problems and frustrations, and then act upon them.

I blame the CPA, first and foremost, and then after them, I'd have to hold the military that operated in that region accountable.

It's not an easy thing to do, I know that, and I'm not trying to oversimplify it. I would not want to be a military commander in a foreign country, having to figure out who's who among the locals, without knowing that area or without having any type of background or expertise in that area.

It's different when you conduct unconventional warfare in the Special Forces. Typically you do country area studies, you know the country you're going into, you speak the language, you know the tribal customs, and in some cases, you've actually been in that country and operated in that country before, so you have a much better feel for what's happening on the ground. For a majority of the guys that went over to Iraq that were in the military, this wasn't their area of responsibility. They didn't speak the language, they didn't know the tribal customs, nor did they know the history of the country. This put them at a tremendous disadvantage. That's why you need to embrace locals, especially the sheiks. They can give you the historical perspective and guidance on everything from economics to religion to political to social issues to problems that relate to the insurgency. They are the knowledge base within the country.

One of the other lessons learned at the operational level of unconventional warfare in Operation Iraqi Freedom was the CPA's handling of the Interim Iraqi Council. I would say, first and foremost, you can't bring immigrants back into a country and then put them in charge. As much as people may think that Ahmed Chalabi is capable of handling the situation, frankly, he's no longer an Iraqi, because he'd been out of Iraq too long. I'm not saying that because I'm a know-it-all. I'm saying that because that's what Iraqis are telling me, they were also saying the same about Dr. Allawi. We can't have a man that's been out of this country for many years come back in and profess to be the king and the ruler of the country. That just doesn't work. So I would say, first of all, the Iraqi National Interim Council should not have had any dissidents on it at all. There shouldn't have been anybody on the council that was exiled from the country or that left the country for many years and all of a sudden was returning to lead Iraq to prosperity. Someone who has come back in a position of authority, such as Chalabi had, won't work. That is a non-starter.

The other problem was the CPA really went against all the principles of unconventional warfare in the establishment of rapport, the way they treated the council members. They were not allowed the same level of access as subcontractors who came into the Green Zone. Specifically I'm talking about the main compound, Saddam Hussein's castle. It really was an atrocity. The fact that they had to be searched, the fact that they had dogs sniff them, and they could watch a South African walk right in, a Bangladeshi guard walk right in, because they had a plastic card. It was a slap in the face to them.

When they carry that kind of message back to their people it resonates throughout the entire community. The amount of rapport that was lost due to that situation was really immeasurable.

Once again, that's because the people within the CPA didn't have a clue about the situation which they were in at the time. If you walked around that building, you'd have noticed a bunch of twenty-five-year-old kids from Georgetown that were politically connected and really had none of the requisite skills required to run an operation like that.

Instead, what should have been done was that the members of the interim council should have come strictly from groups within the country. They should have represented the populations of Sunni, Shia, Kurds, and any other groups of Iraqis. Fair representation by percentage should have been the goal. If 25 percent of the country is Sunni, then 25 percent of the Iraqi council should have been Sunni. These people should have come from very highly respected and recognized families or organizations, people of prominence.

Instead of kicking former Saddam loyalists to the curb, they should have been considered for positions within the council. While at the same time, people who did participate with Saddam Hussein and his sons in business that led to the detriment of the country, or the deaths of Iraqis, should have been held accountable and should have been prosecuted. To this date, the majority of those people have not been punished and this is a major point of contention within the Iraqi community, especially within the leadership of the tribes and recognized businessmen. They really can't believe that these criminals will never be held accountable.

Once the members of the council were selected, they should have been given very high recognition by the CPA and by the military. They basically should have been put on a pedestal, in a palace, an Iraqi palace, and then been given all the honor and prestige associated with anyone that resides in "a palace."

Instead, the CPA moved in, set up shop in a palace, and began to dictate terms from behind twenty-foot walls of concrete that weren't accessible to prominent citizens of Iraq. So we basically looked like Saddam Hussein.

Once the interim council was moved into the palace, they should have been given the authority to make decisions unilaterally, without having to go through the CPA to get permission to deal with the financial recovery of the nation, the oil revenue, if you will. Now that the U.N. Oil for Food Program was no longer robbing the Iraqi people, the Iraqis themselves should have been given the chance to make things right.

Instead, decisions like this resided solely with the CPA. That includes contracting. The interim council should have been allowed to vote on how contracts would be let out and to whom. The majority of the contracts that were let out in Iraq should have gone to Iraqi companies, not to foreign companies.

The interim council should have made all the press conferences and announcements of success and setbacks within Iraq, not Army generals that get on TV and, bless their hearts, and I know they mean well, but they get on and they say, "We've captured Saddam Hussein, God bless America." They completely ignore the fact that Iraq, a newborn country, under new leadership, supposedly going to be democratized, also deserved a blessing from God.

These are the types of mistakes that are made that fall within the realm of unconventional warfare, winning the hearts and minds of people, and the establishing of rapport. You have to get away from the high and tight jarhead, squared-off mentality of crush, kill, and destroy. There's a time and place for that, and when there's a time and place for that, I think the dogs of hell should be released and I have the utmost respect for those organizations that wreak havoc, death, and destruction on people that oppose us on the battlefield.

Believe me, I do. I used to be one of them. But there's a time and place for it. Standing up in front of a bank of microphones and addressing the Arab world is not the time and place for that. It should have been God bless Iraq and God bless the United States of America.

The tactical level of unconstitutional warfare, I think, can simply be summed up as the ability to collect information off the streets, off the floor of the desert, or out of the jungle that allows you to develop a very accurate picture of the enemy, their intentions, and how they plan on carrying out those intentions.

It's all about intelligence. The only way you get intelligence is through human intelligence, having sources on the ground, having local, native, preexisting relationships. This cannot be effectively done by bringing in secret-agent squirrels from the CIA or any of the other alphabet soup organizations that collect intelligence. Now if an agent just so happens to be from that region, and has a history in that region, and has connections and knows people in that region, then, by all means, that's my idea of a perfect collection asset.

But you just can't go in with your typical school-trained, in-the-box-thinking agent and expect to get results instantly. It will take a long time to develop relationships and to get information. Even then, the information that you get is always questionable. The manner in which an agent collects information simply boils down to the fact that he's CIA and he's either paying people for the information or he's coercing it out of them.

Typically, information isn't given due to a long-lasting relationship based on trust with a serious bond. The individual that's giving the agent information will never be concerned that his life may be in danger or that the agent's life may be in danger.

That's the problem with how we collect information. The bottom line is the New York skyline was redesigned for this specific reason. We don't have intelligence networks in countries, within organizations that exist, collecting information for us. No, not because it was neutered by the Clinton administration, and not because we haven't released our agents to go do the right thing. It's because the way the CIA conducts business is flawed. In an unconventional war, at the tactical level, if you don't have forces on the ground, if you don't have the ability to run local sources, and use preexisting relationships, you're never going to get a true and accurate picture of what's going on, which is why I'm flabbergasted. When I heard the secretary of defense, asked by Brett Baier on the fifteenth of April, "Are those forces in Fallujah that we're fighting foreign fighters?" he couldn't answer the question.

I'll tell you why he couldn't answer the question, because he either knows it and he's not saying it, or he has absolutely no idea

Would you like to know who's in Fallujah? I'll tell you who's in Fallujah. The Syrians are in Fallujah. The Iranians are in Fallujah. Zarqawi's al Queda cell folks are in Fallujah with hundreds of agents from Hezbollah. How do I know that? Because I sat down with the sheiks in the al Anbar and they told me of the people that were in the area. The overall scheme at the strategic level is that Syria and Iran are doing the same model of occupation that they did in Lebanon. This is exactly what they're doing in Iraq.

Information collection at the tactical level of unconventional warfare should reside within two areas. First, it should reside within the military and then within a civilian, nongovernmental organization. We currently don't have this capability. What we have, basically, is the CIA and we have the military. It's difficult at times to get both of these organizations to share information in a rapid enough fashion so that it's actionable intelligence.

One of the reasons for that, I've found in the past, is that when you give someone your best information or your actionable intelligence, if you give it to them too early, they may have a chance to corroborate the information themselves. They want to validate that information and see for themselves whether or not it's accurate. If it comes back that it's not accurate, then it's a pie in the face of the people who produced that intelligence. That's why I never used to get timely and accurate information. All the analysts circling the field had to chew on it for weeks at a time before they'd spit it back out.

This is the paradigm that basically facilitated 9/11. Between the lack of information, a lack of actionable intelligence, the dissemination of that information to the airlines, and then the airlines' inability to actually perform security, whether at the gate or on the aircraft itself, left plenty of room for the hijackers to do their deed. They used to show new CIA recruits a film on Pearl Harbor saying that was the main reason for their existence. Never again would it be permitted for an enemy to launch an undetected sneak attack against the U.S. This was a mantra during the Cold War. I wonder if they still show that movie. I bet not after 9/11.

An example of good tactical intelligence in an unconventional fashion is the information that was collected on the whereabouts of Saddam Hussein, which ultimately led to his capture. This was really a good news story, because when you look at the fact that within a country the size of California, the military was able to find one man located in a spider hole the size of a bathtub, it's astounding. Within a country that large, that's an amazing feat.

This was a picture-perfect example of multiple collection assets working nearly simultaneously, passing information back and forth without the red tape that's typically associated with intelligence collection efforts.

The fact that Special Operations forces, nongovernmental agencies, other governmental agencies, and conventional military forces were all working together proved to be a pretty good model for how to catch a bad guy.

A long time ago, when we first started the war in Afghanistan, I said one of the things the military didn't do well was manhunts. I based that on my own personal experience. I spent several months trying to find one individual on the island of Haiti, a very small, very contained area, and we never did find him.

So, when I looked at this and I saw the success that came out of it, I thought we had learned from mistakes we've made. We have learned that by following course of action A and course of action B, trying both ways and then coming out with best practices, best solutions. I think that's what's being applied now in the hunt for Usama bin Laden. It's a different setting because of the terrain, and he's surrounded by supporters where Saddam really wasn't surrounded by as many supporters as bin Laden enjoys. But, I think the point I want to make here is that the military did a very good job in the unconventional mission of finding one individual through the acquisition of sources which, I believe, at the tactical level makes the difference on how to catch a thief.

At the tactical level of unconventional warfare, I truly believe that in the Iraq scenario, the most valuable asset that was needed was a pool of advisors from the prominent families, from the sheiks. The information from them was not valuable for telling the military where to deploy. But, they could have helped with recruiting from within the tribes, within their boundaries of Iraq, to provide advisors to military commanders to assist them with economic, cultural, political, religious, and insurgent issues. The value of this pool of advisors would have been in being able to give the commander a true picture and a snapshot of what was going on in his area. These advisors should have been prominent individuals from the local area, who don't change their profile, and operate as normal. If they wore a certain garb, they continue to wear that. If they never carried a gun before, they should not carry a gun now. They should have been used as a liaison, if you will, to the community. They could provide access and entry to the preexisting business and religious infrastructure, wherever the intelligence resides.

These individuals could also provide access to historical knowledge and institutional knowledge that exists within their area. For example, when a commander walks into a town and he sees a cement plant that's not functioning, one of the civil projects may be, well, let's get this cement plant back up and running, because it can employ several hundred people.

Now the commander would have to do an assessment of that cement plant. He would need to know what it could produce, how many yards of cement it could crank out. He would need to know what size workforce it requires. He would need to know whether or not the plant was functioning on the day it closed, whether or not it had mechanical requirements, whether it was broken down or if certain aspects of the plant needed refurbishing.

Typically, what's done in Iraq for us to get that information is someone does an assessment of the plant. A bunch of white guys then come in and assess the plant. When in fact what should happen is that the commander has the proper access to the community, and to the institutional knowledge and the historical knowledge of the community. He should be introduced to the person who used to manage the plant. That gentleman could tell him everything he needed to know about the plant, including how the employees were paid, when they were paid, how they were treated, the number of hours they worked, and the production capabilities of the plant. All that information could be revealed within a two-hour conversation. This would not only save the commander weeks of waiting for his assessment report from the contractors, but it probably could save tens of thousands of dollars.

Another example of the capabilities of these advisors is in Fallujah. Once the city was encircled, the advisor that was from Fallujah could have facilitated a meeting between the commander of the forces that surrounded Fallujah and the leading sheiks and community representatives within Fallujah.

The agenda of this meeting could have been "How to take care of the current situation within Fallujah in reference to security, and the slaughter of the four Americans contractors."

Given the opportunity, through the proper influence from the sheiks and the community leaders, I feel they could've produced information that would've led to the apprehension, detention, or death of the insurgent cells that existed within Fallujah and the Iraqis that were supporting them. There would have been a little bit of brokering, in that some of the individuals that were involved in supporting these foreign terrorists would probably be related to the sheiks that were negotiating the deal. So, they would want to negotiate some type of terms of release or some type of promise or assurance that their relatives that were going to be turned in wouldn't be harmed, wouldn't go to a kangaroo court, and things of that nature. Big deal, huh? Better than the continuing nightmare which we still see in Fallujah.

This is all part of a negotiation and a compromise that leads to stability. In some cases, where you don't have the ability to reach a compromise, you have to go to the next extreme, which is the use of force.

You can always fall back on your points that were made during the discussions of compromise, and that gives an out to everyone. You have to leave a way out when you back a pit viper into a hole and he has no place to go. Don't be surprised when he lashes out and injects venom into you. It's going to happen.

It's no different when negotiating with a terrorist, a freedom fighter, or a POW. You can't back them into a corner. If they have no way to get out, then they will resort to self-protection mechanisms. It's the same thing with these people. We have to provide an out. Never forget how Kutuzov dealt with Napoleon at Moscow, always leave an avenue for your enemy to retreat. By doing this, the Russians destroyed Napoleon's *Grand Armeé* more completely and effectively than they ever could have by force.

Another great example of the positive use that resulted in hostages being released was when the families of the Japanese hostages pleaded their case on international television. This was viewed by the Sunni clerics within Iraq. The Sunni clerics sat down with the people that had captured the hostages and begged them, or negotiated with them, to release the hostages based on their viewing of the suffering and the grief that these families were showing and demonstrating on international TV.

That's how you negotiate. And there are a couple of things that need to be taken away from this. We tend to demonize our enemies. The fact is that the Sunni have everything to gain by the coalition being defeated. Keep in mind that this is the former ruling faction within Iraq that has everything to gain by bringing Saddam Hussein back into power. The Sunnis sat down and negotiated a deal based on their sympathy toward the families of these people that were captured.

We do have common ground. We all care about our families. We all do care about our offspring. We are all sensitive to the weeping of a mother. These are the issues where we all have common ground. These are the things that can be used and leveraged as bargaining and negotiation devices. If the majority of the people that are currently involved in the insurgency in Iraq sat down at a table and had discussions with people they respected, we would find common ground for universal agreement that would be best for both sides.

It's all about communication. In unconventional war, the way you defeat the enemy is by convincing him that you're right and bringing him to the negotiation table without firing a shot.

One of the most impressive examples of the use of coercion and co-opting individuals that I've ever heard of was from Dick Meadows, who is a former Special Forces officer who served in Vietnam and Korea. He used to run patrols in North Vietnam. They would capture North Vietnamese hard-core regular soldiers. They would keep them for an extended period of time, then they would share their food with them, they would entrust them with certain freedoms, and in the process of doing that, would win them over and turn them and use them as double agents, if you will, to collect intelligence.

This discussion of how to win the low-intensity, unconventional war we are in is meant to serve as a guideline for how to avoid the mistakes we have made in the past. In particular, the weaknesses we have in the collection, analysis, dissemination, and action on intelligence is a deep concern for us all. The next time the terrorists strike, we may not even know who was responsible. Who do we retaliate against? How do we retaliate? The last chapter of this book provides a means for escaping from this seemingly intractable dilemma.

Chapter Six

Intelligence: The Good, the Bad, and the Ugly

One of the key components in winning a war is the ability to collect intelligence against your enemy. You have to be able to determine what your enemy's going to do before he does it. By correctly anticipating his next move, you have the option of either striking while he's conducting the operation or preparing an ambush so once he does make his move you can spring a trap against him.

The United States' ability to collect intelligence is severely limited and our overall intelligence apparatus suffers in a number of different areas. Our inability to understand the cultures of the world and how they operate is made evident by our inability to collect intelligence in Third World remote locations or on foreign soil in general.

The 9/11 catastrophe occurred because of our inability to gather timely intelligence and put a plan together in order to negate or mitigate an attack based on the intelligence we'd collected.

So what do we do? How do we fix it? Well, first, we need to understand what "intelligence" is.

Intelligence is the result of a number of individuals and organizations sifting through raw data that is collected from a number of sources. This raw information comes in and is collected by various agencies, whether it's the CIA, NSA, the Defense Intelligence Agency (DIA) or other government entities, and the information is corroborated against other information that is obtained from numerous sources.

Now, these sources, themselves, go through a source verification process. In order to validate your source and determine the accuracy of the information, there are several different things that can be done.

If I wanted to know whether or not you were providing me with accurate information, I would ask you to go gather information about things to which I already knew the answers. I'd have you go out, collect that information, and bring it back to me and, based on the answers you gave me, I would know whether you were collecting meaningful intelligence or, perhaps, being fed false information by the enemy as a deception.

Information corroboration can also take a long time because it has to be evaluated against other information that's been collected by other sources.

What all this leads up to in this lengthy process is providing actionable intelligence to the user. And that's what this is all about. We don't collect information to provide it to the president of the United States, the national security advisor, the director of the CIA, so they can sit back and feel important because they now know something that no one else knows.

We collect information to give it to the end user so they can affect the outcome of something in the field. If end user is the military, if it's an agent working for the CIA, or if it's an FBI agent working a sting operation that's been set up, you collect intelligence to give it to the end user so they can affect a change in the theater of operation.

This is where the flaw comes in. Most information, I would submit to you, is not actionable intelligence. By the time the source information goes through several layers of bureaucracy to be corroborated, and for the sources to be verified, it is no longer real-time. So much time has elapsed since the information was initially collected it is now dated. Typically too much time elapses between the collection of raw data and the creation of actionable intelligence.

The best way to collect information and turn it into intelligence for someone to use in the field is for the field unit to be directly involved in the collection and corroboration of that information. Provide them with direct assets to collect that information and turn it into intelligence. The shorter the process for information corroboration and the shorter the process for source verification, the more actionable the intelligence will be. The issue with this concept is the alienation of intelligence personnel who will fight tooth and nail to maintain their participation in the intelligence process—even if it is detrimental to the mission.

Yes, field units who run their own intelligence process will hit a few dry holes, they will chase some ghosts, but in the long run, they will be able to hit targets faster, they will be able to get into the enemy's decision cycle faster, and they will find that they have information that is far more accurate and far more actionable than if they had to pass it through the typical multi-layered process.

Intelligence Collection

How do we collect intelligence? How do we get information from the streets? In most cases there are four different ways to collect information. First, there is human intelligence (HUMINT), which is, quite literally, a human being. Second, there is signal intelligence (SIGINT), which is our ability to intercept signals and messages that are either being sent wirelessly, by satellite, or by cell phone. Third, there is imagery intelligence (IMINT), which is gathered by overhead satellites, unmanned aerial vehicles and drones that have the ability to capture imagery, either as still photographs or video streams. And finally, there is cyber intelligence, the ability to collect information using a number of different mediums that are all tied to computer systems such as the Internet. I would also add one more intelligence collection method to this list which is right under our noses and that few people think about. This is what I would call open-source intelligence. This can be material published openly in newspapers, broadcast over TV news, or made available publicly in a variety of other ways.

Did you know that after the northeast blackout in 2003, in the course of investigation as to how it happened, a Web site was discovered that contained a highly detailed analysis and description of the CONUS power grid, including likely failure and attack points? The college student who compiled this information relied entirely on open-source information made available, usually for free, by the power companies. The guy who did this collection as a hobby had placed a very powerful weapon in the hands of potential enemies of the United States, quite by accident.

Another thing about open-source information is that it can be used as a covert means of communication by our enemies. It is widely believed, for example, that Usama bin Laden's audio- and videotapes broadcast by Al Jazeera and other Arabic language news channels contain secret encoded instructions to cells located throughout the world. Soviet spies during the Cold War were frequently given instructions through classified ads in newspapers like the *New York Times.*

Now three of these capabilities, SIGINT, or signal intelligence; IMINT, or imagery intelligence; and cyber intelligence are tied to technology. The United States, because of its incredible access and ability to develop new and emerging technologies has the advantage on the intelligence side of the house for collecting information through technology means.

The one area, however, that provides the most accurate and the most timely information is tied to organizations—what they're going to do, their next move, their decision-making process—and that is human intelligence. We severely lack the ability to conduct human intelligence in Third World and other offshore locations for a number of different reasons.

First and foremost, American culture is a great handicap for the collection of human intelligence. Second, our inability to think outside of the box and collect information in a manner that would be deemed unconventional is painfully obvious. This was illustrated perfectly by the words of the 9/11 Commission's report published at the end of July 2004. In discussing Deputy Defense Secretary Paul Wolfowitz's concern about Iraq's involvement in the attack, the report said the following:

> Given this background, he (Wolfowitz) wondered why so little thought had been devoted to the danger of suicide pilots, seeing a "failure of imagination" and a mind-set that dismissed possibilities.

The worst thing that affects our ability to collect human intelligence is political pressure. Every agency head has to continually worry about being called in to testify before the House and Senate Intelligence Committees. Everybody is always keenly interested in putting forth the best possible image, proving they didn't screw up. The kind of oversight practiced by these committees doesn't exactly encourage creative and innovative thought that could be considered risk taking. So, political influence plays heavily in our ability to collect human intelligence. The devastating effect of this process can be illustrated best by then-House Representative Bob Torricelli's complaint to the Clinton administration that the CIA shouldn't employ people who had engaged in "unsavory activities" or "human rights abuses." CIA Director John Deutch's directive to the agency in 1996 put Torricelli's doctrine into practice. What color was the sky of the planet on which these people were living? Did they beam in here from some sort of parallel universe? This policy could not have come from anyone in the intelligence area in the world I live in. In my world, if you want to recruit someone to penetrate a criminal or terrorist organization, guess what? You have to recruit a criminal or a terrorist. What a concept! In the immortal words of Jack Nicholson in the 1997 movie *As Good as It Gets*, "Sell crazy someplace else. We're all stocked up here."

These four categories of intelligence are impacted by what is known as tradecraft. That is what's taught in classrooms, but more importantly learned on the streets of the real world. Tradecraft is what agents use as their skills in the field, in order to collect information.

The problem that I see in modern-day tradecraft is that it's very narrow-minded, it's very controlled and managed, and it lives within a certain box that we can define. It has cultural limitations, and it's politically impacted by the hierarchy of the system in which it lives, whether it's the CIA, the DIA, or the NSA, there are just too many political influences that hamstring our ability to execute a good, unconventional tradecraft in the field.

First of all, you have to have the ability to go native. The individual that collects the information, "the source," shouldn't have to be cleared through a fifteen-step process, shouldn't have to have a background check, shouldn't have to have a polygraph check, shouldn't have to have a security clearance, shouldn't have to have U.S. citizenship. A source that you use in the field should be based on preexisting relationships through commercial entities and through different civil enterprises. A source should *not* be someone who's been *recruited* by an agent because the agent has a briefcase full of money.

There are agents right now that do have the ability to collect information from sources where they have built relationships over a long period of time, based on trust and a personal relationship. They are not the majority. Those are few and far between.

A perfect example is the CIA's inability to keep agents in country in Iraq for longer than ninety days. It is impossible for an agent that's running sources on the street to build a relationship and establish rapport with the local people in less than ninety days. You will never get true penetration into the insurgency organizations that exist, into economic groups, and into religious groups, if you're only in the area for ninety days. As someone once said about the war in Vietnam, "We didn't have ten years of experience in Vietnam. We had one year of experience ten times." That was because everybody only had to do a tour that long.

So here is a paradigm that has to be broken. If we want to collect information using human intelligence, we must use a tradecraft that, right now, I would submit to you, would be deemed unacceptable by the organizations that set the standards for the tasks, and the conditions on how you will collect intelligence. That's where our intelligence is most flawed right now. The directives and policies, the training, must change. There must be a paradigm shift.

I would submit to you that I can collect intelligence more accurately and more rapidly in the Middle East, in Iraq, than the CIA, because I have the ability to leverage preexisting relationships that are based on business and trust, not based on me carrying a briefcase full of money.

In the Haiti chapter, you'll recall me talking about the CIA providing us with information on the compound, which turned out to be inaccurate, and then later on providing information about the organization or the group of guys that shot one of my guys in the back that proved to be inaccurate.

There are other examples of military blunders that have led to failed operations. One of the more classic ones is the Son Tay Raid.

The objective of Operation Kingpin was to rescue as many as a hundred U.S. POWs that intelligence said were at the Son Tay prison camp, only thirty-seven klicks west of Hanoi. Shortly before midnight on November 20, 1970, at Udorn Air Base in northern Thailand, fifty-six Green Berets boarded three rescue choppers for the mission. They flew over five hundred kilometers to Son Tay accompanied by two C-130 aircraft. A real American hero, Dick Meadows, was on board the lead chopper that actually crash-landed inside the compound. Dick was the man who pinned the Ranger tab on my uniform back in 1988.

But, you know what? The intelligence was bad—there were no prisoners there. While on the ground, they killed two hundred North Vietnamese and Russians, no big surprise there, and, I believe, several Chinese. The assault force was extracted from the area without losing a single person. The bad intelligence which provided the basis for this mission was gathered, of course, through overhead imagery and other human and SIGINT sources. The prisoners had been moved, possibly because a cloud-seeding operation that the CIA was conducting resulted in rivers overflowing. The camp had to relocate its prisoners because of the flooding of a nearby river. There's a little bit of speculation involved in that, but the CIA had not only collected inaccurate intelligence, but had also possibly caused the displacement of the POWs.

Another intelligence failure was about weapons of mass destruction (WMD) in Iraq. You can't convince me to this day that the president was given an accurate picture of our ability to find WMD in Iraq—not whether or not they existed, but our ability to find them. The decision to go into Iraq was partially justified by the need to find WMD. Unfortunately for the White House, this determination was based on severely flawed intelligence.

Most of the folks I've talked to in the intelligence community have all told me the same thing. The terminology used when briefing the president and the national security advisor was that there existed a high probability that we would find some type of weapon of mass destruction—chemical, biological, radiological, or nuclear. It was plausible, according to briefings given to the president and the National Security Council, that Saddam Hussein would transfer some of these weapons to al Queda or other terrorist organizations that would use them to cause grievous harm to the United States. It was possible, in fact, that he had already done so.

But what I didn't hear from anyone was a smoking gun, that they were 100 percent sure at this location you would find canisters containing specific chemical agents.

When I asked a three-star general in the Pentagon during a briefing of the Secretary of Defense's outreach group, (talking heads) if we had a smoking gun, he said, "No. We do not have a smoking gun."

At that point, it became obvious to me and everyone else in the room that we were going to war based on half-baked intelligence.

There was no assurance that we would find WMD. There was no assurance that there were WMD to be found. It was based on intelligence that was provided by Ahmed Chalabi and his organization, which proved to be rather inaccurate, to say the least.

Now, a few words must be said about Dr. Chalabi, leader of the Iraqi National Congress (INC). The INC was set up and funded by the CIA to foment unrest in Iraq and bring about the overthrow of Saddam Hussein. After 9/11, Chalabi, who had all along insisted that Saddam had WMD and would sell them to the highest-bidding terrorist organization, had become the darling of the Pentagon neocons, particularly Paul Wolfowitz. Wolfowitz became a champion of Chalabi's cause and, as a result, began to value the INC's "intelligence" allegedly coming out of Iraq over that of the CIA.

Chalabi's influence over the Defense Department became more pronounced after the summer of 2002 when Khidir Hamza, former head of Saddam's nuclear weapons program, started briefing Pentagon people about the dangers of leaving Saddam in power. Some of you may remember Hamza. He appeared frequently as a guest on Fox News and other cable channels. He had been smuggled out of Iraq by the INC and, thus, his direct experience and his manner of expression made him seem very believable.

In this way, a tremendous amount of pressure was put on the CIA to come up with intelligence as "good" as the INC people were providing. The 9/11 Commission Report is careful to say that there is no evidence that anybody from the White House or the Pentagon ever directly pressured the CIA to manufacture evidence of WMD in Iraq. This is undoubtedly true in my mind, but then, they didn't have to. The pressure came from the overemphasis by the Pentagon and the Bush administration on the value of the INC's estimation of the threat from Iraqi WMDs. The CIA's coinage, its worth as an intelligence-gathering source about WMDs in Iraq, was seriously threatened by the INC. That, my friends, is where the pressure came from.

But wait, there's more, as they say in infomercials. The strange saga of Chalabi continues. When President Bush gave his State of the Union Address in January 2004, guess who was sitting in the row right behind Laura Bush as the Bush family's invited guest? Yes, you got it, Ahmed Chalabi. Yet, four months later, in May, Iraqi police were raiding Chalabi's compound in Baghdad and putting the word out that he was a double agent for Iran. The U.S. intelligence people also agreed that there was rock solid evidence to show that Chalabi and his organization had "extensive ties" with Iranian intelligence. So, Dr. Chalabi goes from White House favorite to enemy spy in almost the blink of an eye. How did this happen? How did this happen particularly after the U.S. funneled $33 million in aid to the INC? Did anybody ever bother to really check up on this guy? Did anybody care that he had been convicted of embezzling millions from a bank in Jordan during the 1980s?

Folks, I don't want to go over the top about Chalabi. I am bringing all of this up to show how poorly run the intelligence services have been under the first three years of the Bush administration. If you want to know how close to collapse the entire intelligence operation in the U.S. was, the Chalabi story is clear proof that we were very near the edge.

Now, also, is the time for a few words about George Tenet, the hold-over director of the CIA (DCI) from the Clinton administration. Tenet was an extremely capable administrator and was exceptionally loyal to the presidents he served. The problem was just that, he was too loyal. He didn't have the guts to tell George W. Bush the truth about what was going on in Iraq because he didn't want to make his agency look less informed and reliable than the INC.

I will say this flat-out. If Bush loses the election, in a large part it will be due to the fact that George Tenet sunk him.

Lesson Learned: It doesn't matter how good your intelligence-gathering capability is if there is a failure at the strategic-political level to use it wisely. Every fact and every estimate can be twisted and turned a thousand different ways. If the man in charge of reporting intelligence to the president is himself threatened or has an axe to grind, then his worth to the country is not only absolute zero, it is a positive and very real danger to the security of this country. This country cannot afford to have anything less than a DCI of complete and total honesty and with the guts to look the president in the eye and give him the really bad news. If we have a person in that job who tempers his judgment according to the political whims of the day, then we are surely doomed.

Another example of a military intelligence failure was our inability to catch Usama bin Laden. Now the military does not do manhunts all that well. If you look at examples of trying to catch key individuals over a long period of time, the only agencies within the United States government that do this and do this well are the FBI and the U.S. Marshals Service. They have an established infrastructure in place designed to track, locate, and subdue fugitives from justice. The military doesn't have that type of infrastructure available to support operations overseas, so they have to do things that are not typical. When you take the military and you put them in that position, our ability to gather that type of intelligence is really limited, because we don't have the necessary assets to collect information that leads to the apprehension of a fugitive from justice.

If you want to know how difficult a real manhunt is even in the United States, think of Eric Rudolph, the 1998 Atlanta Olympic Park bombing fugitive. It took seven years for the feds to track him down. His capture in 2003 only came about because of a lucky break provided by a young local cop who saw him rummaging through a Dumpster in Murphy, North Carolina. Other outlaws have never been captured, including D. B. Cooper, the skyjacker who bailed out of a Northwest Orient Airlines Boeing 727 with $200,000 in cash. That was in 1971 and he has never been seen since jumping out of that plane over a forest in Washington State. In 1998, a massive manhunt was launched for three suspects in the murder of a Colorado police officer. One of the three was found dead at a campsite. The other two have never been found and are still at large. They were last seen in the rugged Four Corners area of Utah.

What I have just described shows how difficult it is to hunt down bad guys right here at home. In Afghanistan, the story goes that we did receive intelligence that bin Laden was at a certain location. It was also likely that key Taliban figures like Mullah Omar were there as well. There was a Special Forces A-Team that was within striking distance that could have hit that target within an hour. They were not given the green light by their commander. Instead, they were put on hold and the Delta Force was brought in to do the takedown, to do the hit. Unfortunately, they were four to five hours away because of the location of their base camp.

Due to that gap in time, and their inability to get into the target as soon as possible, the tactical situation on the ground changed—the intelligence became dated. You have to remember that intelligence is nothing more than a snapshot in a period of time that says, "Bob Bevelacqua is located in this house."

Now there's nothing in place that prevents me from moving. So if there's observation or if there's an asset that's been used to collect information that says Bevelacqua's in this house, and if that asset doesn't stay on station and doesn't continue to collect information on me, when I get in my truck and go to the store, that intelligence is no longer accurate. Unless someone is following me and saying, "He's just left his house, he's in his truck, and he's driving to the store," the intelligence is absolutely worthless.

That is what happened, basically, in Tora Bora. Bin Laden probably was in that area at that moment in time. They could have gathered that information through signal intelligence, phone calls that were being made by cell phones, and triangulation was being used to determine this is where he's coming from, this is his current location. He picked up and moved. And, when he picked up and moved, we didn't have a source, a human source on the ground that could say, "Okay, bin Laden's just gotten into a convoy of vehicles, they're now moving down this path into a canyon and he's getting out of his vehicle and going into a cave."

Five hours later, when the Delta guys show up on the scene, the intelligence has changed, the picture has changed. It was no longer accurate. Geraldo Rivera with Fox News cameras in tow actually walked a mountain trail with the help of local guides from the caves on Tora Bora over into Pakistan. Did bin Laden take that same route? We don't know, but he could have.

For whatever reason, the Special Forces A-Team was not given the green light, and that fact blew our ability to react to what was at the time actionable intelligence.

Lesson Learned: When you get information that you believe is accurate, you have to act on it as soon as possible with whatever resources you have available. I don't care if you have an infantry platoon that's a half a kilometer away. If that platoon possesses enough combat power to take down the target, you let them take down the target. You don't bring in an organization based on its status and its notoriety to give them the benefit of taking down the target. Which Special Operations command gets the prestige and honor of having taken down the target and actually capturing Usama bin Laden is absolutely irrelevant to winning the war on terrorism.

So what have we done right? Have we had intelligence successes? Absolutely! I used the Son Tay raid earlier as an example of bad intelligence. I'll also use it as an example of good intelligence.

Because of our ability to do flyovers and take detailed imagery of the Son Tay prison camp, the team was able to put together an extremely accurate model of the camp. There were two models that existed. One was the life-sized model that was built at a location in Florida. The camp was dismantled whenever we believed a Soviet satellite was overhead and then it was put back together. There was also a small-terrain model that was built. It was extremely detailed and they had developed an instrument that you could use to place yourself on the terrain model and when you would looked into it you would get the view of the compound as though you were standing in it six feet off the ground.

This model proved to be extremely accurate, which led to the success of the strike force going in on the ground. The strike force was led by Dick Meadows, the ground force assault team leader, code-named "Blue Boy." When Dick and his team went into the compound, they knew exactly which huts to go to, they knew exactly what was behind every compound wall, and where they believed the prisoners were kept. This is why they were able to so decisively engage the enemy and successfully extract themselves. So that, really, in itself, was an intelligence success story.

The other success story that we can use in developing lessons learned is the capture of Saddam Hussein. The fact that we were able to catch one man hiding in a spider hole, in a country the size of California, with 25 million people, is truly amazing.

The assets that were used were numerous. Every form of intelligence gathering was used—SIGINT, IMINT, HUMINT, the works. There is an interesting story about the use of cyber intelligence and the capture of Saddam. Various intelligence agencies and now the Army are using a software program called Analyst's Notebook in order to visually display large amounts of information and see the links between elements, or nodes. Every interview, every eyewitness account, every reported overhead image is stored as a node. These nodes can provide a visual web of contacts that can show key nexus points of convergence. In the case of Saddam, interviews with his family members and others close to him proved vital to tracing his location to a particular farm. That location had been visited by the 4th ID before. It was good intelligence that brought them back. They are also using the same software to build up a Web nexus about bin Laden. It will be interesting to see what role it plays, if any, in his final capture.

The 4th ID cordoned off the area, not allowing anyone in, not allowing anyone out, and then the Special Forces teams were sent in to search the farm. If it wasn't for the experience of the operators on the ground and their ability to develop the situation as they conducted operations, Saddam would still be at large If an individual soldier hadn't taken the time to properly search the area, and pick up the piece of covering that was over the spider hole, and then take the time to pull the spider hole cover out, they never would have found Saddam Hussein. So, really, this is a great example of how good intelligence works. Timely, accurate, and actionable. It's not something that you sit on and corroborate and do source verification on for days and weeks on end.

The group that caught Saddam Hussein had the ability to break a paradigm called stove-piping. Our intelligence community suffers from the practice of everyone having a rice bowl, everyone having a stake in the game. Typically, information that's collected by different agencies isn't shared, because they feel like they have to keep their information close to their vests for them to legitimize who they are and what they do for a living. Their intelligence is equivalent to the intellectual property (IP) that Fortune 500 companies safeguard. If they share their IP with other departments or other agencies who may attempt to act on that information or collect against that information, they feel like it may compromise the source or it may compromise the integrity of the information, thus they lose their IP and a portion of their reputation goes with it.

This stove-piping existed on 9/11, and the result was the hijackers being able to take down multiple targets simultaneously.

Some gains have been made within the intelligence community on lowering or reducing the stove-piping.

Recently, there has been a renewed interest in creating task forces. These new organizations have been put together bringing in different assets from the different agencies. This is one possible way to proceed. We have to share information collectively in the community, especially down to the user level. Cross-agency communication is vital if we are going to win the war on terrorism. No one agency by itself in a vacuum will crack the code on terrorist organizations, on insurgency cells, or on sleeper cells. No one organization by itself can act on that intelligence, conduct a raid, or conduct an operation that results in everyone being caught in one fell swoop. It's not going to happen.

The creation of the Department of Homeland Security (DHS) under Tom Ridge has been a catalyst for this new mode of operation. By its charter, DHS is supposed to function as the cross-agency military clearinghouse. It's supposed to have the integrated databases and open access to ALL intelligence information about the terrorists, so it can coordinate an effective response. Let's hope and pray they do their job and that the intelligence bureaucracy has learned its lesson after 9/11.

When you stove-pipe, or when you operate in a limited intelligence collection mode, you don't have the ability to bring in other assets that other organizations typically have. These are national-level assets that exist that will never be directly allocated to the United States Army, which will never be directly allocated to a brigade, a battalion, a platoon, or a Special Forces team that's operating in the field. You have to put these organizations together; you have to integrate all of the different assets in order to come up with a holistic picture of the battlefield. A picture that presents actionable intelligence that somebody can actually go out and act on and get a positive result from the information that was collected.

The CIA needs to update their indoctrination film substituting 9/11 for Pearl Harbor. The intelligence bureaucracy needs to take the bitter lesson of 9/11 and institutionalize changes to the system in order to break down the information-sharing wall that has existed since the now-famous Gorelick memorandum of 1995. In that memo, Jamie Gorelick, a deputy in Janet Reno's Justice Department, strengthened barriers against information sharing between the CIA and the FBI. Here is what the *Washington Times* had to say about this memo in an op-ed piece written in April 2004.

> Attorney General John Ashcroft declassified a four-page directive sent by Ms. Gorelick (the No. 2 official in the Clinton Justice Department) on March 4, 1995, to FBI Director Louis Freeh and Mary Jo White, the New York-based U.S. attorney investigating the 1993 World Trade Center bombing. In the memo, Ms. Gorelick ordered Mr. Freeh and Ms. White to follow information-sharing procedures that "go beyond what is legally required," in order to avoid "any risk of creating an

unwarranted appearance" that the Justice Department was using Foreign Intelligence Surveillance Act (FISA) warrants, instead of ordinary criminal investigative procedures, in an effort to undermine the civil liberties of terrorism suspects.

That memo laid the precedent for nine terrorists to enter the country, enroll in flight training classes, hijack four commercial airliners, crash them into the two tallest buildings in New York City, and brutally massacre three thousand innocent civilians.

But wait, there's more!

What earthly reason did anybody in the Justice Department have to write such a memo in 1995? Did it just pop out of the blue one day because Ms. Gorelick was bored? I should add that Ms. Gorelick was one of the members of the 9/11 Commission and was active in interrogating witnesses and compiling reports. In other words, a member of the 9/11 Commission had a personal stake in making sure that certain acts of hers were not investigated or portrayed in a bad light.

Some have said that she wrote the memo in order to help the Clinton administration hide campaign contributions from foreign countries like China, and foreign companies like the Riadys and the Lippo Group. I have no inside information that points to this as fact, but given the known scandals involving foreign interests this is not an unlikely supposition.

Democratic fund-raiser and Friend-of-Bill (FOB) Johnny Chung told federal investigators that he transferred nearly $100,000 from the communist Chinese military to the Democratic Party in the summer of 1996. The money was given to Chung by the daughter of the commander of the Chinese People's Liberation Army (PLA), General Liu Huaqing. General Liu was also one of the members of the Chinese Communist Party's ruling politburo.

Chung himself was quite ubiquitous around the White House, having visited it forty-nine times. Eventually, after the scandal broke publicly, the Democratic National Committee (DNC) returned $366,000 to Chung, which was suspected of being illegal foreign contributions. Chung later pleaded guilty to campaign-related bank and tax fraud.

But wait, there's more!

In 1996, the Clinton administration removed the State and Defense Departments' oversight of dual-use high-tech items involving advanced satellite and communications systems. This act allowed the Chinese to purchase many items from companies like Loral and Hughes that directly led to improvements in their space systems and military hardware. Now, instead of being able to simply reach Los Angeles with a nuclear-tipped missile aimed to impact within a circular error probability (CEP) of three miles, they can reliably hit targets with an accuracy of three meters. Great work!

> **Lesson Learned:** Well, you have been waiting for a good example of great intelligence work, so here it is! The bag-job that the Chinese and other foreign interests did on the Clinton White House is a classic example of getting into the pants of a country's leadership and manipulating that leadership to serve your agenda. In addition to changing the Pearl Harbor indoctrination film to 9/11, the CIA should consider doing a textbook case on how to penetrate the highest levels of a foreign government using Chung and the PLA operation as an example, you know, kind of like a Harvard case study. Just kidding here, folks. It will never, ever happen.
>
> It all begins and ends with corruption, lack of integrity, and greed. That is how the evil creeps in. It's through an open door.

As a change of pace, I'd like to give you a close-up and personal look at what it's like to collect intelligence and apply it to specific operations in our current war against terrorism. The best way I can do this is to give you a synopsis of an interview I conducted in June 2004, shortly before my deployment to Iraq, this time as a civilian contractor. (Maybe more about this in my next book!)

I interviewed a guy named Michael McInerney. Some of you may be familiar with this name. His uncle, Lt. General Tom McInerney (USAF, retired), appears frequently on Fox News as a commentator. Mike and I served as lieutenants in the 8th Infantry Division and later as officers in the Special Forces. Mike is currently an FBI agent and spent about a year in Afghanistan with the 20th National Guard Special Forces Group. He is an American hero who won a Silver Star in Afghanistan and, in addition, he's a very close friend of mine. If you want to know how to collect intelligence and act on it at the tactical level, here it is.

Mike: Okay, so you want to know about successful use of intelligence in the battlefield and some of the successes I've personally had while over in Afghanistan. One example that comes to mind is one night in August 2003, when we were searching for one of the Top Ten Most Wanted in Afghanistan. We were canvassing his village and the general area. We had set up a checkpoint, a vehicle patrol point outside his village.

As the villagers were passing through all day, we were questioning them, asking them if they'd seen this individual, and trying to meet any family members or close contacts. I knew eventually we would come across somebody who had a beef with him and would provide us with actionable intelligence, something that we could use quickly. By about 16:00, as we were sitting down eating dinner, a gentleman came along and talked to us and said, "I've got information on that man you're looking for, but I can't give it to you here. I can't be seen talking to you. Meet me down the road about three miles at this crossroads at 20:00 tonight."

So at 20:00 we went down there, we linked up with this individual, and he said he would be able to point out the man's house and where he was staying that night. We picked him up, we put him in the back of the vehicle, and we explained to him that if he was driving us into an ambush, then he was going to be the first one who was shot. We put him in the back of the vehicle with our interpreter to give directions. We also had a man with a weapon guarding him.

As we drove into the village he directed us right to the house where this guy was, we surrounded it, and kicked in the door and were able to grab this man. The reason why we were successful is that we had intelligence that we could operate on instantly. Now, what we learned from our informant was something that was not verifiable. Yet we knew that if we spent more time checking it out, or if we passed it on up to higher headquarters to receive confirmation and approval for our operation, it would generally take another twelve to maybe forty-eight hours. They would get the overhead, have a Predator unmanned aerial vehicle (UAV) do an over flight, get satellite imagery, spin up the guys from the Joint Special Operations Center (JSOC), the Delta troopers who were there, or Seals, put them on hold, fly them down in a helicopter, God knows what else, and it would just take too long. We operated on information that we knew was time-sensitive, that that guy was going to be there that night, but we didn't know if he was going to be there the next night or the night after. That's one example where we were successful.

Another example occurred in August 2003 when we were fighting around Dai Chopan, Zabul Province. We received intelligence from our local scouts, who worked for the Afghanis. They were able to provide us with information about Taliban and al Queda, their numbers, and what they're doing, even the *names* of the people there. We were told we had to move to a village approximately fifteen kilometers north of us and seize the village because there was a suspected Taliban hospital and training center there. We passed this on to an Afghani general and he informed me that his local scouts had spent the last four days escaping and evading through that territory. He told us exactly where they'd set up an ambush waiting for us if we drove into the valley to reach that village. We passed this on to higher command and said, "Look, if we drive in there we're gonna be ambushed. What we recommend is use of helicopter assets to leapfrog forward and hit the village via helo insertion."

We were denied the assets and told to move directly into the valley approach to the village. Subsequently, we were ambushed. We managed to fight our way out of the trap after ten hours. But that was an example of where our intelligence gathered from the locals was dead on.

We also utilized what was generally described as "the hearts and minds method" of gathering intelligence. Doing that, we would spend time moving to a village, setting up a medical facility, basically bringing in a lot of doctors and veterinarians to take care of the villagers and their animals. While we did this, people would always come forward and bring us information on the bad guys in the area.

Compare this approach to the CIA's, which historically in Afghanistan was to show up and try to to buy their way in—buy their intelligence. We also noticed in our area that we were gathering more accurate intelligence just by going downtown on a daily basis. We would drive through the town, stop, maybe have our vehicles worked on, have some lunch, buy some food, buy some rugs, whatever, and get to know the people in our local area. By doing so, it allowed them to approach us. Perhaps not that day or not that week, but they would see us around and eventually someone would come up and say, "Hey, I've got information on so-and-so," or "somebody's got weapons here." "The guy who's been firing rockets at you works for this guy."

As we built rapport and trust with them, they realized we weren't the bad guys coming in a raping-and-pillaging role. We were spending money, we were helping their economy, we were there protecting them. They willingly brought information to us which allowed us to pacify their area.

One night, I was talking with some of the other intelligence operatives in the area. They told me that basically they relied on information given by people walking into our compound. They did not go out and actively seek it themselves.

Well, we would seek it, as I said, through the means of going out and meeting with the locals and helping a guy out when we could. We were driving down a riverbed one day and saw a farmer that had his tractor stuck in deep sand. We pulled him out of his predicament, and then just talked to him for a couple of minutes. We gave him some of our big pancakes that we had with us. These are MRE-type cakes in a metal sealed pan. As we fed him, he provided us intelligence on some of the local bad guys, because some of the questions we asked were, "Are you from the area?" "Do you know what's going on? Have you heard of this? Are you aware that people have been firing rockets at us? Putting improvised explosive devices (IEDs) in the road? Do you have any idea who's doing this?"

Most of them would start with, "I don't have any idea." But generally, as you talked to them over time, and they built that trust, you'd see them come forward and say, "Uh, I don't know exactly who did it, but my understanding is that it's from this village," or "There's this number of compounds in this area." This allowed us to pinpoint and pick up information and focus our collection efforts.

The CIA and the DIA had people in our area. I would watch them work and their intelligence was generally based on, "Yeah, some guy named Hassan walked into the compound today and said, so-and-so is up here." Nine times out of ten, this information was incorrect and if it did actually have any credibility to it, it was generally because the guy was ratting out somebody that he didn't like, maybe even a family member. "Ah, Hassan's got fifteen AKs up here."

Well, you go up there and, sure enough, Hassan's got fifteen AKs. But that didn't mean that he was Taliban or a bad guy. He was probably just trying to sell them to whomever.

Bob: Mike, explain the benefit of having been an FBI agent and learning a different form of field craft, and how that may have assisted you in what you had to do in Afghanistan.

Mike: I had a perspective that was different from probably 90 percent of the military. Most of them have never had to work their field craft—gathering information, vetting sources, setting up routes, doing surveillance and countersurveillance. They had probably studied it sometime in the military, but they never had a chance to practice it in reality. I have talked to and interviewed thousands of witnesses, thousands of subjects. We call the interviewees "subjects." I've had people who didn't want to tell me anything. But after talking to them for hours on end, they would usually come clean and admit to a crime.

I utilized these skills by talking to the people and using multisource verification of intelligence. I paid close attention on how to gather it and how to put it together. I got better results than the military guys did; based on the fact that the military guys really don't have any experience in going out and talking to people.

Bob: Mike, what's your opinion of the interrogation techniques that were used at the Abu Ghraib Prison in Baghdad based on the success you've had in the FBI getting information out of people without having to violate their human or civil rights?

Mike: I've gotta look at what has occurred at Abu Ghraib and say, "This is—I'm trying to think of a good word—it's aberrant behavior by some kids who are basically white trailer trash, who had no leadership, left alone, and then saying to themselves, "Look, this is our job here. Our job is to break these people and gather information from them." Our job is not to sit there and try to embarrass them or take pictures showing that we're the guys in charge. I mean, naked pictures of guys doesn't do anything. Now, having them stand around naked in a cold cell and hosing them down with water, depriving them of sleep, depriving them of warmth, depriving them of food to get information, you have to create leverages. I agree with that.

The fact that they took pictures and you have some female who seems to be glorifying in the fact that these guys are naked and that she is the one who is causing them this embarrassment, I find that to be ridiculous.

It has no value in gathering intelligence. It's done by kids who have no respect for themselves and have no leadership. They needed somebody who was a trained interrogator to say, "Okay, look, these are the methods we're gonna use." And then the stair-step approach. You try to break the guy as quickly as possible with something like food deprivation, sleep deprivation, or water deprivation. You do that over a twenty-four-hour period and generally, you start getting information from them. If that doesn't work, then you take it to the next level.

You remove their clothes, you have them stand in a cold cell hours on end, you hose 'em down with water. You're trying to break one down little bit by little bit. I think the examples of them strung up with wire and mock executions and having dogs bark around them, yeah, that's nothing more than instilling some fear. But, you're not gathering any intelligence; you're not breaking them down.

Bob: So, Mike, given the intelligence failure of 9/11 and some of the successes that you've experienced as an FBI agent fighting the war on terror in Afghanistan, in short summary, why do you think 9/11 happened? Then follow it up with how you think it could have been prevented.

Mike: There were a number of failures in our intelligence-collecting ability prior to 9/11. There were indicators that something was going to occur. The FBI failed, the CIA failed, all of our intelligence apparatus failed to protect the United States. When these indicators came up, they should have been addressed. It's easy to say that and spot them now. At the time, there were so many indicators coming in it's very difficult to get the signal-to-noise ratio adjusted so you can figure out what is going on.

I think that 9/11 occurred not just because of our inability to stop them, but because under the administrations prior to this, not four years ago, not even eight, but ten years ago this was a growing problem and nobody addressed it. The problem was the growing fundamentalism under Usama bin Laden, creating an us-versus-them mentality—the jihadists versus the West. I think that was the biggest failure. We should have looked to address these issues a long time ago and that's why 9/11 occurred. They had to take a stand and do something to the United States. This was their only means of doing so. If they'd been able to get their hands on nuclear weapons, I think they would have utilized them during 9/11.

Bob: Mike, recognizing the failure of events that led up to 9/11, what do we need to do in order to prevent another 9/11 and are our actions right now in Afghanistan and Iraq enough to prevent another 9/11 scenario?

Mike: You know that's a very good question. How do we prevent another 9/11? A lot of people, especially a lot of liberals, say we need to get an understanding and sympathize with this fundamentalism, and I would bet and say that is a nice, colorful approach, but it's not going to solve it. It's a little bit like taking pity on some kid because he's an orphan, forgetting that he was the one who killed his parents.

We can understand the fundamentalists and what they believe in, but it's not going to change their belief system. The way that we prevent another 9/11 from occurring is we do what we're doing now. We fight this war on terror.

Our first step was to go after those people who struck us during 9/11, al Queda, specifically. But they are just part of a terrorist web, a network of terrorists throughout the world.

We went after them in Afghanistan, we've been successful there. Our successes will continue to grow there, but we also need to bring in other people, a coalition of the willing, who will stand with us and be involved in this war on terror. The fact that the French just vetoed NATO going in to help Hamid Karzai in his election in September is ridiculous. It shows that the French care more about themselves. We must have more countries willing to say, "You know what? We want to be successful in Afghanistan, we're getting successful there but we need to continue. We have to help them rebuild."

We went into Iraq for all the right reasons. A lot of people say, "Well, there are no direct ties to al Queda there. There was no evidence of weapons of mass destruction." I say to all that, there are ties, there are examples of WMD. But what was more important is the message that we sent to these other rogue nations that are involved in terrorism—to Syria, to Saudi Arabia, to Libya, to North Korea, to the Chechens, everybody. We told them we are willing to go into a country and remove somebody who sponsors and supports terrorism. And we did so.

We are going to be successful in Iraq, I think, in this war on terrorism for a couple of reasons. Number one, economically, we're helping now but we have to provide them with the ability to grow economically, to become stable. We must have the staying power to push these people forward. Militarily, we can stay there and fight for the next twenty years and never get anywhere, but if we use the economic sword, by which I mean, we assist them, we help them grow. That's where we're gonna see a change. We're seeing it today in Iraq and I think it's gonna continue to grow.

The problem with Iraq is that it's become a focal point for all the jihadists and fundamentalists who do not want us to be successful. So they're doing their damned best to keep us from being successful. They're sending in people who try to disrupt everything that we do. They want to disrupt the convoys, disrupt the election process, and disrupt the media.

Bob: Now, Mike, this is no different from what we experienced back when the Soviets were fighting and occupying Afghanistan. The world's jihadists came together and actually formed a province in Waziristan, in Pakistan, to rally the then-mujahedeen to go into Afghanistan and overthrow the Soviets. Is this a lesson that we should have learned and maybe done a little bit better prior planning before going into Iraq? Should we have recognized the fact that these nations were probably gonna bring in some of their more aggressive fighters and kind of create the same type of environment, and if that was the case, where was our intelligence capability that should have identified that? Who should've been advising the president? "You know, sir, what you're probably gonna end up having is a very large insurgency." Do you think we should have seen that one coming?

Mike: Bob, I think that, as you brought up, is why we were not aware of what was going to occur. I think the reason behind that is nobody looked at it historically and said, "Okay, what's going to happen here? What are we doing? What is the plan that we have in place to address these issues?"

We know that in Iraq, for these jihadists to come in, they have to have some means. We never shut off the borders with Iran, Syria, and Saudi Arabia. If we had done so, we could over-fly with Predators; our satellites could look down and search for these people, preventing them from getting in there. Then we wouldn't be dealing with the issues we're dealing with today. You're right about the model of what occurred in Afghanistan. There the jihadists sat up along the eastern Pakistani border and developed training camps and a whole terrorist infrastructure. The Soviets never went after those training camps.

For us to be successful, if we identify an area, say in Syria, or within Saudi Arabia or in Iran, where they're developing a base of support, a base of operations, we need to go after that. We need to hit these people, hit them as hard as we can militarily. I also think that the way we'll be successful is utilizing the Iraqi people to identify the foreigners. They know who they are. But they have to have some type of carrot over their heads, which is, "Hey, these guys are coming in. They want to disrupt the economy. You're the sheik; you're in charge of this tribal area, in charge of this village. Either fix it, or the weight of it will fall on your head."

We're not going to, you know, buy your groceries, we're not going to buy your food; we're not going to spend all this money in this area if it's not safe.

Well, economically, it's important for the sheik to have that ability. Is he going to trust somebody who has dared to disrupt that process and take money away from him? Take food out of his family's mouth? No, he's going to support the people who provide a secure environment so he can put the food on the table. The jihadists can't put the food on the table.

Bob: That's a great point, Mike. I want to wrap this chapter up in talking about leadership as it pertains to the intelligence community. What kind of guys need to be in charge of these organizations that are responsible for collecting intelligence? Describe to me the type of leadership that you want to see as heads of these organizations, and what kind of power and authority do they need to possess?

Mike: To address that, number one, who do we need at the head of these intelligence organizations? Who needs to be in charge? My recommendation is that we need to have somebody who has had experience in the intelligence community, yet is not a politician. We can't put a politically elected person there. Or somebody whose entire focus is, "What is my next job gonna be after I finish this one?"

We need somebody who is basically beholden to no one, someone who has very few oversights. The oversights will come from the president, himself, or his inner staff. We need somebody whose focus is, "What does it take to get the job done," not, "What does it take to make sure the senators on the Oversight Committee are happy, to see that the people who give us funding are happy." We need somebody who's beholden to no one and is willing to go all the way. This is a war on terrorism. We need somebody, perhaps a former military man who's not politically motivated. We need somebody who's entire thought process is, "Well, what am I doing for the good of the nation?" not, "What am I doing for the good of myself?"

That is the type of person we need to put in charge.

Bob: How much power and authority do these individuals have? I mean, if you were gonna be the director of the CIA, should you have the ability to conduct missions unilaterally without having to go through a series of individuals in order to get permission?

Mike: Well, especially for the CIA, the director needs to have the ability to authorize an operation independent of any oversight, other than the president. Being able to say, "Mr. President, this is what we've got occurring, this is what I'm doing." We need somebody who's willing to put it on the table, but in doing so; you also have to have somebody who's willing to accept responsibility if there's a failure. He accepts responsibility for it.

The American public always wants to know what's going on with their intelligence organizations, but it doesn't do any good. The American people generally do not have a need to know. They just need to be safe. Our intelligence apparatus needs to operate independently of the American public's awareness. If we don't do so, what we create is, once again, what do the people want to hear? How will this look if it gets out? Well, that's not how we should be operating. An intelligence operation by opinion poll is not the way you want to go.

Bob: Mike, do you think the media has had a negative impact on our ability to collect intelligence? I mean, it seems like we're flooded with "everybody wants to know." They want to have information. They get twenty-four-hour news. Everyone feels like they need to be briefed. Is the media affecting our ability to collect intelligence?

Mike: I believe that the media is adversely affecting everything on the war on terrorism. The American people, as you say, have this need to know. They know what's going on, what the CIA's doing, what they're not doing, and so on.

And all that does is destroy our ability to gather intelligence, because you have these media networks out there, basically disrupting our ability to work, trying to get deep inside the CIA, trying to utilize moles within the FBI and CIA to pry out information so that they can gather ratings, and gather viewers.

That we don't need. Our intelligence community needs to be able to do its job without worrying about the public opinion. The media is driven by one thing and that's ratings. They want to get people to watch, so they sensationalize every tidbit of information on the CIA, on the FBI, especially failures. If an organization doesn't do something correctly, they're gonna jump on it. Why? Because that makes great headlines. It doesn't help solve the problems of our war on terrorism; it doesn't make anybody any safer at home or feel any better about it. It just lets everybody know that, "Hey, we're all people, intelligence organizations are based on people, their bureaucracy, they do have failures. There are also hundreds of successes that nobody's aware of. And never should be.

Bob: So, Mike, one of the things that I advocate throughout my book is using unconventional means to collect intelligence, or to affect the battlefield, to change perceptions, things of that nature. Do you see possibly using a media platform like Al Jazeera as either an intelligence-collecting tool or a way of changing the mindset of people within their audience?

Mike: Well, Al Jazeera has such an impact in the Arab world, you know. It's one of a number of the Arab media stations, but it's probably in it's primacy with most of the Arabs for gathering information on what's going on throughout the world. They have a huge impact. My recommendation is we can certainly gather some intelligence from them, if it's verifiable and it conforms to the recordings we have. But, my recommendation is we utilize Al Jazeera to influence the rest of the Arab world. We can put pressure on the people who run Al Jazeera, like Wadah Khanfar in Baghdad, or some of the other individuals who are owners of that and let them know, hey, it's in your best benefit to stop catering to the Wahhabis and jihadists and the fundamentalists and start working with the rest of the Arab world to say, "Hey, you know, we need to come to an understanding of what the West is doing. They're not here trying to take over the world, they're just trying to protect themselves."

Bob: And would you say that the influence that we need to put on them goes back to your earlier statement of wielding that economic sword within Iraq, I mean, is the dollar truly what counts here?

Mike: The economic sword is the greatest weapon that we've got in this war on terrorism. We can utilize it to influence all of the Arab nations to either have regime changes or a change in their values, their fundamentalist values.

You can believe in anything you want to believe in, but if it's taking food off your table and it's starving your family, you're not going to believe in it. You're going to go with whatever it takes to put food on the table and food in the mouths of your children.

Bob: So then we really aren't all that dissimilar as a race, as a human race, between the different cultures and the different religions. It all does boil down to quality of life and family, doesn't it?

Mike: Exactly. Once you take out the differences in religious values, which are really not that dissimilar, once you put them side-by-side and you get people talking about it, I think that the problems especially being utilized by the fundamentalists are pretty simple. They believe that we are inferior to them and that we're exporting our inferior pornographic and degenerate culture and that we're replacing their culture. We're not attempting to replace their culture. What we're trying to do is create a mindset within them of, "Hey, you can accept our values if you want, but you don't have to take them on." We have to give them a choice. There are children who are growing up in Iraq and Jordan and Saudi Arabia who want to wear Western clothes. It's changed. And it's difficult for a lot of people growing up to see this change. Hell, we have the same thing here in the United States. We see kids running around, they have different values, different clothing, etc., and we don't understand it, but we accept the change. They have to be willing to accept change.

Bob: We'll probably go ahead and end it with that. And that's good.

What we have done here is set the table and prepared you for the last, or ultimate, chapter of this book. It will be an experience for you, something like you have never read or seen before.

In the 1995 movie *Seven,* if you will recall, Kevin Spacey is sitting out in an open field in the middle of nowhere, with nowhere to go and no place to hide. What makes the moment so terrible is that suddenly down this dusty road comes a delivery van. The delivery guy has a box for the Brad Pitt character. By this time, the other cop, Morgan Freeman, has pretty much figured out what is in the box and doesn't want his partner, Brad, to look inside. Brad, too, has it figured out, but he looks anyway. The audience never sees what's in there, but we all know just the same.

All of us know what is at the end of the last chapter. Let's hope we never have to look in the box.

Chapter Seven

The Middle East: The Emergence of Islamo-Fascism, and What Lies Next

In order to understand the problems that we have in the Middle East, it is essential that we understand how Israel became a state and how the Arabs were involved in that process and where the deep-rooted resentment began and how it has grown to the point of contention that we have today. The Arab-Israeli conflict is a situation that plagues us in every area within the Middle East and on a global scale. This conflict has provided the backdrop for many of the continuing problems we have had in Iraq.

If I were to compare Israel to any other country, I'd have to pick Sicily, because Sicily has been invaded and conquered and used as a launching platform for the invasion of Italy and southern Europe by numerous armies over many centuries. Israel has been used basically in this same way. Since biblical times, Israel has been conquered and re-invaded and if you look at the amount of times that the land was turned over from the Jews to invaders and back to the Jews again, it shows nothing but a continual struggle over a long period of time, with several governments being involved and trying to "fix the problem."

Roughly 1,250 years before the birth of Christ, one of the four Semitic tribes, the Israelites, settled in the area then called Palestine, in the land of

Canaan on the eastern Mediterranean coast.

This led up to the reign of King Solomon and the establishment of the temple in Jerusalem. Solomon's reign was immediately followed by what became commonplace in the area of Palestine, which was the division of the land into two kingdoms.

About 586 years before the birth of Christ, the seventh kingdom, Judea, was conquered by the Babylonians, who basically drove the Jews into exile. Their king, Nebuchadnezzar, destroyed Solomon's Temple in the process.

Approximately sixty years later, the Jews returned to the area and rebuilt the Second Temple only to see it again completely destroyed by the Romans in AD 70.

The Jews have always been drawn back to this area in Palestine and no matter what the decade, the era, who is in political rule, they always saw this as their true homeland. This was the land promised to them by God through the person of Moses.

In roughly AD 630 the Muslims had taken over this area and in the early eighth century built a mosque at the site of what is now the al-Aqsa Mosque in Jerusalem. This area is regarded as particularly holy to Muslims, being the site from which the prophet Mohammed ascended into heaven. The al-Aqsa Mosque is located on what the Jews call Temple Mount. The Dome of the Rock covers the rock from which Mohammed went to heaven. With the exception of about ninety years during the Crusades, that area has remained under Muslim control until the eventual fall of the Ottoman Empire in the early twentieth century. So for twelve hundred years, this land known as Palestine was dominated by *Arabs* who were one of the four Semitic tribes.

Starting in the late 1800s, the Jews began to pour into Palestine and purchase land. A fund was set up that allowed monies to be collected for financing the purchase of land from the Arabs. Most of the landowners at the time that owned property in Palestine were more or less absentee landlords. They weren't located in the area and the land that they *did* own was currently being farmed by very poor Arabs.

So with the beginning of the Zionist movement and the creation of the Jewish National Funds, the Jews were able to acquire land at an amazing rate and the prices for land skyrocketed in the 1930s. This was equivalent to the prices you see in Monterey, California, in Los Angeles, and in northern Virginia. The common Arabs that were farming the land didn't have the ability to pay the steep prices and leases or rents for that property to their landlords.

British involvement in the Middle East centered around their need to keep open the Suez Canal and its pathway to India. For this reason, they were only too happy to play a major role in the administration of Egypt after the collapse of Ottoman Turkey's power there. By the early 1880s Britain had become the defacto ruler of Egypt. During the First World War, 1914–1918, Britain's influence grew throughout the Arab world due partly to the successful leadership of the Arab revolt against Turkey by T. E. Lawrence (Lawrence of Arabia). By the fall of 1918 British General Allenby occupied Palestine shortly before the war ended in November. Although the Sykes-Picot Agreement of 1916 had generally delineated British and French spheres of influence in the Middle East, Britain remained the dominant power in the region.

The Balfour Declaration of 1917 committed Britain to support a national home for the Jews in Palestine. Even though this territory had been controlled by Muslim Arabs for centuries, British and world opinion was swayed by the Zionist Movement. In 1896 Theodor Herzl, an Austro-Hungarian journalist, set forth the argument for a Jewish state in his book, *Der Judenstaat (The Jewish State)*. By the end of World War I this movement became unstoppable, as it was fanned by the desires of Jews worldwide to end the *diaspora,* the dispersal of the Jews that occurred after the destruction of the Second Temple. After the suppression of the Jewish revolt against Rome, Jews were banned from living in Jerusalem and in the province of Judea. Thus, the reestablishment of Israel as a nation had religious and political significance for Judeo-Christian societies in the West far beyond any Arab nationalistic arguments that could be made against it. In an ironic way, one of the greatest reasons Israel exists today is Adolf Hitler. The Nazi Holocaust resulted in the deaths of six million Jews in Europe. By 1945 the horrors of this mass murder had become burned in the collective consciousness of the civilized world. Newsreels of the liberated death camps at Buchenwald, Dachau, and others with the unforgettable scenes of emaciated human beings being thrown into piles of dead bodies was too much for public opinion to take. The gas ovens convinced even hardened opponents to the Jewish state to say, "enough is enough."

Ethnic Conflicts Far and Wide

At some risk of having your eyes glaze over at the above dose of history, I have felt it necessary to lay before you the background, the context, if you will, of how and why Israel became a nation. Understanding this will let you know why the solution to the problems of modern Israel and the Palestinians is so intractable. Minds much greater than mine have been unable to truly come to grips with this problem and solve it to everyone's satisfaction.

It's because we can't enter a time capsule and travel back through the centuries and right the terrible wrongs of ages past that we are so frustrated today. By the way, in addition to Palestine and the Arab conflict with Israel, there are several other knotty problems that the world has never solved, including: the patchwork of settlements and centuries of hatred in the Balkans, in Serbia, and in Kosovo; the division and separation of the Kurds across Turkey, Iraq, and Iran; and the suppression of the Shia Muslims by the secularist Sunni minority in Saddam Hussein's Iraq. Potentially the biggest explosive ethnic conflict of all is going on full blast in Chechnya. Chechnya is located on the southern periphery of Russia in the Caucasus Mountains region. The population there is predominantly Muslim and fiercely independence-minded, wanting a complete separation from Russian rule. Al Queda has been particularly successful in recruiting Chechen fighters. They were in the front lines of the Taliban army in Afghanistan and are now operating in the wild tribal areas of northwest Pakistan. The Chechens have been responsible for several really nasty terror incidents in Russia, including the seizure of a Moscow theater where 129 hostages were killed. Other recent incidents, including bomb blasts at rock concerts and in the Moscow subway system, have led to rising panic in Russia. This panic has greatly increased due to the hostage taking of the school in Beslan, Russia, where hundreds of schoolchildren, parents, and babies were brutally slaughtered. In latest developments, the Chechen war has spilled over into the neighboring territories of Georgia, Ossetia, Ingushetia, and Daghestan. All of these problems exist today and will continue to haunt us to varying degrees in the future. The final explosive ingredient for trouble in this tortured region, if one were needed, has been the emergence of radical Islamo-Fascsim throughout the Muslim world, but particularly in the Middle East and most specifically in Saudi Arabia and Afghanistan under

248

the Taliban. How did Islamo-Fascism come about? What are its roots? How can it be combatted?

In an indirect way, the roots of Islamo-Fascism can be found in the emergence of the Palestinian cause and the struggle against Israel. I say "indirect" because of the peculiar way in which the Palestinian cause is used by Arab governments and intellectuals as an instrument of social control.

How Did the Palestinian Refugees Come to Be?

The withdrawal of the British from Palestine in 1948 ended its mandate there and Israel declared itself an independent nation. This declaration was reinforced by the United Nations and by 1949 truce agreements under U.N. auspices had been signed by Egypt, Jordan, and Syria. A lasting peace was, however, not possible and Israel fought and won two major wars with her neighbors in 1967 and in 1973. The area known as Gaza or the Gaza Strip was occupied by Israel after the end of the 1967 war.

The acute problem for Arab Palestinians who lost their homes and land during the initial foundation struggle to establish Israel as a nation in 1948 was only compounded by Israel's occupation of Gaza and the territory west of the Jordan River known as the West Bank. Squalid refugee camps were set up in many places including Jenin, Khan Younis, and Beqa'a. In the initial phase of Arab displacement in 1948, according to U.N. estimates, some five hundred thousand Arabs were turned into refugees. How exactly did this happen?

Of course, there are two versions as to why this forced displacement of Arabs from Jewish Palestine took place. The Arab version is that the Jews took over the land at gunpoint and made the Arab population either flee or be killed. The Jewish version of the story is more complex, but it does have a direct bearing on how the situation developed in the future and persists until our present day.

In 1958, the novelist Leon Uris in his novel *Exodus,* told the story that Arab leaders forced the evacuations because they intended to send their armies in to drive the Jews into the sea and didn't want to have to be concerned about killing innocent Arabs. There is documentation that proves Arab refugees were told they could return to their homes in Palestine after Israel had been destroyed. Uris's novel was later made into a Hollywood movie and the sound track by Ferrante and Teicher proved quite successful in the music world.

Again, the choice is yours as to which side you want to take on all this. I will simply say that the arguments as to why the Palestinian Arabs were forced into refugee status is beyond my power to untangle or even attempt to definitively explain. I will say also that in a very peculiar way some irresponsible Arab leaders like Syria's dictator Hafiz al-Assad have callously used the Palestinians to prop up their own corrupt states and blame the Zionists and the Jews for all of their problems.

Since the end of World War II, there have been many instances of mass refugee migrations. After the end of World War II, at the Yalta Conference, it was agreed by the major powers, the U.S., Britain, and Russia, that the German populations in the Baltics, East Brandenburg, East Prussia, Pomerania, Silesia, and in the Sudetenland, some ten and a half million people overall, would be forcibly driven out of their homelands and moved mainly into what was left of Germany. German towns, communities, and families had lived in some of these areas for a millennium, but the punishment of Germany for the war and compensation to the Soviet Union and Poland for the suffering they had endured was deemed to be the greater good. For good measure, other peoples were forcibly evicted including hundreds of thousands of Hungarians (Hungary had been a German ally in the war) from territories now in Romania, Poland, and Slovakia. Many of the mass expulsions were carried out under fierce winter weather conditions and under fire from the advancing Red Army.

Another very large-scale migration of peoples took place after the partition of India in 1947 led to the creation of modern Pakistan. In this huge population exchange, largely compulsory, some five million Hindus, Sikhs, and other non-Muslims were forced to move into India. Going the other way, some six million Muslims were packed up and moved into Pakistan. It is estimated that in these migrations and the resulting communal violence some one million people died.

Finally, our short but by no means exhaustive list of mass expulsions must include the invasion, occupation, and forced colonization of Tibet by the Chinese after 1949. Events in Tibet have largely been hidden from Western eyes, but there are numerous accounts of genocide, suppression of Buddhist monasteries, the killing of religious leaders, expulsion of Tibetans from their land, and large-scale importation of Chinese settlers.

Now, native Tibetans are a minority in most of their former territory.

In none of these cases has the refugee problem persisted to the present day, in any significant way. In no case other than the Palestinians has a permanent U.N. commission been established with the sole purpose of looking after their welfare. Why is this? Why is this situation "permanent?"

What the Palestinian Cause Really Means to Others

How is the Palestinian cause useful to the Saudi monarchy? Why did Saddam Hussein send $25,000 to each family of a homicide bomber who blew him- or herself up on an Israeli bus, inside a seaside nightclub full of teenagers, or in a pizza parlor?

The answer is that so many social, economic, and political problems exist in Arab lands that it is a very convenient thing for radical Islamic fundamentalists to blame everything on the Zionists, the Jews, and, due to guilt by association, the Americans. They claim that you and I are to blame for all the ills of the Middle East, the poverty, the lack of economic opportunity for young men, education, and whatever else you can think of.

Instead of reforming their own societies, irresponsible leaders choose to blame whatever outsiders are convenient. If the outsiders appear to be more affluent, successful, technologically advanced, better educated, and more powerful, then it's even easier to blame them for your own failings.

In the middle ages, Arab societies made tremendous advancements in science, astronomy, mathematics, exploration, and commerce. Today, in spite of the vast oil wealth they have amassed, the hereditary princes can point to virtually no inventions or innovations that have led to the benefit of mankind. Their feudal infrastructures have led them to educate their young men in Wahabi madrassas, schools where they can learn to memorize the Koran and to hate Zionism, but they learn little else that will prepare them for a life and a career in a modern society. This problem also has sadly affected former communist countries. My co-author of this book once was approached by the daughter of a famous Russian mathematician who wanted to know if he could help her with admission to an American graduate school. He looked over her transcript from Moscow State University and found that much of her course work included such gems as "Applied Marxist-Leninist Theory," "History of

Socialism," and "Contradictions of Modern Capitalism." He told her that, unfortunately, she would get no credit for any of these classes in an American university or anywhere else in the West and that instead of being a university graduate, she would probably rank no better than a junior-level student. An anti-capitalist, anti-American education is not an asset when you start looking for a job in a real-world economy.

At a point in time not long after the establishment of Israel as a nation, the feudal monarchies, warlords, and radical fundamentalist clergy in the Muslim world figured out that here was a great opportunity to keep control over their own people. Use Israel and the West as an unimaginably great horror to strike fear into the hearts of your people. Convince them that the evil Jew and Westerner wanted to harass their women, banish their religion, steal their wealth, their oil, and use them as slaves to further the foreign interests. They could point to the depravation and poverty of the Palestinians to help nurture the hatred and fear of the Jews and the West. They could teach young boys in school to devote their lives to destroying Jews and Americans. They could have grade-schoolers play games with mock suicide explosive belts.

Let's be real honest here. The Iranians could CARE LESS about the plight of the Palestinians. The Palestinians are Arabs, the Iranians arePersian. Arabic is a Semitic language, Farsi is Indo-European. The Palestinians are largely Sunni Muslims, the Iranians are Shiites. Do I need to continue? This would be like the American government getting concerned about the people living on the Kamchatka Peninsula (far eastern Russia for you geographically deprived). It isn't going to happen.

Why then does the radical Iranian regime support Hezbollah and try to cause so much trouble for Israel and the West in general? Again, keeping the terror going is a very predictable way to get Israel to retaliate. One of the Palestinian terror groups, Hezbollah, the Islamic Jihad, the al Aqsa Martyrs Brigade—whatever—blows up a city bus in Jerusalem. Then, Israel retaliates, taking out a weapons factory and several other houses in the neighborhood. Innocents are killed, babies are dead. There are more riots and demonstrations in the streets of Gaza, all great TV for Al Jazeera in Teheran and Damascus. Thus, the stories about Jews killing Arabs and America supporting the Jews get constantly, continuously, and brutally reinforced. What more do they need to keep their people constantly on edge, worried about themselves and their families, and ready, willing, and able to provide fresh recruits for the cause of jihad?

Radical Wahhabi fundamentalism is charismatic. It promises simple solutions. It captures the hearts of the oppressed. Arabs and Islam are not bad, but the virulent brand of Wahhabism sponsored by the Saudis until quite recently has proven to be a very useful tool for directing frustration and pent-up hatred in closed oppressive societies outward toward the Zionists and the West.

Throughout human history, hatred of others, outsiders if you will, has been the great unifier of evil, dictatorial regimes. It's almost axiomatic to say that you CAN'T have a brutal oppressive regime WITHOUT an external threat. For Hitler it was the Jews and Bolsheviks (largely the same in their eyes), for the communists it was the capitalists and fascists, for the Japanese it was British, American, and Dutch colonists who wanted to strangle Japan by depriving it of rubber, steel, and oil. For just about every tinhorn, corrupt, and evil dictator in the world today from Castro to Kim Jong Il, the Great Satan is the United States of America and anybody that is allied with it. Hey, man, we are in a tough, lonely league here.

I'm not trying to be flippant, but they all hate us. For different reasons they hate us, but who cares why? I wish we could make them all happy and be cozy and friendly to the U.S. and to Americans. I wish any American with a Visa card could travel freely without fear for his safety anywhere in the world. I wish every big town had a McDonald's and a Kentucky Fried Chicken. It's a big world, but heck we'd all be better off if they did.

The Roots of Islamo-Fascism

In many ways, the rise of Islamo-Fascism in its most radical manifestation can be interpreted as a backlash against the encroachment of modern technological societies into feudal Muslim states. Nowhere was this more evident than in Iran, where a rapid injection of American industrial and military technology into the country happened much too quickly for society to absorb. The radical clergy there appealed to the masses with the popular cry to rid the country of the unclean and immoral elements of the West and all their trappings. No more equal rights for women, no more American movies and television, no more satellite dishes to the world, no more much of anything outside of Iran that they didn't control.

Few societies and cultures in the world can withstand modernization without a huge, profoundly paralyzing shock. Institutions and infrastructures have to be changed when modernization occurs. Schools have to be established that teach real subjects—math, physics, engineering, chemistry, business administration, you name it. What happens to the education monopoly of the clerics? What happens to their control over national life; everything from politics and economics to culture and family life?

Well, if you start to lose control, your family monarchy starts to get questions about why there isn't a parliament. Your economy starts requiring things like cell phones and a real judicial system to enforce the rule of law, to regulate contracts and business relationships, a real banking system with investment credit—anything you can imagine. What do you do then if you are medieval-minded cleric with your power and influence deeply rooted in religious intolerance, aided and abetted by an equally feudal political system? What you do is stage a counter-revolution and drive out the alien influences. You grab everything around you and put it back where it belongs.

There are other historical examples of fascism arising out of culture shock. Studies have been written that show convincingly that the Nazi appeal to the working class in Germany in the 1920s and '30s was largely due to the displacement of many families from rural communities who were forced into large cities to find jobs. This process had begun in the 1890s but it rapidly accelerated after the end of World War I in 1918. The Nazi storm troopers found a rich supply of dispossessed recruits, ready to join a cause to end the ravages caused by defeat in war and by a cruel, grinding capitalism that had no feeling for the working man.

Don't forget, the German acronym "Nazi" actually stands for *Nationalsozialistische Deutsche Arbeiterpartei* or "National Socialist German Workers' Party." Blaming the Jews for Germany's woes was easy for Hitler. In his book, *Mein Kampf (My Struggle),* he perpetuated the myth of the *November Verbrecher,* the "November Criminals" who stabbed the Kaiser and the German Army in the back (*Dolchstoss*). Many of these November criminals had communist and Jewish backgrounds. When the Weimar Republic was established after Germany's signing of the Versailles Treaty in 1919, the stage was set for blaming the Jews for the defeat, for the humiliation of Versailles including onerous reparations and disarmament—for everything wrong in Germany. The leap from blaming the Jews for Germany's shame in the war to the Holocaust was a short one.

Karl Haushofer, Alfred Rosenberg, Julius Streicher, and other Nazi theorists popularized the ideas of *Lebensraum,* "Living Space," meaning more room in Europe for the ascendant Aryan race. The idea was that living space would come at the expense of the Slavic-occupied territories in the east, mainly in Poland and the Soviet Union. Connected closely with this theory was the myth of *Blut und Boden,* "Blood and Soil." The German *Heimland* or "Homeland" had special significance for the Aryan race and its ascendant superiority over other human beings.

This had particular significance for the "stateless Jew" who by contrast was only interested in subversion of countries and manipulating them for their own use rather than founding a nation of their own. Many of these ideas were fashioned into a bizarre occult philosophy which Heinrich Himmler used to wield a pathological social control over his elite SS *(Schutzstaffel)* units, which later became the instruments of destruction in the death camps. German propaganda at home rested on the pillars of hatred for the Jews and on the myth of a German-Aryan super race which, in fact, existed only in Wagnerian operas and in the weird minds of crazies like Rosenberg.

It doesn't require deep thinking to see many parallels between Hitler's Nazis and Usama bin Laden's al Qaeda. Let's discuss a few of these.

The idea of a *Herrenvolk* (Master Race), so central to Nazi philosophy, is not all that different from radical Wahhabism, the particular strain of Islam preached throughout the world and promulgated by the Saudis. Wahhabism was the mother's milk fed to Usama bin Laden in his formative educational years in Saudi schools and universities. The idea that Jews are no better than apes and pigs and that Western infidels are a constant threat to Islam and an enemy to be overcome is at the center of the hate-filled teachings that Wahhabism has for Israel and the West. Any time you set yourself up as being superior or more worthy to live than your fellow human beings by virtue of your race or religion you are, by my definition at least, a fascist.

It is not my intention to get into a detailed discussion of Wahhabism. Others more knowledgable than me have already done that. I'm just drawing the parallel here between Wahhabism as it exists in the minds of terrorists today with the Master Race theory of the Nazis. There really is a pretty close fit.

Now let's take the Blood and Soil, Homeland, and Living Space myths of the Nazis. How do they apply to our current crop of terrorists?

If you accept the idea that Jerusalem specifically and Palestine in general is a very special place for several major religions of the world, Christianity, Islam, and Judaism, then you can see that the concept of "Homeland" is extremely important to them. Christianity certainly established a legacy for itself during the Crusades to capture the Holy Land from the Muslims and Jews during the eleventh and twelfth centuries. The modern-day struggle for control of Judea or Palestine does have similarities to the Homeland myth. Both religions attach special religious significance to Jerusalem. Islam reveres the place where Mohammed ascended into heaven on a horse, the Dome of the Rock. The Jews worship and pray at the "Wailing Wall," the last remnant of the Second Temple destroyed by the Romans in AD 70. Both of these are sites are centered around the Temple Mount in Jerusalem.

Christianity gave up on Jerusalem as a homeland in the Middle Ages. The Jews have been willing to share ownership of the sites, being quite content to let the Muslims have their holy shrine. For the Islamo-Fascists, however, the concept of Homeland is quite real. For them, the Jews must be purged from this region and the Israelis driven into the sea. There is no compromise with them, the Jews must be expelled from Palestine or be killed, no other solution is allowed.

Again, I am not about to try and untangle all the religious and historical reasons for the return of the Jews to Palestine and the establishment of Israel as a nation. I will have to say, look, like it or not, Israel is there, it does exist, it can and has defended itself, it has nuclear weapons, it is not going away. So, we have to deal with it and we have to help protect it from being overrun and its citizens slaughtered. Make no mistake, if Saddam had the warheads, he would have put sarin gas on those Scud missiles fired into Tel Aviv during the first Gulf War in 1991. If Usama bin Laden could get his hands on the population of Israel, there would be another Holocaust, make no mistake about it.

The Living Space idea for the Islamo-Fascists is very simple. Only the Arabs have a religious and historical right to the land of Palestine, modern-day Israel. The Israelis are interlopers and occupiers. Now, given the amount of available land in other nearby Arab countries, Jordan and Syria for example, you might think that resettlement of the Palestinian refugees wouldn't be much of a problem. But, it is. It is because of the reasons we discussed earlier. Arab leaders as well as the radical Iranian ayatollahs have concluded there is no better way to subjugate their own people than by waving the bloody shirt and using the Palestinians as a rallying cry for jihad.

A third parallel that the modern-day terrorists have with the Nazis is that both groups relied on a large pool of dispossessed, rootless, jobless, hopeless men to provide a large supply of recruits. Both parties needed recruits ready, willing, and able to carry out ruthless and barbaric acts against Jews, communists, Westerners, basically anybody who didn't agree with them and got in their way. The Nazis had this opportunity handed to them in Weimar Germany after World War I and the onset of the Great Depression. The Islamo-Fascists have this opportunity among the hopeless men in the refugee camps, among the ill-schooled men in the madrassas in Saudi Arabia, Pakistan, and other places where the economies are medieval and there is little work beyond menial tasks, the military, or government-bureaucratic jobs.

Here, both the Nazis and the Islamo-Fascists share a belief in inculcating the nation's youth with the proper party or religious views. The Nazis created a large network of youth groups, most notably the *Hitler Jugend* (Hitler Youth). The communists created the Young Pioneers and all of the known Islamo-Fascist terrorist groups have programs encouraging children in *shahada* (dying for the sake of Allah). Many of the homicide bombers in Israel and Iraq have been seventeen years old or even younger.

Fourthly, both the Nazis and Islamo-Fascists have a mystical-religious belief in the ultimate God-ordained superiority of their own cause. It was not just the right, but the DUTY of the Nazis to kill or enslave the Slavic peoples in the east, to take their land and settle it with Aryan Germans. This was a mystical concept rooted in the imperatives dictated by a host of Nordic gods and other occult predeterminations that make no sense to explain here. The Islamo-Fascists also believe in the Allah-ordained superiority of their cause. Martyrdom is the highest form of sacrifice. Mohammed Atta's final letter before he drove United Airlines 767 into Two World Trade Center is proof of this. After shaving his body hair and anointing himself with perfume, he was ready to be received into paradise with its virgins and other accompaniments which make paradise, well...paradise.

Finally, as an instrument of social control, Naziism and Islamo-

Fascism have had no equals on earth. The Nazis ruthlessly and bloodily eliminated all of their competition, politically, socially, and religiously. The German election in the fall of 1932 had a lot of excitement in it. There were basically three major political parties in Weimar pre-Hitler Germany: the communists, the Nazis and the Catholic Center Party. The spice in the election was that the communists knew that if the Nazis won the election, then they all would be rounded up and killed. The Nazis knew that if the communists won, then Stalin would send agents to Germany and convert the country into a slave-satellite of the Soviet Union. They, too, would be quickly rounded up and killed. As fate would have it, no party won a clear advantage in the Reichstag. The Center Party made a pact with the Nazi devil and convinced the doddering President Hindenburg to make Hitler chancellor, thinking that he could be controlled and managed. Hah! We know how that turned out.

In much of the Middle East, a lot of the religious strictures and rules are meant to apply to the masses, not the elite. I know there are things which go on behind palace walls which are not allowed for the public at large. The stories of princely journeys to Las Vegas, where whole floors are cordoned off for fun and games are legendary. Legends, of course, cannot be repeated here. Uday Hussein's mountainous collection of pornography might be a clue.

The leaders in the Muslim world have permitted nothing more than a mock democracy in their countries. They have no intention of sharing power with anyone else. Even in countries where there is a veneer of democracy, like Egypt, appearances can be deceiving. There, the ruling National Democratic Party runs things with an iron hand, make no mistake. Saudi Arabia? Forget it, forget a parliament, forget a free press, forget everything. Do we need to discuss Syria, Libya, the Emirates, and the rest of them? I think not, you get the point. We will get back to this later, but it does make one wonder what chance democracy will have in Iraq. I guess we will soon find out, but the prospects from an historical and sociological perspective are not good. Iraq may make Putin's Russia, also allegedly democratic but not, look like Athens in its Golden Age.

I have spent a little time in discussing some of the Nazi theories because no one actually teaches anything about them anymore except in very obscure history courses in some rarefied universities. This is really a pity because once you understand the roots of Nazi theory and how it struck a sympathetic chord in the German population you might better understand what has shaped modern-day Islamo-Fascism.

U.S. Foreign Policy and its Support of Israel

This is a difficult section for me to write because, as most Americans, I believe in fairness and it is obvious to all that the U.S. has a completely one-sided approach to the Arab-Israeli conflict. Our country has strongly backed Israel with aid, military equipment, intelligence information and with whatever else it needs to survive.

Having said this, are we doing the right thing? Could our actions be modified in a way that chances for success in building a true peace in the Middle East could be achieved? In short, is it our fault that Israel exists, that there is no peace and that the Arab peoples pretty much hate us? The man in the Arab street perceives the U.S. government as being lackeys for Israel, captive to the powerful Jewish political and media lobbies here in this country. They see absolutely no chance of the U.S. ever being fair to them and understanding their pain. Decades of propaganda about the justness of the Palestinian cause, decades of pictures, film, and videotape of Israeli warplanes launching missiles into refugee camps, of Israeli soldiers kicking in doors, bulldozing houses, and streets littered with the bodies of innocents, including women and children, have all taken their toll. You can argue that the situation is hopeless, that if there were only two people left alive on earth, one Arab and one Jew, they would be at each others' throats. Is this true? Is there any ray of hope? Is the U.S. hopelessly and helplessly locked into a situation of which it can't get out? Is there a win-win solution anywhere?

The short answer is, if I knew the answer to these questions then I would be operating at a considerably higher pay grade. But, in my view, there is some hope and a way out, as risky and fraught with peril as it may be. So, with all of this in mind, here goes.

In the first place, the playing field of the U.S. versus Israel and the Arabs is a great deal more level than it might appear on the surface. The reality is that since 1978 the U.S. has given Egypt $1.3 billion a year in military aid and another $815 million a year in economic assistance, mainly food grains. In all, since 1975 the U.S. taxpayer has forked over $50 billion in aid to Egypt. As part of its aid program, the U.S. hands over $200 million in cash for the Egyptian government to do with as it pleases. This money is supposed to be used for encouraging deregulation, privatization, and free trade, but there really are no strings attached to it. According to U.S. government information, in fiscal year 2003 the U.S. gave $95 million in aid through the U.N. to Palestinian refugees. I could go on with this, but I'm sure you get the picture.

The point is that, God knows, we are trying. We are trying as best we can to move all the parties along in the Middle East to a point where they can all live together without killing each other—or us! What keeps Colin Powell optimistic and trying and pushing and never giving up trying to find a peace in the Middle East is beyond me. Trust me, the man doesn't need the grief. He could write another book, he could work the lecture circuit, he could run for office, he could do anything he wants and write his own ticket. God bless him for not giving up. Hopefully, he will remain in the Bush administration if there is a second term for them, but there are persistent rumors he will retire. I hope not.

If you have read this far, you know by now that I am not a fan of Bill Clinton. There has been nothing the man did as president that I found admirable. No, I haven't read his thousand-page memoir, and I won't. I know that I couldn't find anything in the book that I could believe or admire—except for one big thing.

The next-to-last big thing that our friend Bill did before he left office (the last thing was pardoning Marc Rich, Susan McDougal, and some other buddies of his) was to flame out, spectacularly, in trying to get Ehud Barak, the prime minister of Israel, and Yasir Arafat, chairman of the Palestinian Authority, to agree to a lasting peace at Camp David. I would like to spend a little time here and explain what the deal was and how and why it failed. All of this will be very instructive about the mess in the Middle East at large and explains, in a very clear way, why U.S. policy is as "unfair" as it is.

Toward the end of the Camp David negotiations, with Bill Clinton himself personally present, his own legacy and the prestige of the U.S. on the line, Barak caved in to virtually everything the Palestinians had asked for. As Barak was the leader of Israel's Labour Party, Clinton instinctively knew that any further concessions by Ariel Sharon's Likud or Conservative Party, the likely winner of the next Israeli election should Barak fail, would be impossible. As a result, Clinton leaned on Barak and twisted his arm beyond the point of pain.

Here, in a nutshell, is what Barak agreed to. First, he agreed to the establishment of a Palestinian state, their own real country. Next, he agreed that the capital of the new Palestine could be in Jerusalem and that they could keep the territory that included the Temple Mount. He agreed that all of the Gaza strip should be given up by Israel and that he would pull the settlements out of about 95 percent of the West Bank. Finally, a package of $30 billion in aid for the Palestinian refugees was presented to Arafat.

The most revealing and informative commentary on the Camp David negotiations and Arafat's ultimate rejection of the plan was published in *The New Yorker* in March 2003 in an article by Elsa Walsh. In this article Prince Bander, the longtime Ambassador of Saudi Arabia to Washington and a close observer of Camp David, was quoted as saying that Arafat, by his rejection of the offer, had "committed a crime against the Palestinians—in fact, against the entire region." After this, everybody pretty much washed their hands free of Arafat. Nobody trusted him any more, not the Americans, the Europeans, the Saudis, or other friendly Arabs—nobody.

At this point, take a deep breath and ask yourself what else do they want? What else can we as Americans do for them? What can anybody do? What can Israel do? The answer, my friends, is pretty plain— NOTHING!

Look, there are Arabs who love us in Iraq and those that hate us. God knows I wish they all loved us. I want the Palestinians to love us, too. But, there is a limit to the blood and treasure that we have. You have to eventually get to a point and say, "This is it, it doesn't get any better, take it or leave it." Going on, Prince Bandar was upset because our boy Bill didn't screw up the courage to level a real ultimatum against Arafat and absolutely force him at the point of a proverbial gun to yield and take the deal. But, that was not Bill's way. Bill would rather make love than war so to speak. Stop it! Get me off this subject. Now!

Well then, what was in Arafat's mind? What caused him to balk and not take the deal of the century, the true win-win-win…solution? Those of you who have been paying close attention to the horrible *tour de force* in this essay probably have guessed by now why Arafat did what he did, or didn't do, actually.

Yes, you have it. The terror groups in Palestine, most certainly Hamas, Hezbollah, the al Aqsa Martyr's Brigade, Islamic Jihad, and who knows how many others probably including al Queda, had told Arafat's people back in Ramallah that if he took Barak's deal he was a dead man walking.

That's it, end of story. If Arafat signed, he died, no question. Well, my friends, this is the crucial question of our age; what would you have done had you been in Arafat's position? Would you keep your life safe and continue to hole up in your office while padding your Swiss bank accounts with U.S. and U.N. aid money or would you show a bravery and a courage that you had never shown in your life and do something that would really help your people for now and ages to come? Come on, the answer is too easy.

There is an old story about the Middle East which I would like to repeat. It goes like this: Once there was a scorpion who wanted to cross the Nile. He saw a frog who also wanted to cross but was afraid to because he couldn't see high enough out of the water and asked him, "Could we form an alliance and cross the Nile together? I can stand on your head and give you directions."

"Of course not," said the frog, "I would be at your mercy, if you sting me I would drown."

"And why would I do that?" said the scorpion, "If I sting you I, too, will down."

After thinking it over a little bit the frog agreed and the scorpion hopped aboard. Midstream the scorpion's nature overcame him and he drove his stinger deep into the frog. As they both started to sink beneath the waves the frog said, "Why did you do that, now we both will die?"

The scorpion replied, "There is no reason, this is the Middle East."

What Is the Enemy's Strategy?

As a tactician and wargamer I have learned how to put yourself in your opponent's shoes, to really think and believe like he does. You cultivate this skill by playing the enemy side from time-to-time. So, bear with me for a little while and let's see if we can discover what Usama and friends really want. What were they hoping to accomplish by hijacking four planes in the United States and crashing them into high-value targets? Briefly stated, here is a list of bin Laden's goals.

- To annihilate the crusader enemies of Islam led by the U.S. and its allies.

- To restore Muslim dignity, the purity of the holy places, and lost territory.
- Expelling the U.S. completely from all Muslim territory.
- The complete return of Palestine to the Palestinians to include the expulsion of the Jews and the destruction of Israel.

Bin Laden capitalizes on what many Muslims believe is Western aggression against their people, religion, and culture. Although it would be wrong to characterize him as a deep thinker, it would be a serious mistake to underestimate the power his words can have over ordinary Muslims. An independent poll taken in 2003 showed that almost half of the Saudi population had a favorable opinion of Usama bin Laden.

Okay, Usama is a very bad guy, we know that. Despite his bad acts, his rhetoric is popular among many Arabs. There is an increasing number of people here in the U.S., mainly left-wing Democrats, who believe that we deserved 9/11 because of our support of Israel, because we have a strong presence in Saudi Arabia, the home of the holy places Mecca and Medina, and because, in general, we have a foreign policy that is too aggressive and too prone to make war.

But, still, where does that leave us? Suppose the anti-war people are right? Suppose we just get Usama on the phone and tell him we surrender? First, how exactly would we do that? Secondly, what would that lead to? What we need to do here is figure out what an al Qaeda victory in the war on terror would look like. If they win and we lose, then what happens? Are you ready? I'm about to tell you.

First, understand that Usama bin Laden knows that he can never militarily defeat the United States of America. He will never have enough power to accomplish the destruction of our armed forces. Understand that the attacks on 9/11 were designed to defeat us psychologically and economically. The U.S. economy was already headed toward a recession by the end of 2000, but the attacks on 9/11 greatly accelerated the downward trend. The airlines and the stock markets were the first to suffer, then all sectors of the economy went into retreat. Trillions of dollars were lost, investments, IRAs, and careers disappeared overnight. Usama was thus able to create a huge negative shock in the U.S. economy with a cash investment of less than $500,000. This, as we say in military terms, is a great force multiplier, getting much more damage out of your firepower than the enemy can possibly afford.

On the psychological side of his strategy, Usama counted on the secular and isolationist American public to turn against U.S. involvement in the Middle East. He hoped for little or no military reaction against the attacks and he hoped for the political climate in the U.S. to turn against Israel. After all, how often has the case been made that if it weren't for our support of Israel, then all of our problems in the Middle East would go away?

Okay, so we agree to pull all of our forces and our company people out of the Middle East lands, then what happens? What happens then is that the Saudi ruling family quickly disappears and Usama establishes a power base there. Iraq would be sure to follow in short order. Within a few months Usama bin Laden would have his hands around about a third of the world's known oil reserves. Then he would not have to shock the U.S. economy anymore, he could CONTROL it. We would pretty much have to do whatever he wanted in order to sustain ourselves with petroleum and all it means to us, our economy, our jobs, our families, everything.

But wait, there is more. The next thing to occur would be the assassination of President Musharraf in Pakistan. An al Queda-led coup there would quickly establish control over the Pakistani armed forces—and its stockpile of nuclear weapons.

Within a year, Usama bin Laden would transform himself into a world superpower. This superpower would straddle a territory from India to the Mediterranean. It would have monopoly control over all of the oil in the Middle East and it would have nuclear weapons.

This is what your basic left-wing, let's leave Iraq pacifism will lead to. If you think that it would have been impossible to really negotiate a peace with Hitler, then wait and see what will happen with Usama in power. From that position Usama would be able to dictate to the world.

One of the problems I have with the neocons and the Bush administration is that we need more plain talk from them. Why do I have to draw you this picture? They should be doing this, not me.

What Should our Middle East Strategy Be?

By now you should realize that the answer to this question is rather simple. We have to stay the course in Iraq and help transform it into a stable, prosperous, friendly, and, if possible, democratic country. There really is no other thinkable option to this. Anything less at this point would be a disaster for not only the U.S. but the civilized world.

Next, we have to do everything in our power to keep the Saudi ruling power from going down the tubes. The seizure of power in Saudi Arabia by Usama bin Laden would be a worldwide disaster.

In the 1975 movie *Three Days of the Condor,* Robert Redford plays a CIA agent on the run from rogue plotters within his own agency. They are trying to kill him because he has uncovered a plot for the U.S. to invade the Middle East. Here is some dialogue from the final scene in that movie between Redford (Agent Turner) and Cliff Robertson (Higgins), his boss.

Turner: "Do we have plans to invade the Middle East?"

Higgins: "Are you crazy?"

Turner: "Am I?"

Higgins: "Look, Turner…"

Turner: "Do we have plans?"

Higgins: "No. Absolutely not. We have games. That's all. We play games. What if? How many men? What would it take? Is there a cheaper way to destabilize a regime? That's what we're paid to do."

Turner: "Go on. So Atwood just took the game too seriously. He was really going to do it, wasn't he?"

Higgins: "It was a renegade operation. Atwood knew 54-12 would never authorize it. There was no way, not with the heat on the Company."

Turner: "What if there hadn't been any heat? Supposing I hadn't stumbled on a plan? Say nobody had?"

Higgins: "Different ball game. The fact is there was nothing wrong with the plan. Oh, the plan was all right. The plan would have worked."

Turner: "Boy, what is it with you people? You think not getting caught in a lie is the same thing as telling the truth?"

Higgins: "No. It's simple economics. Today it's oil, right? In ten or fifteen years food, plutonium. And maybe even sooner. Now what do you think the people are gonna want us to do then?"

Turner: "Ask them."

Higgins: "Not now—then. Ask them when they're running out. Ask them when there's no heat in their homes and they're cold. Ask them when their engines stop. Ask them when people who've never known hunger start going hungry. Do you want to know something? They won't want us to ask then. They'll just want us to get it for them."

The problem the left has had with this dialogue, and it's been frequently discussed, is that everyone deep down recognizes the innate truth of what Higgins said. It's like the law of gravity. You may not like it because you weigh too much, but you can't change it.

Here is my message to our Arab friends in the Middle East, to people of good will who would like to be friendly to the U.S. Give us a break on your problem with us and Israel, did we not try our level best and do the right thing at Camp David in 2000? What more do you want us to do? So, cut us some slack here and we will continue to try and do the right thing. We will pay you a fair market price for your oil and we will thus vastly enrich your countries. It's up to you and your leaders as to how you spend the money. You can build universities, highways, and shopping centers or you can build palaces and store the excess in Swiss banks. It's up to YOU to figure out how to run your governments. My best advice is start democratizing and let the people vote. You might be surprised at the results if you are not corrupt and honestly try to help them.

But, and there is always a "but," DON'T F*** WITH OUR OIL SUPPLY! If you do, then we have no choice but to fulfill Higgins's prophecy.

Where does that leave us? No one cares much for Ariel Sharon's unilateral plan to withdraw from Gaza, partially pull back the settlements and build a security wall. Even members of his own party, Netanyahu in particular, are a thorn in the Israeli prime minister's side. But, and here's the "but" again, he's the only game in town. As Charles Krauthammer wrote in the *Washington Post* in June 2004, "Sharon's campaign against the intifada is working, the wall, though only partially complete, has significantly reduced the number of terrorist acts." Eventually, if enough fellow Arabs come around to the truth, Arafat will be gone and a settlement will follow, probably pretty much on the basis of Camp David. Don't give up on Bill's legacy yet, there may still be time to save it.

I would say we have to stay the course in the Middle East and finish building a nation in Iraq. I would totally disagree with John Kerry and others who continually cry for more international troops, U.N., NATO, whatever, to help us in Iraq. As I have said many times on the air on Fox, no, folks, we don't need French, German, Swedish, or Russian troops in Iraq. We need IRAQIS to run Iraq. Only they can run the police and provide security in their own country. We can give them all the assistance in the world, but only they can gather the intelligence and carry out the operations on a daily basis that will bring safety and security to their people. We have to trust them. Listen to me, there is no other choice.

What Should our Strategy Be to Fight Global Terrorism?

If you thought this chapter has been horrific, brutal, and tough to take, then fasten your seatbelts. You just thought I had offended people and sowed panic and disorder up to this point. Honestly, I thought long and hard about what I am about to write. There are people who will no doubt classify me as a first-class Dr. Strangelove after this. What I am about to do is ask you to take a fantasy trip with me into a world which you can't and don't want to imagine.

Again, I have a problem with the Bush administration for not doing enough to adequately prepare the American people for what they are about to face. SOMEBODY needs to tell the God-awful truth here. Again, why me, Lord?

There is an old joke, you know you are about to have a bad day when you turn on the TV in the morning and they are showing evacuation routes out of your city. Folks, I wake up fearing that nightmare every day. And, yes, it's not a matter of "if," but "when." A goodly portion of this book has shown you how soft a target we are, how vulnerable our entire infrastructure is to a truly devastating attack from chemical, biological, radiological, or nuclear weapons.

I'm not going to take the time here to go through what the dangers are from each of these threats. The prospect of mass casualties and severe economic disruptions for years to come are quite plausible in the environment we live in today. So, what do we do?

First, I have given you many ideas in this book about how to make ourselves less vulnerable. Re-read the section on corporate security and understand at least a little bit about some very simple things you can do in the way of getting trained or informed about how to react if an attack occurs.

The Department of Homeland Security, other federal agencies, the airlines, the trucking and shipping industries are doing some things right, but much, too much, is left undone. It is largely up to the individual citizens of this country in all walks of life to be aware and be prepared to alert authorities when something potentially threatening is noticed. We know now about people from the Middle East taking flight training and only being interested in how to steer the plane, not take off or land it. What else is there you have seen? Do you attend a mosque, have you heard suspicious conversations, has someone tried to recruit you to perform illegal or questionable acts? It may be socially and culturally not okay for you to talk to the FBI, but do you want your kids to go to school when a car bomb might kill them? You live here, too, help us all by taking care of yourselves.

Finally, and here is the really tough part, what do we do if something really bad happens in one of our big cities? Let's say a small tactical nuke, one or two kilotons goes off in Chicago, or say a large amount of plutonium-contaminated dust gets released from a radiological bomb in LA, what do we do then?

Believe me, folks, I don't have ANY inside knowledge as to what our war planners and Homeland Security people will do in case of such an event. But, I will guarantee you that there are real live people coming to work every day who are making plans for these kinds of horrors. Again, I really fault the Homeland Security people and the Bush administration for keeping us in the dark about all of this. I know they don't want to panic the stock market and they don't want people to live their lives in fear, but it is way too late for that.

How would or should we react to a major catastrophic event with resulting mass casualties and untold economic damage in our country? Well, the options as I see them are not very good.

First, even knowing where the attack came from, who ordered it, and who takes responsibility is a huge issue. What if al Queda takes credit? Where are they, what cave do we drop a bomb on? Even worse is the likelihood that no one might take credit for it. It could be al Queda, the North Koreans, the Iranians, or even some kind of home-grown crazy like Timothy McVeigh. Even after some period of time using our best intelligence assets, it might be impossible to know who was responsible for the attack. What should we do then, sit back and wait for the next one? That is not an option.

In 1962 a futurist at the RAND Corporation, Herman Kahn, wrote a book, *Thinking about the Unthinkable*. In this book he described what the results would be of a global nuclear war. This book came out at the height of the confrontation between The U.S. and the Soviet Union over the Cuban Missile Crisis. Fallout shelters became a big concern in those days and people lived in fear of nuclear war. Afterward, as the full strategy of mutually assured destruction (MAD) took effect, the world rested a little easier because no one but a madman would launch those weapons. Well, this brings me back to Usama bin Laden. Enough psychological studies have been done on the man to at least leave the question open about him being that madman with a nuclear trigger that underlies our deepest fears.

Some of you by now may have figured out where I am going with this train of logic. I say "logic," because in the ultimate sense there may be no other way out.

Suppose we had our intelligence people informally contact Iranian intelligence, North Korean intelligence, Syrian intelligence, and a few others and tell them something like this:

"One of these days a weapon of mass destruction will be used against our population. We may not be able to determine where it came from and who was responsible for this crime against humanity. Because of this, we have selected your country as a random target for total thermonuclear obliteration. Depending on the nature of the attack, it may be more than one country or the capital city in one country, but it will be at least one. We are sorry to have to do this, but it will happen, we guarantee it. Our response will come without any warning and it will be devastating and total. You and all your people, your country, your history, your genes, and your DNA will be blasted into atoms. We suggest at this point to avoid this fate that you apply all your resources, all of your intelligence assets into helping us find the terrorists who want to harm us and aid us in destroying them."

My guess is that very soon you would see a totally different kind of cooperation from all of the rogue and terrorist states, President Bush's Axis of Evil if you will. This is the only way I know to make OUR problem THEIR problem, too, in a way they can personally identify with. Some might view this as the road to Armageddon. I hate to tell you folks, but we are already well along down that road. The solution I offer here may be our only way out.

Lesson Learned: We had to bomb Nazi Germany and Imperial Japan back into the Stone Age in order to bring total defeat to them and end their wars of destruction and genocide. In order to similarly crush Islamo-Fascism and other terroristic ideologies that threaten our civilization we will have to carry out this level of total destruction again. God has given us a "terrible swift sword" to use to conquer evil. If we do not use it when we must, then we will be relagated to the dustbin of history and evil will triumph and rule the world. We cannot and will not let that happen.

God bless America, and God bless all of you.

Acknowledgments

This book would not have been possible if it wasn't for the persistence and support of several people in my life. Special thanks to my mother and father whose constant support and caring have given me a strong foundation on which to grow. My coauthor, Bryan Fugate, and his ever faithful and dedicated assistant, Donna Delvy, brought this project to life by sacrificing months of their free time to the painful process of listening to my stories and ramblings on tape and transcribing them into print. If it weren't for Bryan reaching out to me and pushing me in the direction of writing this book and sharing my stories and opinions, I would have never taken on this venture. I would be remiss if I didn't thank my longtime friend, mentor, and former company commander, Doug Wisnioski. Doug is ultimately responsible for my "talking head" career on Fox News and simply got me where I am today. I am fortunate to have two incredible friends and both of them have taken an active roll in my life and I would entrust my life to them—Mike McInerney is one of them. Mike's input into the intelligence chapter is priceless, his real-world experience and no-nonsense style add credibility to this effort.

Lastly, I want to thank my wife and little girl. Once again my family took a backseat to my career and my wife displayed the ever-faithful support that only an Army wife can understand—thank you, Jen and Jessie.

All inaccuracies and faults within this book are a direct result of my own actions and I accept full responsibility for them.

About the Authors

Bob Bevelacqua

Bob was born in Attleboro, Massachusetts, on September 11, 1965. He moved to St. Augustine, Florida, during his junior year in high school where he enrolled in Junior Reserve Officer Training Corps. Bob attended Georgia Military College and Georgia College in Milledgeville, Georgia, graduating in 1987 with a BS in Political Science and Public Administration. He then went on to active duty in the U.S. Army as an infantry officer. Bob's assignments included serving as an anti-tank and scout platoon leader in the 48th Brigade (GA National Guard), rifle platoon leader, anti-tank platoon leader, and company executive officer in the 8th Infantry Division (M), battalion S4 in the 3rd Armor Division, battalion assistant S3 in the 7th Infantry Division (L), special recon & direct action detachment commander, SCUBA A-Team detachment commander and headquarters and support company commander 3rd Special Forces Group (A). Bob also served on the U.S. Army staff in the Pentagon as an executive assistant to the director of strategy, plans and policies and as the secretary for the Joint Action Control Office for the Army G-3 (Plans and Operations). Following his resignation from active duty Bob performed consulting work for the U.S. Marshals Service, the Defense Information Systems Agency, the U.S. Army Space and Missile Defense Command, and the Army G-3 Pentagon. Bob has served in real-world deployments during Operation Desert Storm, Operation Garden Plot (LA Riots), Operation Uphold Democracy (Haiti), JTF-Six (Counter Drug) Foreign Internal Defense Missions in Benin and Ghana, and continues to serve as a project leader for special support to coalition forces during Operation Iraqi Freedom. Bob has also served as a military analyst for the Fox News Channel since September 2001.

You can contact Bob through his Web site: http://www.majbob.com.

Bryan Fugate

Currently, Bryan is president of J & B Imaging Services, Inc., Austin, Texas. Bryan has an earned doctorate from the University of Texas–Austin (1976). His doctorate is in European history and he is fluent in Russian, German, and Spanish. Presidio Press has published two of his books, *Operation Barbarossa Strategy and Tactics on the Eastern Front* in 1984 and *Thunder on the Dnepr: Zhukov-Stalin and the Defeat of Hitler's Blitzkrieg* in 1997. Bryan's books have been translated into Russian, Polish, and Czech.

Bryan founded J & B Imaging Services, Inc. in January 1993. The company, better known as JABIS™, in its early years concentrated on document conversion and data acquisition. Recently, JABIS has focused on high-quality electronic publication, CD and Web publishing, and hyperlinking families of documents.

You can contact Bryan through his Web site: http://www.jabis.com.